early
childhood
identity

# Rethinking Childhood

Joe L. Kincheloe and Gaile Cannella
*General Editors*

Vol. 35

PETER LANG
New York • Washington, D.C./Baltimore • Bern
Frankfurt am Main • Berlin • Brussels • Vienna • Oxford

RITA CHEN

# early
# childhood
# identity

## construction, culture, & the self

PETER LANG
New York • Washington, D.C./Baltimore • Bern
Frankfurt am Main • Berlin • Brussels • Vienna • Oxford

Library of Congress Cataloging-in-Publication Data

Chen, Rita.
Early childhood identity: construction, culture, and the self / Rita Chen.
p. cm. — (Rethinking childhood; v. 35)
Includes bibliographical references and index.
1. Early childhood education. 2. Identity (Psychology) in children. I. Title.
LB1139.23.C47    372.21–dc22    2008043860
ISBN 978-1-4331-0162-5 (hardcover)
ISBN 978-1-4331-0161-8 (paperback)
ISSN 1086-7155


Bibliographic information published by **Die Deutsche Bibliothek**.
**Die Deutsche Bibliothek** lists this publication in the "Deutsche
Nationalbibliografie"; detailed bibliographic data is available
on the Internet at http://dnb.ddb.de/.

Cover design by Sophie Boorsch Appel

The paper in this book meets the guidelines for permanence and durability
of the Committee on Production Guidelines for Book Longevity
of the Council of Library Resources.

© 2009 Peter Lang Publishing, Inc., New York
29 Broadway, 18th floor, New York, NY 10006
www.peterlang.com

Printed in the United States of America

# Contents

# Foreword

Readers of this remarkable ethnography by Rita Chen should prepare themselves for some intensely emotional moments. Chen succeeds in vividly capturing many features of elementary school life from the child's perspective, so that one cannot help but feel the joys and pains of her young participants. Readers will also find that forgotten or repressed memories of their own years in the first and second grade waken as they follow Chen's account. A reader will feel herself taking a variety of positions when reading this ethnography. Many times one feels like a child, a child with indignation at the unfairness of teachers in giving awards and punishments, with high self-esteem when a writing and drawing project is "published" for all the class to see, with pain when other children are rejecting and negating, and most often with boredom due to required classroom activities that take fun out of living. The reader is also often in the role of parent or older sister or brother. The accomplishments of these students fill one with pride and wonder, the injustices of classroom life with a desire to intervene and protect. And readers are very often in the position of fellow theorists and colleagues with Chen who includes many enlightening discussions of concepts and many insightful and original sections of analysis.

Chen's own role as fieldworker and writer defies any simple label. She spent two full years in a mixed first and second grade classroom in the United States, and managed to establish a very high degree of rapport with the children. Although Chen grew up in Taiwan and was of adult age, one senses from the text that she succeeded in many ways to become accepted by these young people as one of them. She deliberately taught herself much of the consumer-driven features of children's culture as we find it in many diverse nations today by watching popular shows on TV, reading popular children's books and playing Nintendo and computer games on her own. And she was able to talk with the children about their favorite games and characters just as an enthusiastic child would do so, not as a kind but condescending adult. She openly shared her unfamiliarity with both other features of the children's culture and particular uses of English expressions so that the children would explicitly teach her about ways to use words, toys, candies, classroom rules and peer culture norms. One gets a sense for the kind of person Rita Chen is from her text: unpretentious, humble, interested in anything and everything, smart, easy and fun to be with. Surely this is how the children found her. They invited her to their "secret spots" in the classroom, they drew pictures with her and liked to sit by her during various activities, they gave her recommendations for writing up the field notes and even reminded her when her tape recorder batteries were running low.

And the result is an ethnographic account that truly gives a child's perspective of elementary school life. As I have already mentioned, much of this account is painful to read. A young boy breaks into silent tears because two girls he had hoped to join at a table stand books upright between them and him, like a wall to keep him out. A girl repeatedly tries to talk with several boys about her Nintendo gaming at home, only to be continuously rebuffed, disbelieved, belittled, kept-out of their young "masculine" conversation. Working groups of two set up by teachers to encourage cooperative learning actually formed into strong dominant-subordinate relationships experienced as negating and oppressive by those in the subordinate roles. Many readers will be reminded of fears and pains we learned to hide from others and to some extent even from ourselves when growing up in school. But much of the account is inspiring as well. Chen's ethnography shows us positive, supportive friendships, a love for the free expression afforded in drawing and writing, and young enthusiasm for knowledge. We find acts of support and kindness that breach gender lines, struggles between power and justice in which justice occasionally wins.

This book delivers much of the full complexity of classroom culture, personal identity formation and learning processes. Chen innovates continuously in her analysis of these things. Her novel analyses range from methodological issues pertaining to studies of young children to broad themes and issues in social theory and philosophy. I will mention only a few of these insightful and important contributions.

Chen's analysis of personal identity in relation to classroom culture takes an original track by relating identity claims to existential questions that underlie them. These questions differ specifically for different participants in the study, but they can be understood to be specific manifestations of core questions faced by all human beings: "Am I okay? Am I good? How am I the same as and/or different from others? Is it okay to be different? Is it okay not to be popular?" These questions came up within this classroom in different ways for different children, related to their social positions within an exceedingly complex set of classroom and friendship cultures. Two central themes structured most identity concerns: being popular and being successful in the classroom. Chen writes:

> Being popular is a complex social construct and identity involving discursive power relations and privileges that are only available for certain groups of people. Its complexity is also illustrated in the linguistic structure of the children's narratives in which a convoluted thinking process cuts across the normative culture, the self, the other, and the search for "truth." While explaining being successful, the children regarded it as straight-forwardly following rules, doing "what the teachers say," and just doing what everybody else does. Being a successful student becomes a static and mechanically rule-governed identity that is regulated through sameness. Interestingly, it is with the meaning of being popular that the children gave more concrete experiences, expressed their feelings, denied the norms and challenged inequity in school, and thus shed light on the meaning of unique identity that is neither merely being successful nor being popular as defined by the school culture.

Interestingly, all the children, even those who called themselves popular and were identified as being popular by others, differentiated themselves from the "*really* popular." "Really popular" students were uniformly described as being boastful and "snotty" and *other* than each student who described them. No child identified her or his self as "really popular." As Chen's analysis shows, this is a clear example of how generalized other positions form and work—they are idealized, shared constructions that enable a cultural set of sameness and difference relations which make it possible to be an acceptable person in only limited ways. By reconstructing sets of questions underlying self-descriptions and the implicit identity claims carried in action, Chen shows us how children struggle with tensions between what they would like to be and how this is constrained by cultural milieu. In many cases awareness on the children's part of unresolved questions about themselves was stimulated by their sense that the identity claims they *could* make were not in harmony with their true recognition needs and desires.

Chen's analysis extends from identity issues to the formation of official and unofficial cultural domains within the classroom. With identity concerns as a chronic motivation and driving force for much of the classroom activities we are led to understand how informal friendship groups are created, "secret spots" constructed with special discourses to use within them, and patterns of conformity and nonconformity produced and reproduced in the daily classroom activities. Chen writes:

> An obvious consequence of the harm done to children's identity is when they are caught in the web of cultural reproduction, contesting the social norms constraining their sense of the self and yet keep reproducing that discontentment unknowingly.

Chen makes sophisticated and extensive use of social theory in her analyses of these patterns of cultural contestation and reproduction, along with how these processes are actually experienced by the children. Giddens' theory of structuration is extensively used at a level of specificity that one rarely sees. Rules and resources, social reproduction in distinction from system reproduction, etc. are convincingly and sharply employed. Social encounters are discussed by Giddens as involving "enclosures" and Chen uses this to bring out children's efforts to enfold their interactions within small groups protected from teacher surveillance and other children in the room. There is also a smooth integration of Giddens with Habermas with respect to many analytically useful concepts. And she makes an excellent use of front/back region distinctions within co-presence relations. Front regions are those under strong surveillance, requiring more norm-conformity, and back regions are those associated with enclosures where unofficial culture can be made dominant. The children were adept at managing both at once:

> In fact, the back and front regions often co-exist and intersect with each other in a complex way. For instance, even in the front-regional setting of the formal class instruction in which children are under intensive surveillance, they somehow manage to find a way to "communicate" back-regionally, such as making faces, winking, kicking each other under the table, passing notes to each other, whispering and so forth. .... Both the official and unofficial reinforce each other to reproduce the causal coordination between them—the official regulation controls children's action in time and space while children try to re-gain their control by doing all sorts of things back-regionally in which their own unofficial culture is enabled and produced by the official agenda.

Many aspects of the classroom studied by Chen show it to be progressive and to extend choice and power to children in ways that exceed what we find in more traditional classrooms. Yet from the children's point of view, much of daily classroom life is experienced as boring, as robbing them of having fun, as involving relations with other children structured by relations of domination and subordination, and as having encounters with teachers that seem unfair in terms of the rewards and punishments handed out. One official classroom activity, however, was reported by all the participants to be greatly rewarding for intrinsic reasons and to be a high motivator for taking part in learning activities: drawing and writing.

Chen's analysis of writing and drawing is again original, insightful and something of much value for educators and educational researchers. She draws upon theories of human expression and Bakhtin's theories of narrative, heteroglossia and the author-hero relation as these things pertain to written texts. Chen examines the books and drawings of many of the children to analyze the expressive processes they display. She finds a different *order* of thinking to characterize the creative-expressive processes of different children. Some think in images first, some in words. Some move from a holistic grasp of the product they wish to produce to the finished book or drawing, others begin with a vague notion of where they are going and develop their goal along the way. Chen's analysis includes the different genre's children employ and the different subject matters that interest them, from portrayals of themselves to action stories involving heroic fights with monsters and enemy forces. Some children incorporate highly self-reflective symbols and linguistic expressions into their work and others leave themselves as more implicit references in straightforward descriptions of what they have done and what they own. Interesting gender differences are evident in the material.

In a special chapter on drawing as related to human expression, Chen questions the widespread belief that drawing is a natural and early interest in developmental processes, which must be replaced with full linguistic expressions. She asks why it is that drawing, among all the activities children take part in, is usually the favorite. Why do teachers subtly discourage drawing and push children toward privileging writing? She asks:

> Has an important part of children's identity been taken away or alienated in the process of transferring their natural and creative semiotic power, focusing only on one particular sign system? Is this a "normal" process every child has to go through as he/she learns and uses more verbal forms to mean? Are we, as teachers, parents and researchers, simply considering it as a "developmental" passage when children use more words and less drawing? Or, are the children abandoning drawing for other ways to mean on an involuntary basis as they grow?

As Chen shows, drawings convey complex ideas that the children could not have written out in words. And drawing is a high motivator for children. Are we making a mistake in our schools by moving children away from drawing too quickly and by not paying enough attention to the meanings conveyed by drawings?

There is much more in this book, such as different forms of power used by girls and boys and the early formation of subtle patriarchal structures in classroom culture. But I leave these many other gems of insight for the reader to discover on her own. This book makes valuable contributions to many areas of the social and psychological sciences, and it is an excellent illustration and model of what can be done in an ethnographic study.

Phil Francis Carspecken
Indiana University, Bloomington

# INTRODUCTION

### A day in the classroom

First we have D.O.D (i.e., writing the Discovery of the Day journal). Then we have song time. Then we have morning meeting. Next we have team reading. Then we have a story web to work on. Then we have morning work time, and then writing workshop or invitations. Next we have recess and lunch. Then we have D.E.A.R. time (i.e., Drop Everything And Read). Next we have read aloud. Then we do some activities.

—Chris (a 2nd grader) and Oliver (a 1st grader)

*A day in the classroom*, written by Chris and Oliver in their classroom newspaper, depicts the general routine in a school day. Seemingly mundane, familiar, predictable, and perhaps a bit mechanical in tone, a day in the classroom may show us what the children did, but it does not tell us much about what really happened in the classroom. Comprising children's stories describing their daily social practices, contentment, discontentment, accomplishment, frustration, transformation and hopes about their school life, this study invites teachers and educators to see beyond the children's daily school routine and unpacks problems that many children have to confront in school. Some of the stories are told; some are written; some are drawn; some are real and some are imaginative; some need to be inferred from their interactions with their friends and teachers; some are embedded in the school norms; some are acted out intuitively; some are created unknowingly through the curriculum. By exploring different moments of children's classroom life, literacy events, and instances of negotiating the curriculum, their voices offer us great opportunities to learn from their schooling experiences.

Almost every child in the United States is mandated to attend school at the age of 5, and many of them start even earlier at the age of 1–3 in the daycare center or preschool. Despite the prolonged process as well as the universality of schooling in which children are educated and socialized to fully participate in our culture, not every child benefits equally from schooling. Nor does schooling provide the same impact on every child's life in general. Different levels of impact made by schooling on children's learning as well as identity formation need to be explored further so that we know what we can do to make school a place that truly appreciates each child's differences and values each individual's background and ways of learning. However, little effort is put into the exploration of children's thoughts about their schooling experience. Nor do we examine why children react to schooling differently. We simply think that it is normal that every child reacts to and benefits from schooling differently, but we rarely dig further about the important meaning of these different reactions to and benefits from schooling for each child and the possible impact or damage carried into young adulthood.

Two possible reasons for this common ignorance toward children's perceptions may be: (1) the assumption that children are too young to make decisions for themselves in learning, and (2) the policy of education framed largely under the surveillance of standardization and accountability. Because we do not trust children in making their own learning decisions, we think children need to be told what to do in learning. The curriculum objectives, thus, focus narrowly on particular knowledge systems and make sure that each child learns all the skills they need to maximize the achievement result within those knowledge systems. Meaningful learning, active engagement, ample freedom to explore, and precious experience open to the individual child become subordinate. Any children who cannot meet curriculum expectations are easily categorized as "troubled" or "struggling" learners. Any action taken to negotiate with the curriculum or to challenge the authority is identified as defiance. Schooling seems to become a deadly cycle of producing and fixing problems made by the school itself. Nor do children have much say about their learning; nor do we pay much attention to what their real problems are from their perspectives.

I do not deny the fact that children need guidance and help to achieve their academic goals and to keep making progress in their learning. However, I want to point out the dilemma embedded in the schooling system that confuses children's sense of the self in terms of *sameness* and *difference*. Although cultivating individual difference is a core value of schooling, it seems to contradict its major policy of maintaining sameness through standardization. This has essentially become a problem many children in this study face in school that triggers doubts in their minds about themselves. Not every individual difference is valued equally in school; even if one achieves academic expectations, conforming to the sameness of schooling seems not enough to really fulfill one's unique sense of the self.

To some degree, children are, in Althusser's term, "interpolated" into the schooling system where social norms and cultural structures are already in place to define who they are. Many doubts are embedded in their stories: Who am I? Can I really be myself in school? Is school a place for me to be myself? Why are some children more popular than the others? What does it mean when I am not popular in school? Do I have a choice to just be myself? All these questions have inspired me to conduct this study and explore the meaning behind these questions, especially as they concern how schooling affects children's identity formation.

One major and pressing statement organizes my argument in the study: Children's voices need to be heard and brought to the center of reforming our education system. This may not be a new argument, and yet we still see that the children's side of the story is easily ignored or sacrificed in education policy. An instructional decision without acknowledging children's opinions and without paying attention to their individual differences marginalizes children and places them outside the center of the curriculum. A curriculum theory that ignores the significance of children's voices alienates and insults their intellect. An educational policy excluding children's perspectives limits their learning experiences and undermines the quality of school life. If we agree that children should be in the center of a curriculum, that children should be in control of their learning, and that school should be a place to provide individual needs and support for every child, then listening to what children have to say about their school life is a logical place to start reflecting on the potential problems we may unknowingly create in our instruction, and so is reexamining problems that we are familiar with but simply consider them as "normal" in school.

In Bakhtin's (1976) words, "research becomes inquiry and conversation, that is, dialogue" (p. 104). To initiate the dialogue, my inquiry was prompted by the following questions: what do children know about school? How do they live through their school life? How do their perceptions of a curriculum differ from the teacher's instructional goals? What kind of changes do they want to make in school? Why are children enthralled by some activities while bored with others? What is "it" that makes such a difference? What is "it" that we can learn from children? In order to find out what "it" is and what makes a difference in children's school life, our exploration must be guided by the core conceptual mechanism of "identity construction." Four aspects of identity construction constitute the conceptual framework of the study: (1) the emergence of the self, (2) the classroom culture conditioning identity formation, (3) identity construction and literacy learning, and (4) expressing the self. I will briefly review each aspect by linking them to identity theories and research and then explain how each is applied to unpack children's school life.

## The Emergence of the Self

Drawing on American Pragmatism (Mead, 1934), identity is conceptualized as action as well as a situation in which social actors encounter and develop ways of solving problems in life. Unlike Descartes whose presupposition of human rationality and knowledge considers a self as an individual product rather than as an intersubjective one, Mead provided a theory of socialization as well as identity formation and considered the two to develop reciprocally and dialogically. His definition of the self is developed from social interaction that is linguistically mediated and normatively regulated in nature. Different from poststructuralism, which regards a self as an absolute cultural and linguistic subject discursively produced and fragmentally defined by discourses and power relations (Foucault, 1997) and a boundless range of signification (Derrida, 1973), Mead's philosophy suggests that human identity is not exclusively a social product, but that it also contains the innovative part of the human mind that is ready to negotiate, make changes, and create new solutions to problems in life. Thus, Mead placed human identity in a social relation and theorized the development of the self through incorporating structure and agency.

The emergence of the self, according to Mead, presupposed a social process and one's self derived by "taking the attitudes of the others" toward oneself when interacting with the other. This is the way we experience our own self indirectly from the standpoint of the other members in a society that we belong to. Piaget's (1954) idea of *decentering* (Sugaman, 1987), Vygotsky's (1978) social construction of learning (Wertsch, 1985), and Bakhtin's dialogism (1981, 1986; Holquist, 2002) also presuppose the social context Mead talks about for a child to develop her/his identity as well as to become a social being. Without the other, there is no self; the self emerges only through social processes in which one can role-take with the other and generate meaning based on the other's responses to one's act. Thus, the normative binding power in school becomes the key to understand how children develop a self in relation to the other. Mead explained the workings of norms through his concept of the generalized other, an abstract socially contingent position that actors take in relation to their won actions.

Habermas (1987) linked the generalized other to Durkheim's (1984, 1995) concept of social solidarity and collective consciousness in that social norms possess moral authority as a law-binding obligation that enables each member in a society to follow norms responsibly and willingly while also enabling critique of norms. In school, the law-binding obligation is constituted by a set of rules, regulations, and expectations that a good student should follow and achieve. However, not every student in the classroom agrees with all the rules and regulations. Nor does every student achieve all the expectations. Thus, the normative power of the generalized other is a crucial construct to examine what sort of cultural norms children internalize and how they react to these norms. Particularly, I want to know (1) what part of the school norms were already assumed that constrained children's sense of the self, (2) whether or not the children agreed with these norms, and (3) how they positioned themselves in relation to the others in the classroom.

## The Classroom Culture Conditioning Identity Construction

To understand children's school life is to explore what kind of classroom culture shapes who they are. I applied Giddens' (1984) sociological theory of structuration and Corsaro's sociology of early childhood as the major frameworks to reconstruct the complexity of the classroom culture. Giddens's (1984) theory of structuration allows one to examine how social actors—mainly teachers and students in the case of this study—interact, conflict, and support each other through routine social practices and how the consequences of these social practices discursively reproduce social systems implicated in school that serve as trajectories for children's identity construction. According to Giddens, the concept of society and culture is mainly defined by two terms: structure and system. As he explains, systems are sets of reproduced relations among actors, organized as recursive social practices while structures are both *rules* constraining social action and *resources* drawn by social actors to persistently sustain social practices. Framing under the theory of structuration results in two planes for the exploration of school culture: first, the re/production of school culture, and second, the re/production of the broader social systems through educational institutions. The former focuses on the coordination between the official (i.e., the official regulations, standards and curriculum design) and the unofficial (i.e., gender issues, children's peer culture, and their ways of working the system) culture in school and how both conflict with and sustain each other in the process of reproduction. The latter links the school culture to the broader socio-cultural systems (i.e., class, race, gender, etc.). In this study, I will emphasize the first plane and assemble a broader picture of the classroom culture through tension and interaction between the official and the unofficial culture.

Moreover, based on the tenet that "kids are deserving of study as kids" (Corsaro, 1997, p. 95), Corsaro's (1985, 1997, 2003) sociological view of early childhood considers children to be a unique part of the social structure that produces its own peer culture, co-constructs the cultural milieu with adults, and contributes to the cultural reproduction of a society. Corsaro defines childhood as a structural form in which children creatively "appropriate" the adult rules in constructing their own social world for their own purposes.

Briefly speaking, several features of children's peer culture can be drawn from Corsaro's intensive studies about preschoolers in America and Italy that provide crucial insights for conceptualizing children's collective identities in school. First, the notion of "ownership" for young children evolves from being possessive to embracing the idea of "sharing" with friends to meet the interactive demand in school. Second, "friends" become more and more important for a child in which many school activities, official and unofficial, result in cooperation with each other. These activities include, according to Corsaro, playing together, protecting an enclosed space, and forming groups.

Third, an important part of peer rules is constituted by the shared rituals among children. Corsaro uses "the loss of baby teeth" as an example to show how the notion of "growing up" or "becoming more mature" is highly valued in peer culture. Different kinds of rituals, such as chanting nursery rhymes, for starting and solving problems in games are important too.

Fourth, "childhood material culture" for creating children's artifacts, as Corsaro (1997) notes, includes "clothing, books, artistic and literacy tools... and, most especially, toys" (p. 109). However, media culture and technological devices should also be included, as these are becoming more and more dominant in children's world. Kress (1997, 2003) and Dyson (1989, 1993) have conducted studies about how children incorporate media culture as their major resource in making meanings and in creating various forms of artifacts (linguistic and graphic).

Fifth, gender identity is one of the major developments and discourses that dichotomize peer culture into the boys' world and the girls' world. Gender differentiation becomes more and more obvious and important as children age. The gender issue also works as an implicit rule in peer culture for making "boyfriends" or "girlfriends" among young children.

Finally, peer culture is hierarchical in nature. As Corsaro (1997) proposes, differentiation within groups functions as a way of how children "compete with and attempt to control one another using a wide range of interpersonal and communicative skills" (p. 154). The social hierarchy in children's world is closely connected to literacy capacity, which I will discuss in the following section.

All the above themes provided by Corsaro will be reexamined in the subsequent analyses in terms of how children's resistance is developed, supported, contradicted, and distorted under institutional resources and regulations.

## Identity Construction and Literacy Learning

Literacy has been defined, re-defined, and expanded to include multiple disciplines, such as social anthropology (Street, 1984), sociology (Freebody, Luke, & Gilbert, 1991; Luke, 1988; Corsaro, 1985, 1997, 2003; Cook-Gumperz & Corsaro, 1986), ethnography (Heath, 1983; Bloome, 1987), socio-linguistics (Gee, 1992, 1996, 1999; Halliday, 1978; Kress, 1997; 2003; Fair-clough, 1992; Lemke, 1988, 1995), and critical pedagogy (Giroux, 1981, 1983, 1988, 2000; McLaren, 1993, 2001; Apple, 1979, 1999; Lankshear et al., 1997). These fruitful and multi-dimensional perspectives from other disciplines provide literacy theories with different approaches to address sociocultural dynamics, globalization, media, technologies, and new capitalism. Literacy theory and the study of identities show us how rapid sociocultural change has influenced the way we live and how we use literacy to present ourselves in the modern world.

Current literacy research offers us various approaches to examine learners' identity formation in school. The curriculum-based research argues that students' identities emerge from different literacy activities, such as literacy discussion (Bean & Moni, 2003; Denyer & LaFleur, 2001; Atwell, 1998; Graves, 1994), the Vygotskian sociocultural views of collaboration in reading and writing (Jordran, Jensen, & Greenleaf, 2001; Dyson, 2000; Forman & Cazden, 1994), reader response (Galda & Beach, 2001; Marshall, 2000), literacy narratives (Williams, 2003/2004), the writing workshop (Lensimire, 1994; 2000; Rowe, Fitch, & Bass, 2001; Graham, 1999; McCarthey, 2001, 2002), and multiple texts including art (Busser-Webb, 2001; Hamilton, 2000). The above research focuses on how to implement a literacy curriculum to engage learners and meet their needs in assisting and expanding their literacy capabilities. It also shows how students position each other through texts and how their emerging identities inform us of what literacy means to them.

Research focusing on rapid changes of other meaning-making sign systems in the modern era calls for new perceptions and reconsiderations on how literacy has changed and become more diversified and how these factors should be implemented in current education (Kress, 1997, 2001, 2003; Kress & Jewitt, 2000; Finders, 2000; Myers & Beach, 2001; Britsch & Meier, 1999). As Kress (1997) reminds us, globalization and technology (i.e., computers, Internet, medias, movies, video games, popular music, etc.) have changed "the landscapes of communication" (p. 6); relying solely on studying language and ignoring uses of other sign systems are not enough to understand the multiple manifestations of texts and meanings in the modern world. By exploring how other sign systems have been manipulated and permeated within the dynamic changes in society, we will better understand what new ways of meaning-making and new forms of communication students are using and the direction of their identities.

Moreover, there is research emphasizing social issues such as gender division in literacy learning and meaning-making (Godley, 2003; Gallas, 1998; Broughton & Fairbanks, 2003), learners' active construction of meaning and representation of the self through various texts in official and unofficial school life (Dyson, 1989, 1993), and how identities are mediated through making personal connections with reading and writing (Heffernan & Lewison, 2003; Ryan & Anstesy, 2003; Kamler, 2001; Comber, 2000; Comber & Wells, 2001; Burgess-Macey, 1999). This body of research incorporates broader sociocultural aspects into school curriculum and values what learners bring to school as a way of enacting their personal experiences in constructing meanings and identities through texts.

In line with focusing on social issues, research of critical literacy radically highlights voices unheard, messages hidden, subjects marginalized, and actions and changes untaken in the current educational system (Lewis, 2001; Janks, 2000; Lewison et al., 2002; Heffernan & Lewison, 2000; McDaniel, 2004). Critical literacy centers on empowering the marginalized and the subordinate as well as on transforming existing social inequalities and injustices. One goal of critical literacy is to unmask and challenge the role of schooling as a cultural, ideological, and historical process in which race, gender, and class are divided and reproduced. Furthermore, critical literacy emphasizes the moral dimension of education to promote equal opportunities and access to critical thinking. Another aspect of critical literacy is dedicated to the emancipation of education and social transformation. Finally, critical literacy seeks to relocate teacher-student relationships and disrupt assumptions taken for granted in socio-cultural norms, classroom discourses, teacher ideologies, and aspects of school policy (McLaren, 2003; Giroux, 1983, 1988, 2000; Giroux & Shannon, 1997; Freire, 1970, 1973; Freire & Macido, 1987).

From the above research, it is clear that literacy has shifted from the neutral set of conventional reading and writing skills to more radical views that take personal, local, everyday, social, and power aspects into consideration, thereby broadening literacy to a multifaceted knowledge base that questions current assumptions about literacy and whether or not current literacy education really addresses learners' needs. This has great significance in the exploration of identity formation: students' learning, meaning-making, social interactions and cultural production are profoundly intertwined with how they represent their identities through multimodal literacy practices in schools.

With all the above literacy research and theories framing how literacy learning connects to children's identity development, in this study, I particularly focused on the kind of literacy activities that many children in this classroom like the most and investigated how these favorite literacy activities were related to their identity formation. I also applied Bakhtin's (1981, 1984, 1990) aesthetics of author-hero relationships and dialogism to explore the meaning-making process when children were engaged in their favorite literacy activities, and thus I elicited the kind of experience they were longing for from reading and writing.

## Expressing the Self

What I mean by "expressing the self" is a kind of experience children had in the process of action. This kind of experience creates a unique feeling toward one's self by acting out certain forms of meaning-making. Craib (1998) proposes that human identity is best considered as how people *experience* both the world and themselves. Despite the fact that each of us carries multiple identities or roles within a complex social network of relationships, one does not experience him/herself as a different person when taking different positions attached to different roles. A person could be a woman, a mother, a sister, a daughter, a doctor, and more, but usually one does not feel oneself to be a different person every time one switches to a different role.

Derived from the Marxist notion of *totality* and Lukas's concept of *experience*, Craib extends the scope in viewing identity by locating it in the wider social structure as well as in historical processes. Although the rise of a social class contains its interests and consciousness supported by social organization as its resources, the experience making this development possible is the concept of *praxis*–the attempt to transcend the subject/object dualism and the impetus to unite "'abstract thought', on the one hand and the 'concrete', the world of structures, appearances and experience, on the other, into a developing totality that transcends each" (Craib 1998, p. 20). The notion of praxis is the motivation of children's identity formation that they are eager to express themselves in their imaginative way, to penetrate reification, and to create new experiences in trying to grasp the sense of the self.

To further explore children's unique experience through expressing the self, I focus on meaning-making that is spontaneously, creatively, and effortlessly self-made. What I mean by "self-made" is that children choose their own media to design texts that express themselves in a full, rich and creative way, that is, drawing. Drawing is a major way young children use to make meaning. By "drawing," I mean broadly how children create texts, using words, shapes, colors, graphics, numbers, objects, and the like, and how they orchestrate and order these media not only to communicate with others but also to express themselves. Kress's (1997) study shows that young children do not differentiate drawing from writing when making meaning. He argues that children *draw* concrete objects as well as *draw* words that are composed by letters. The theoretical constructs for examining children's drawing include American Pragmatism (Dewey, 1934; Mead, 1934; Joas, 1995), Kress's (1997, 2003) semiotic theory of "representation," and other semiotic theories (Peirce, 1958–1960; Borgaard, 1999; Sebeok, 1999; Lakoff & Johnson, 2003). Specifically, I would like to raise two questions: (1) if one sign system is applied creatively and effortlessly in making meaning, how can we create a literacy curriculum that takes advantage of this natural flow of learning? (2) What happens to children's identity construction when their creative way of expressing the self is ignored and gradually replaced by another mainstream sign system in school?

## Organization of the Book

The book is divided into seven chapters. Chapter One introduces the methodological constructs and portrays an authentic and often complex process of conducting a study in a big classroom with 45 children. In this chapter, in addition to describing the labor-intensive process of data collection and analysis, I also provide readers with some guidelines for doing fieldwork, explaining how I hermeneutically prepared myself before going into the research site, how the techniques of collecting data changed in the process, and the unexpected problems and challenges that appeared when my role as a researcher and my relationships with the children evolved.

Chapter Two examines the two crucial norms embedded in the children's narratives that shape their identity in school—being a successful student and being a popular student. Applying Mead's (1934) theory of the self (i.e., the generalized other, the "I," and the "me") supplemented by Habermas's (1987) theory of communicative action (i.e., the possibility of rational agreement in the illocutionary bonds formed between actors), this chapter explores how children actively construct a valid self by (1) criticizing the norms defined by the generalized other in school, (2) constructing a fair ground for the meaning of who they are, and (3) struggling between the "me" who is socialized to fulfill the expectations and responsibilities as a classroom member and the "not me" in which part of the self is beyond their social identities (i.e., they are more than just being successful or popular).

Chapter Three maps the larger picture of how children's identity construction is conditioned in this particular classroom. Giddens's (1984) theory

of "structuration" and Habermas's (1987) concept of lifeworld and system relations are applied to theorize and guide the inquiry. I sketched a produc-
tion/reproduction loop of three components of the cultural structure in the
classroom that conflict, sustain, and connect with each other in complex ways:
(1) the school's official agenda; (2) the discrepancies between the teacher's official rules and the children's comments when carrying out these official rules;
and (3) the children's own unofficial culture developed under the rubric of the
official regulations as well as the resistance to such constraints. The findings
point out challenges teachers are facing to design a curriculum that engages
every child in the learning process and to provide for the needs of different
learners.

Chapter Four focuses on one of children's favorite literacy activities in
school—creating their own books in a writing workshop—and examines why
being an author is such a fun and important identity-building activity for most
of them. I review Bakhtin's early philosophy about the aesthetics of the author-
hero relationships when creating a novel and his later theory of discourses and
genres to assist in my analysis of young children's work of "verbal art." As
Bakhtin asserts, the novel or the work of verbal art is the artistic "contact
zone" where the self interacts with the other. It can appropriate the other's
utterances as well as contest, synthesize, recreate, and hybridize various discourses into one's unique authorial and novelistic discourse. Three types of
stories representing the most common styles in children's story writing are
analyzed. I probe the connection between particular genres of writing that
these young authors chose to foreground in their stories and how their identity as an author was actualized through text construction.

Chapter Five shifts the focus to another way of meaning-making that children love to do and are capable of doing whenever and wherever they can in
school—drawing. Attention is paid not only to what children have achieved
through drawing, but also to a holistic view of the significance of this particular action affecting children's learning and identity as meaning-makers. By incorporating different disciplines in understanding such drawing, including
Kress's semiotic theories, Marxist praxis theory, Herder's expressionism,
Mead's I-Me relationships, and Dewey's aesthetics of expression, children's
fondness for drawing and the creative process are theorized as a unique expression and experience wherein the self is fulfilled in a full, rich, and creative
process of meaning-making.

Significantly, I challenge the developmental and ideological assumptions
that consider children's drawing as simply something that they often do when
they are young and that it is "normal" to draw less as they age. Instead, I question why it is regarded as "normal" if such a rich and innovative semiotic

power dwindles or is largely replaced by another sign system as children advance in school. By analyzing what children have achieved in meaning-making through drawing, I compare and contrast the rich meanings conveyed and the materials used in their drawings that illustrate written texts. I argue that part of children's identity is gradually thwarted by acquiring the "legitimate" form of literacy in school. They may implicitly learn to think that what they can achieve and create by themselves through multiple sign systems is not important while accomplishing the schoolwork assigned by the teachers is far more significant in reaching the goal to become successful. Moreover, graphic literacy can be just as important as verbal literacy. This is especially true in today's world of computer technology and media culture.

Chapter Six accentuates the investigation on gender identity and re-examines how children construct gender under the conventional binary structure of female versus male. Other insights can be drawn from their ways of doing gender that deconstruct our stereotypical assumption that girls are subordinate to boys in the power structure, or that girls are submissive and boys are dominant. Based on Foucault and Butler's definition of gender as a cultural construct, I explore how the "body" serves as a primary site for doing gender in the children's world. Particularly, the meaning of physical size, appearance, and cultural materials and resources from media culture is applied differently in boys' and girls' worlds when establishing their charismatic power. Moreover, the gender division is strictly monitored by peer rules, particularly in the boys' world. In a sense, boys try hard to secure their male territory from the girls' invasion while girls actively attempt to break through the gender barrier. Another finding indicates that boys and girls exercise power differently when responding to the official authority in school: boys challenge the official authority while girls share the teacher's authority. The girls' compliance to the official standards is their major way of constructing identity as well as asserting power. The teacher is their most powerful "ally" in school when confronting boys.

Chapter Seven summarizes the findings and significance of each chapter, contributing to current knowledge in education as well as to identity theories. I place the children's versions of the "wonderful school day" they wish to have along with a summary of the study and thus provide a dialogic interaction between readers and these children, teachers and students, policymakers and those who struggle every day in school. It is also an invitation for all of us to contemplate the kind of educational institutions we create and the kind of learning environment these children want to have. Finally, a curriculum framework that supports children's identity construction has emerged from the study that invites researchers and educators to join the conversation for deepening our current understanding of the relationships among literacy learning, classroom culture and identity formation.

When you read Chris and Oliver's *A day in the classroom*, I invite you to read between the lines through my exploration and detailed documentation about different moments and structural aspects of children's school life. Before starting the journey of understanding children's identity construction, let me impart to you Ian's suggestion to the class before reading his story:

> *If you can't understand my story, just use your imagination.*

# CHAPTER ONE

# Understanding the Children's World

Field notes January 16, 2004 (9:30–9:45 A.M.)

While every child was writing and drawing in their D.O.D. journals as soon as they came into the classroom in the morning, Julia and Gina were helping the teacher pass out the children's graded math assignment. Ian and Peter were drawing monsters in their journals and discussing about what they did yesterday. Jeff was having an argument with Kate about who wrote better and faster. Bill and Chris were reading their books after they were done with their journal writing. Andy asked Tammy, "How do you spell 'shark'?" Suddenly, Mrs. Jones, one of the teachers, turned on the music, indicating that she was about to make an official announcement. After turning the music off, Mr. Smith, the other teacher, said, "Ok, that's a nice freeze. Oh, man! Oscar's still talking." The whole class was supposed to be quiet when they heard the music. Mrs. Jones announced, "It should be pin-drop quiet every morning. Ian, Edward, shh... Ok, let's put our D.O.D. journals away and quietly move to the rug. Let's start our morning jobs. The weather reporters? The poem readers? The number readers? The song leaders?" The children moved toward the rug area and those who were in charge of the morning jobs were ready. Several parents came in to help the teachers. Some helped them enter information into the computer; some cleaned and organized the books on the bookshelves; some checked the cubbies; some helped children read in the couch area. After the morning jobs were done, the whole class sat on the rug to construct a story web (i.e., a way of brainstorming ideas before writing) with Mrs. Jones. They also took turns reading with Mr. Smith on the other side of the classroom during the story web writing. On the rug area, Oscar crinkled his nose and said, "Whoa," indicating that there was a foul smell. Ted pinched his nostrils together with his fingers and said, "Somebody farted." The rest of the class giggled and covered their noses with their hands. Nick interrogated those sitting around him, "Was that you? You? You?" Tammy warned Nick, "That's very rude." Mrs. Jones stopped talking until everyone was quiet.....

As usual, it was a busy morning in Mrs. Jones and Mr. Smith's multi-aged (1st and 2nd grade) classroom. Within this 15-minute moment, my pen was flying through the lines of my notebook to jot down as much as I had observed in the classroom. A child, Tammy, peeked at my field notes and commented, "You have very bad handwriting." I concurred. Another child, Jeff, leaned forward to read my notes and asked, "What are you writing about?" I told him, "I am writing about your school life." "What! You are writing our school life?" he shouted as if he could not believe that there was someone who was interested in their school life. I said, "Yeah, I am..." Without letting me finish my sentence, Jeff continued persistently, "Why?" I explained to him that I wanted to know more about their school life and to learn from their school experience. Jeff concluded, "So you are writing a story about our school life." I nodded. Tammy asked, "Can I read your story?" I said, "Sure." She tried to decipher my wiggly sloppy handwriting that probably only I can understand.

Jeff was right that I would like to write a story about their school life, but the story was told by the children themselves. This study lasted two years in Mrs. Jones and Mr. Smith's multi-aged classroom with 45 1st and 2nd graders. The elementary school is located in a college town in the Midwest. All participant children are native speakers of English and most of them are Caucasian with the exception of one African American and three Asian children. I had many opportunities to talk with the parents about their children and got to know their family backgrounds when they were on their regular volunteer duty in the classroom. Most children come from middle or upper-middle class families. Some parents were university faculty; some were lawyers; some worked as doctors or nurses; some were school teachers.

It had been a wonderful opportunity for me to conduct the study in this classroom. I appreciate the classroom teachers' support for this research; their generosity and willingness to share their classroom life made the process of field entry easy for me. This class is an interesting research site to study because of its rich literacy activities, emphasis on collaboration among children, and strong community bonds in the curriculum design. The classroom is open for visitors (including parents, student teachers, researchers, guests, etc.) to come and join in the children's literacy activities. Many volunteers take turns coming to the classroom and help children read and write.

The teachers and many parents commented that this was a very busy classroom. "A lot of busy beavers" was the constant praise Mrs. Jones gave to the whole class to encourage the busy spirit in the classroom. Moving from area to area in the classroom, the children were busy doing different literacy activities throughout every school day. Some of these activities are assigned by the teachers and some are generated by the children themselves. Accompanying the different classroom activities is a mixture of various frictions, conflicts, arguments, jokes, playful teasing, and occasional mischief.

As Jeff interpreted, my study is composed of the children's stories of their school life. Collecting and understanding their stories is a rewarding journey strung with continuous challenges, difficulties, uncertainties, surprises, and excitements. In the following discussion, I would like to address four aspects of understanding the children's world:

(1) The theoretical constructs that guide the methodology of conducting the study
(2) The evolving process of entering the children's world
(3) Data collection
(4) Data analysis

## Theoretical Orientations

The theoretical matrices guiding the methodology of conducting this study include cultural studies, narrative inquiry, and critical ethnography. Each theoretical orientation addresses sociocultural issues through various dimensions of human interaction, cultural mediation, and discursive ideologies and thus provides multiple perspectives to understand the relationships between culture and agency as well as identity formation. I roughly sketch each theoretical orientation and explain how each provides methodological implications to this study.

### Cultural Studies

Cutting across issues of gender, class, race, cultural media, textuality, sexuality, ethnicity, and critical pedagogy, cultural studies has developed as a critical discipline to investigate the relationship among culture, power, politics, and knowledge. In terms of critical pedagogy, cultural studies attempts to challenge ideologies existing in educational institutions that create dominant forms of cultural capital, legitimate the usually stratified social identities, and silence the voices of those who are marginalized and oppressed (Giroux & Shannon, 1997). Moreover, cultural theorists also incorporate the hegemonic theory (Gramsci, 1977, sited from Morrow & Torres, 1995) as a way of interrogating the meaning of cultural texts that constitute public discourses and production of knowledge as well as identities that people are struggling with (Giroux, 2001). Holding a strong postmodern insight about human identity, Stuart Hall (1996a) asserts that the dislocation or decentering of the subject is the crisis of identity that constitutes social struggle within a cultural site. Trying to theorize this complex question of the postmodern incoherent self within this fragmented modern cultural landscape becomes one of the main tasks of cultural studies.

In terms of cultural production, as Kincheloe and McLaren (2002) suggest, cultural studies is "an interdisciplinary, transdisciplinary, and sometimes counter-disciplinary field that functions within the dynamics of competing definitions of culture" (p. 111). It seeks to detect the tacit rules that guide cultural production as well as to investigate the linkage between diverse forms of culture produced in different social contexts that affect our ways of living, thinking, and coordinating our interactions with each other. For instance, the representation of signs and images in cultural media through TV, video games, movies, advertisement, computers, and so forth has a profound impact on our way of meaning-making, communicating, shopping, reading, viewing, and learning. Thus, when studying children's school life, it is impossible to avoid the production of popular "kinderculture" because "education takes place in a variety of social sites" (Steinberg & Kincheloe, 1998, p. 4). The existence of the hyperreality and power in Disney (Giroux, 1998), Warner Brothers, and McDonald's and all kinds of game/toy companies produce fashion, pleasure, and desire that colonize children's consciousness, control their social identities, as well as diminish their reflective ability for critical thinking. Fiske (1998) also points out that " cultural studies attempts to be multilevel in its methodology and in particular to explore the interface between the structuring conditions that determine our social experience and the way of living that people devise within them" (p. 376). Thus, when studying children's school life, whether literacy activities or peer culture, cultural studies provides a methodology that peels off, layer by layer, permitting analysis of children's texts and actions, linking the meanings embedded in these texts to their identity construction and other socio-cultural phenomena that affirm their identities, and questioning the kind of world we make, consume, and live in.

## Narrative Inquiry

Following Bruner (1990, 2002) and Freeman (1993), narrative is a primary way that human beings construct order and make sense of their lives. Telling sequential stories is a way of using language to make meanings in our daily interaction with each other. Through narrative, human emotion, desire, memories, imagination, reasons, positioning of self and others, spatial regions, temporal sequences, cultural referents, and the like are all woven into a fabric of memory as well as life stories (Freeman, 2002; Josselson, 2004). Embodying self in stories told, narrative inquiry is one of the crucial ways to study human identity and subjectivity because its methodological orientation focuses on human agency and creativity through persons' interpretations of their life experiences. When people tell their stories, they "enact a characteristic type of self, and through [narrative self-construction], they can become that type of self" (Wortham, 2000, p. 157). As Widdershoven (1993) indicates, the implicit meaning of life experience is made explicit in the stories people tell; what they select to emphasize or to omit carries epistemological implication in exploring both the self and the identity.

In Wortham's (2000) study, he finds that his participant describes her life experience as a way to reinforce as well as recreate who she is by moving from "repeated victimization to active and even heroic self-assertion" (p. 181). When people tell stories about themselves, they construct a new and more fulfilling self in which their identities get established and maintained. Constructing a new and usually a positive self through narrative has applications in the field of counseling psychology and psychotherapy (Schaefer, 1992; Crossley, 2000). In Schrauf's (2000) study of three carnival directors' narratives about their experiences of losing the carnival contest, the three directors engage in the "narratives of identity repair" through repositioning themselves and others "in new plots that exonerate them and repair their threatened social identities" (p. 127).

In Hanninen's (2004) model of narrative circulation, three modes of narrative meaning structures are introduced: (1) the told narrative (the empirical phenomena: the symbolic representation, most often verbal, of a chain of human events); (2) the inner narrative (the narrative organization of experience in how we think, position, imagine, interact, and make moral choices); (3) the live narrative (the real life events containing the sequential quality of narrative—beginnings, middles, and ends). To summarize Hanninen's three narrative models, they aim to explore the relationships among people's narrative expression, internalized experience, and real life itself.

The implications drawn from narrative inquiry affect my study in two aspects: first, collecting the narrative data, and second, reconstructing counternarrative. One of the main purposes of the study is to explore children's identity formation in their school life. Thus, their narrative of school life becomes crucial data in understanding how self is constructed and manifested through their own versions of stories and what sorts of purposes or motivations are conditioning their storytelling (i.e., complaining, boasting, informing, teasing, clarifying, excusing, justifying, questioning, etc.). This also implies that the techniques of getting children to talk about themselves and share their stories are important when collecting narrative data. How much and how deeply one is able to understand children's school life depends on how well one can engage and encourage children to talk. For this reason, interviewing techniques are critical to gaining access to children's perception of themselves and their school life. One way of conducting a successful interview is to adopt the pattern of narratives that construct flexible interview questions and to then blend these questions into the natural flow of children's stories. I will explain more about interviewing skills in the section on data collection.

The second methodological implication for this study is related to data analysis, what many theorists call counter-narrative—that which is not told based upon what is told. In children's narration, they selectively jump from the past to the future or connect both to the present. They intentionally—

consciously or unconsciously—include and exclude parts of their life history and weave those chosen parts into the narrative fabric of self-representation. To put it more precisely, the absent parts of their life history in their narration may not be purposely excluded, but rather become the unreflective, habitual, taken-for-granted conventions that constitute their cultural horizon (Gadamer, 1982; Allen, 1993). As Allen (1993) suggests, "we make ourselves by how we use what is provided for us" (p. 37). This also echoes the critical insight of cultural studies that, in a sense, we are what we consume. Therefore, what children are provided for in school that establish their cultural horizon and condition their identity formation are the implicit aspects of their narrative that the researcher wants to reveal and contemplate.

The idea of counter-narrative is also connected to processes of resisting culture that people, particularly those who are oppressed, develop to challenge the dominant cultural narrative (Andrews, 2002), resist the pain of exclusion, and thus empower themselves through constructing positive identities in a distorted way. In other words, counter-narratives implicitly told by children provide us with different versions of the same story, and thus, may suggest the embedded version of "truth."

## Critical Ethnography

The theory of critical ethnography by Carspecken (1996, 1999, 2001, 2002, 2003) brings the concepts of culture, power (in cultural studies), resistance, positioning, and counter-narrative (in narrative inquiry) into another level of understanding. All these concepts are dimensions of meaningful actions in which human identities are embedded. As Carspecken (2002) implies, the ultimate goal of conducting research is to not only articulate the power relations that produce a certain cultural form for maintaining actors' identities but to also try to reveal human needs and motivations behind their actions that constitute a reciprocal relationship "between institutional orders and self-maintaining, self-adapting systems" (p. 26). I will briefly summarize Carspecken's reformulation of the praxis theory based upon Willis's (1977) *Learning to Labour*, an ethnographic study that provides a profound approach to penetration of human actions, cultural production, and identity formation.

In Willis's ethnographic study, working-class youth develop and produce their own counter-school culture, which gives them both recognition and pride as members of their working-class community. Not only does their resistance affirm their working-class status, but also, more importantly, their action is oriented toward constructing positive identities for maintaining their dignity (Carspecken, 1996, 1999). In this sense, their resistance to power unintentionally produces and reproduces their working-class culture, which in turn reinforces that culture, creating a dialectic responding to the external conditions and environments (i.e., the social constraints) as well as to their internal social needs (i.e., a sense of belonging and being recognized).

Carspecken's reformulated theory of praxis, therefore, provides an added level of understanding of the internal relation between power and praxis that relocates the postmodern and post-structural notion of power. That is, power structures manifested through economic relations, political institutions, and dominant cultural ideologies constitute the conditions of human actions. Yet those who are marginalized in a cultural site would develop and produce their own subcultures to maximize the few opportunities available to them for self-expression and a positive sense of self. This act of producing their own subcultures for maintaining positive identities is the act of power and the driving force motivated by human needs and desires to be recognized by others. By placing power within human agency, this reformulated praxis theory keeps postmodern and post-structural themes while reconceptualizing notions of power and subjectivity. Moreover, the reformulated praxis theory offers a "nonocular-centric theory of knowledge" (Carspecken, 2002, p. 67) that avoids the error of simply applying metaphors based on visual perception in concepts of knowledge, which reside in both traditional mainstream epistemologies and the post-structural critique of them.

Drawing from Husserl's (1962, 1970) phenomenology and Derrida's (1973) deconstruction, we may conclude that truth is unattainable through visual perception or any subject-object relationship. The idea of "observation" prevalently used in most research methodologies is actually more related to our experience through actions than to visual perception. Husserl's analysis of subject-object forms of knowing phenomenologically displayed the extent to which things are *added* to perceptual knowledge through what he called unconscious synthetic activities of consciousness. This problematizes observation-based knowledge to a certain extent but Husserl took "presence" for granted. Derrida (1967/1978) deconstructed presence, partly by showing that we never have an object of knowledge present to consciousness at the same time that we *know* we do. Carspecken's critical ethnography also rejects the belief in presence, regarding it to be an unreachable limit case in three central epistemological relations: self to objective world, self to other selves, and self to self. Carspecken's use of communicative action over subject-object relationships in epistemology draws upon Habermas's theory of the internal relation between validity claims and meaning

Moreover, the reformulated theory of praxis elucidates the dialectic between structure and agency and broadens Marx's praxis theory that is based solely on the materialist orientation of self-production (e.g., the human praxis need for self-expression and self-maintenance is expressed in the production of material objects). Praxis is expanded to self-production through social relations mediated by culture rather than limited to material production. Simply put, cultural structures provide stability as well as resources for people's actions, which are in part motivated by praxis needs. At the same time, people also bring changes into their existing cultural structures and add new elements. The relationship between cultural structures and human agency is like a circulating loop in which cultural structures condition and resource people's actions and people's actions contribute new substances to the existing cultural structures (also see Giddens 1984, pp. 281–348).

Carspecken believes that most human actions contain a "motivating 'identity claim'" that is "praxis or praxis-relevant" (p. 65). Moreover, "human-to-human relations are most immediately involved in praxis; the need to produce a self through social relations and the desire for recognition that is attendant to this need" (p. 64). These praxis needs, thus, constitute the motivational structures of communicative action for the emergence of a self. This "motivating identity claim" deepens Habermas's (1984) theory of communicative action in terms of the three ontological relations (subjective, objective, and normative) embedded in each speech act.

By applying Carspecken's critical epistemology, this study not only seeks to explore children's identities from their routine actions in school, their versions of life stories, and their resisting counter-narrative to the dominant values, but it also aims to investigate why they position themselves in a certain fashion, why they choose one way over the other to solve their problems, what motivations underlie their assertive acts, and what sorts of meaning embedded in their actions constitute their sense of self. Moreover, the problems in current educational institutions, the systems that condition these problems in the cultural site, and the kind of society we create and live in are reflected through the individual child's life experiences, stories, and actions. Ultimately, the purpose of this study is to link the micro-level findings in this classroom to the macro-level socio-cultural structures, challenge the current knowledge of education, and explore other possibilities for improving our schooling.

# Entering the Children's World

## The Process of Exploring, Noticing, and Surprising

Entering the children's world is a long process, and it requires patience, perseverance, respect, and sensitivity to get to know them as different individuals, understand their culture as a whole, and be accepted in their world. However, studying children is peculiarly difficult because of physical, social, cognitive, and political differences between children and adults (Graue & Walsh, 1998; Holmes, 1998; Lancy, 2001). Adult researchers are never fully accepted into the children's world, but this does not mean that children are not capable of sharing their experience with adults or that adults cannot understand the children's world. Gaining access to the children's culture requires special ways; finding these ways is at the core of collecting valuable data. After data collection, making trustworthy analysis is the next responsibility. I roughly divide this process into three parts: (1) sketching the process of getting to know the participant children—*Getting Hermeneutically Prepared*, (2) finding ways to minimize my adult status in the children's world—*Encountering the Unexpected*, and (3) taking cues from the children's discourse when interacting with them—*Noticing the Unnoticed*.

1. *Getting Hermeneutically Prepared*: Before having direct contact with the children, I prepared myself through exposure to typical "kids' culture," particularly pop culture, such as cartoons, video games, toys, and child-related media culture. It is like reading a travel guide about a new place before the trip. However, I consider myself to have a certain advantage in understanding the children's pop culture, because I have collected comic books, especially Japanese *manga*. I am also familiar with video games and other media products imported from Japan. When I watched Cartoon Network, many of the Japanese cartoons were not new to me (i.e., Pokemon, Dragon Ball Z, InuYasha, etc.). I also got to know many American cartoons, such as Scooby Doo, Powerpuff Girls, Dexter's Laboratory, Sponge Bob, and so on.

The purpose of this kind of hermeneutic preparation is to reduce the communicative barrier between the children and me. By having this preparation, I am more ready to understand what might appear in the children's conversations, which may increase the possibility for me to join their conversations. In fact, this hermeneutic readiness for kids' culture does help me in some way to connect with them and understand what I have observed in this class. One example is when I saw Peter drawing on his table. He drew a human figure that looked very similar to the character Gokuu in the cartoon Dragonball Z. I asked him, "Are you drawing Gokuu?" He stared at me for a while and seemed surprised. Then he asked me, "Did you watch it [Dragon Ball Z] yesterday? Gokuu fought with this monster uh I forgot." I answered, "You mean Majin Buu?" He replied excitedly, "Oh, yeah. Majin Buu and Baby Buu." And we continued discussing the details of it.

Examples such as this are many. Being familiar with kids' media culture helped me know how they applied it in their daily interaction and literacy activities. This also allowed me to laugh with the children when someone was imitating a particular cartoon character. Getting hermeneutically prepared is helpful in the early stages of data collection. Knowing what children know builds up the channel to learn what I do not know yet about them.

2. *Encountering the Unexpected*: The previous section discusses how I prepare for entering the children's world; this part reveals those situations for which I am not able to prepare in advance. As I indicated in the beginning of this chapter, studying children is challenging and exciting. It is challenging because children are more unpredictable emotionally, intellectually, and socially compared to adults. It is also exciting for the same reason because this unpredictability leads me toward many aspects of children's life that I was not aware of and thus deepens my understanding about children's world. Moreover, I notice that I am, vis-à-vis the children, not only the observer, but also the observed. This helps me see the reciprocal process involved in building up relationships between the children and me. I will share two unexpected events in the early stages of my observation to show how I get to know the children more and how children get to know me in their own way.

The first event happened when recess ended at 12:30. Because I spent recess time talking to the teachers to clarify my observations and to finish my field notes, I quickly grabbed my chocolate cookies and was about to start eating. Two children, Nicole and Oscar, ran into the classroom from the playground and saw me eating cookies. Nicole pointed to my cookies and yelled, "Oh, we are not supposed to bring snacks to school and eat in the classroom." Oscar concurred, "Yeah, the teachers say we cannot bring candy or cookies to school unless it's your birthday or there is a party." For a moment, I stopped chewing and stood there with one cheek bulging with cookies and one hand holding the unfinished cookie. I was not prepared for this accusation. Nor did I know the rule of no food in the classroom. Without knowing what to do, Nicole suddenly held her palm facing up toward me and asked, "Can I have one?" Oscar followed her and asked, "Can I have one, too?" I gave them each a cookie. They dashed into the closet and closed the closet door. I could hear them giggle inside.

Another event happened when I had a Ricola cough drop. Kate came to me and said, "I smell something minty. What are you eating?" I told her that it was a cough drop not candy. She replied with several coughs, "I also feel a bit of pain in my throat." I explained that cough drop might not be suitable for children under age six as indicated in the warning section of the bag. Kate insisted, "I can eat it. I am seven years old now." Again, not knowing what to do, I gave her one. She opened her pocket and leaned toward me with her eyes looking around the classroom as if indicating that I should "secretly" put the cough drop inside her pocket. When I put it in, she patted and pressed her pocket as if making the bulge in the pocket lie flat.

These two events show that first, I am observed, and second, my role is defined by the children in their own way. One thing that I am aware of is that my adult status seems to carry little authority that would threaten their "private" activities. My presence as an adult in the children's world does not seem to intervene in what they usually do among themselves. The children acknowledge my adult status but they treat me according to their rules in the children's world. Nicole and Oscar are surprised to see me violating the rule, and yet they do not really want to accuse me for this mischief. Instead, they want to "join" me, as they usually do in their peer world. Kate negotiates the cough drop with me and feels safe to do so with me because she knows that I am different from the teachers. My unintentional violation of the classroom rule in some way connects with these children and brings me closer to understanding the children's culture.

3. *Noticing the Unnoticed:* In the early stages of the study, I spent most of my time recording the class routines and paid much attention to the physical or tangible artifacts in the classroom. After becoming familiar with the classroom routines, environment, and concrete artifacts, I shifted my attention from the visible to the invisible, making a move from passive observation to active participation in the classroom. Building up good relationships with the children is crucial to accomplish this transition.

Noticing the implicit rules operating in the children's culture is critical for entering their world. This is what I call noticing the unnoticed: to notice the ways children interact among themselves that are usually not obvious to adults. Once these rules are discerned, they become channels leading to the children's world. Here I list three kinds of channels that brought me closer to the children's culture:

(1) Sharing: Sharing is a common interactive way and a major norm in school. It is also each child's responsibility as a member of the classroom to share their works, knowledge, ideas, and opinions with each other in both formal class contexts and in private activities among peers. Most children like to share and some are even eager to share. There is a "sharing time" block in which the children are allowed to bring their favorite toys, interesting collections, or something meaningful for them to school and share with the whole class.

Sharing is also one way that many children express themselves and connect with each other in the class. To enter their world, I adopt the norm of sharing and the first thing I share with the children is what I had been doing in the classroom. Fasoli (2003) argues that making research practices more transparent to children can assist them to participate more effectively in the research. Children are eager and competent to help construct the research practices. They are collaborators rather than mere subjects in the research. Whenever they came to me and checked my field notes, I let them know what I wrote in my notebook. Many children enjoyed reading my notes. One time, Ted opened my notebook and read aloud to the other children:

9:30–10:00     *Poem reader (My Tooth in Loothe)*
               *Two song leaders*
               *The writing workshop demonstration*
               *The authors talked about their favorite book Harry Potter*
10:00–10:30    *Team reading and group interactive reading with Mr. Smith*

They liked to read my notes because they were familiar with these routines. Checking my field notes became part of the routine interaction between the children and me. They sometimes gave me suggestions about what I should include in my field notes. Julia reminded me, "You should write about our field trip to the zoo. It's called Exotic Feline Rescue Center." Vivian said, "Oh, yeah, my mom will come with me." Max added, "We donated money to the Rescue Center." I was well informed by the children about what was going to happen in this classroom and also about what they deemed important and interesting in their school life.

They were also curious about my tape recorder. I explained to them that it was a device to help me remember things that I was not able to write down immediately. Ian nodded and said, "I write slowly, too." Edward joined our conversations and said, "I can write very fast. I write like shooooo..." He made this flying jet sound to describe how fast he could write. Ian argued, "No, you don't write fast. You spent like two hours to finish your column." The two started arguing. Instances such as this provided me an opportunity to observe and know more about children's peer culture.

My tape recorder seemed to be personified by the children as someone they could interact with. Jeff pressed his ears against the tape recorder and then said "hi" to it. Ian examined it for a while and then moved it closer to his mouth and said, "Hello, my name is Ian." He laughed aloud. Edward also leaned forward toward the recorder and said, "Hi, I am Edward. My favorite color is green." Jeff grabbed the recorder and placed it in front of his mouth, "Hi, my name is Jeff. I have an identical twin brother. His name is Nick." They were excited to record their voices and played with my tape recorder until the teachers nudged them to do their work.

The children got used to me writing in my field notes and carrying the tape recorder with me whenever I was in the classroom. Some of them even reminded me, "Your batteries are almost dead," when they saw the battery indicator blinked. The initial sharing between the children and me is the icebreaker that eliminates their confusion about my work in the classroom. At the same time, making my work transparent to the children also in some sense engages them to participate and helps to co-construct the research practices.

(2) Drawing: Drawing is another specific way of sharing among children that I notice in their everyday life. The children love to draw. They draw in their journals, their pen pal letters, their storybooks, and any piece of paper they can get in the classroom. "I am gonna draw a tank," Ian claimed and started drawing on a piece of paper. His neighbor Peter put his pencil down and walked toward Ian. "Let me see," Peter said. Then they began talking about all sorts of weapons, military bases, and the war movies they had seen. "I'll draw a big gigantic monster that can smash any tanks and jets," Peter claimed. Ian said, "Ok, your monster can join my army force." Then they continued drawing more and talking more about their cooperative plan. The Pokemon fans in this class constantly get together and draw their own version of Pokemon. Some girls like to draw their imaginative fairies and some like to draw their family members. There are also children who love to "draw" their stories. Through drawing, they build up friendships and form their own peer groups.

Children share their fantasies and imagination through drawing. They like to show each other their pictures and tell each other the stories contained in their pictures. Noticing drawing as a common social event among the children, I start drawing with them, first, to build up closer relationship with them, second, to understand how children use drawing to interact with each other and third, to understand drawing as an important part of their text construction (see Chapter Five for more discussion). Drawing seemed to be the fun part of many literacy activities. In their dinosaur project, each child gathered information and drew dinosaurs to make their dinosaur book. I too did the project and shared my dinosaur sketches with the children. Many children gathered around me and checked my sketch pad during the project time. I was often surrounded by a lot of dinosaur experts and amazed by their knowledge of prehistoric life. They showed me their dinosaur books and how they compiled information from the library, the Internet, and their own book collections. They borrowed my color pencils, markers, erasers, and sometimes even a piece of paper from my sketch pad. They liked to see me sketching and I listened to them talking about dinosaurs, themselves, their imagination, and their school life.

(3) The secret spots: Children tend to behave differently in the adults' presence to avoid interference with their activities. These activities are usually carried out secretly by children either individually or with their peers. Finding out the particular regions in the classroom where the children carry out their private activities is challenging because they do not want to be seen. I respect their privacy and observe their secret activities only from a certain distance. Most of them are not afraid of letting me know their private activities. Some of their secret spots are the places where I interview the children. Before interviewing, I usually ask them, "Do you know any good place to talk?" They would choose a place where "nobody would listen to us." This helps to engage them to talk freely and express their feelings safely.

The following are some of the children's secret spots during reading time that I observed one afternoon. Instead of reading, some children were finding places to do their own things. Ted and Andy hid under the teacher's desk and talked. Sally, Michelle, and Winnie sneaked into the closet. They tried out different kinds of hand lotion in their backpacks and then commented on different fragrances. After a while, they came out of the closet with their book opened and pretended as if nothing had happened. Meanwhile, Winnie hid behind the couch. She carefully opened the little purse that she carried around her neck and took out a glowing lipstick. She applied it on her lips as if quickly drawing a circle and then put it back in her purse. Allen and Pat were under the fish tank discussing their collection of Yugioh cards. Then, they moved toward the closet. Allen saw me observing. He put his finger in front of his mouth and said to me, "Shh." In the closet, he opened his backpack and showed Pat the Yugioh cards he collected. Pat whispered, "You are supposed to wait until sharing time." Allen replied, "I know. Shh..." Later, Allen explained to me, "We cannot bring any toys to school, but I did not take my cards out." He defended his action and claimed that he did not break the rule yet as long as the Yugioh cards stayed in his backpack.

These secret spots—under the table, behind the couch, in the closet and inside the backpack—are usually places where children negotiate privacy, appropriate the classroom rules, and enjoy the risks of doing their own things in school. Noticing what they do in these places also contributes to my understanding of children's school "underlife," which reflects the other side of "truth" about their school experience. I will discuss these back-regional settings more in Chapter Three.

(4) My *Shifting Roles*: The relationships between the children and me continue to change, and my role, too, shifts as our relationships change. I roughly divide the process of how my roles have evolved into three stages. At the first stage, I was more or less like a classroom guest and a stranger. There was limited interaction (i.e., eye contact, smiles) between us. I was a passive observer documenting and familiarizing myself with the children's school routines. Several months later, we started to interact more through talking and sharing. Besides doing my fieldwork, I volunteered to help the children with math and writing, but I did not take on an active role. Rather, the children came and asked me to help them. Our relationships are more than merely the researcher-participant rapport. Thus, the second stage of my role is like an adult friend for most of the children. It is similar to Corsaro's (1985) *reactive role* or Mandell's (1988) *least adult role* in their studies.

After building up friendship with them, I was gradually accepted in the children's world. At the same time, my adult role was under constant challenge from the children. Some children invented a word and asked me to spell it. When I said I never heard of that word, they would laugh and show me how to spell it. Sometimes, they would tease me about things I do not know in children's culture. One time, Max told me he got three "Musketeers" from his neighbor. I asked him, "What's that?" Max was surprised that I did not know what "Musketeers" was and quickly spread the word among the other children.

In a sense, my adult role is an incapable one in the children's world, but that does not mean that they treat me without respect. They can understand that I do not know everything about their culture. Some gaps between children and adults are expected in the children's world. Moreover, studying children does not mean that the adult researcher needs to behave like a child or become a child. Rather, the adult researcher applies the children's ways to understand and explore their routine actions without intrusion. In the later stage of the study, especially during interviews, I found that my somehow incapable adult role provided some advantages, for I was easily exonerated from asking naïve questions, requesting detailed explanations, and inquiring about concrete examples in the children's school life.

At the third stage, my role changed from a passive observer to an active participant in the classroom. I was involved in and invited to join their class activities, such as watching their drama performance, joining their music concert, participating in various parties (i.e., pizza, Halloween, birthday, Valentine's Day, etc.), and going for field trips. I also joined the school-wide activity Reading Across America, in which the children and I wore our pajamas, and brought our sleeping bags or blankets to school for a non-stop reading day. My role as a researcher was pushed more and more into the background as my relationships with the children were getting closer.

# Data Collection

I like Graue and Walsh's (1998) vivid description of the researcher's routines during data collection: The researcher "must go out and look and listen and soak and poke and do it all again and again" (p. xiv). Spradley (1980) uses "explorer" as a metaphor to illustrate an ethnographer who tries to "map a wilderness area …begin with a general problem … identify the major features of the terrain… [gather] information, [go] first in one direction, then perhaps [retrace] that route, [and] then [start] out in a new direction" (p. 26). Their description as well as metaphor suggests that collecting data is labor-intensive because it requires researchers to "look in avoided places and in unfamiliar ways" (Graue & Walsh, 1998, p. xvi). Exploring avoided places through unfamiliar ways usually leads to finding out new questions. During data collection, there are two interrelated processes: (1) forming new questions and (2) adjusting ways of finding out possible answers to new questions. I will briefly discuss each process in terms of how it relates to the kinds of data I collect as well as some techniques involved.

## Forming New Questions

Forming new questions involves revising the old ones. This process, in a sense, is very much related to Carspecken's (1996) critical methodology in compiling the primary record with "thick description" of the cultural site in the early stages of the research. Forming new questions is exciting and yet contains a great uncertainty. New phenomena and/or unexpected situations continuously emerge that challenge my previous assumptions about children's school life and expands my views, thus encouraging me to examine my old beliefs. My research questions start from simply exploring the children's literacy activities and then go on to reconceptualizing literacy—as discursive social practices, ways of language use, as well as means for constructing identities—and uncovering the meaning of their school routine through their perceptions. This organic process starts from one question as a seed. It continues to grow, branch out, and reach multiple layers of the children's school life; it then develops diverse perspectives in understanding their concerns and incorporates various social contexts involved in their complex school experiences. As Gadamer (1982) indicates,

> [T]he horizon of the present is conceived in constant formation insofar as we must all constantly test our prejudices...the horizon of the present does not take shape at all without the past...understanding is always a process of the fusing of such alleged horizons existing in themselves... For there old and new grew together again and again in living value without the one or the other ever being removed explicitly. (p. 289).

This continuous accumulation and fusion of the new and the old constitute my comprehensive understanding of the children's world. New questions generated in the process require new ways to finding answers.

## Finding Out Possible Answers to New Questions

Once the new questions emerge, the ways of finding out possible answers to these questions need to be adjusted as well. Simply collecting children's literacy artifacts, recording their literacy activities, or observing the explicit classroom routine is not enough to understand the deep structure of their school culture and the meaning of constructing their identities. Thus, it is necessary to explore the new and implicit territory in the classroom where children's camouflaged actions and the embedded problems are derived.

Data that would provide more direct access to the children's perceptions, become crucial as well. Interviewing children is one way to find out possible answers to new questions. Interviewing young children, however, is difficult and demands a lot of practice and patience. The major techniques involved include asking children comprehensible questions, restating and clarifying children's seemingly contradictory statements during the conversations, and, the most important of all, maintaining great flexibility to improvise whenever possible. Children's linguistic abilities vary and their ways of processing information or interpreting the interview questions are very different from that of adults. This also means that not every interview question works for every child or that it may work very differently from what the researcher has expected. Therefore, flexibility and improvisation presuppose what the researcher has planned for interviews. This includes: (1) adjusting the questions as soon as sensing children's difficulty in understanding these questions, and (2) allowing children to digress from the questions.

One thing that I found difficult when interviewing young children at the beginning was that, because I focused so much on what I wanted to know, I forgot about what the children wanted to say about their school experience. After all, the ultimate goal of conducting interviews is to get deep understanding about children's life through their perceptions. Interview questions function only as a rough plan to achieve that goal. Researchers should not get stuck in their own structured questions.

Moreover, some children are not used to interacting through a formal structured way. For instance, Kate and I built up a good friendship, but she does not want to be interviewed in a one-on-one situation. Rather, she likes to talk and draw with me and seems to feel more comfortable to interact in a natural classroom setting. Thus, the interviewing data I collected are not just children's conversations but also informal talks and drawings. Furthermore, paying attention to the interview setting is crucial for some children. As I mentioned in the previous section, some children choose their comfort zones (their secret spots) in school during interviews. I also tried out doing pair or group interviews in which two or more children are interviewed together. Usually, they would like to be interviewed together with their friends and help each other answer the questions. Of course, sometimes, they would argue during interviews, which not only provided rich information about their complex school life but also helped me notice other questions that I was not aware of.

Despite the difficulties and skills involved in conducting interviews with young children, the process is fruitful and rewarding. After conducting the first interview, I was constantly asked by many children, "When are you gonna interview me again?" Some even made an appointment with me on a specific date for their interviews. I ended up interviewing them more than I had planned to. They are eager to talk about themselves, and I can sense their joy when they talk about themselves and share their experiences.

I would like to conclude this section by summarizing my interview experience and other child specialists' insightful suggestions (Poole & Lamb, 1998; Zwiers & Morrissette, 1999; Wilson & Powell, 2001; Daniel, Beaumont, & Doolin, 2002) in conducting interviews with young children:

(a) Beware of adult assumptions that might prevent us from understanding children's social meanings in their world.
(b) Try to adopt the language of the child and keep the level of questioning accessible.
(c) Use semi-structured interviews with more open-ended questions and allow digressions.
(d) Be careful not to overreact to their responses, either positively or negatively, so that it will reduce potential effects from the interviewer's behaviors.

(e) Encourage children to use alternative ways they feel comfortable with to express what they intend to say, such as demonstrating with actions, drawing, or singing.
(f) Pay attention to physical setting when conducting interviews. For instance, talking privately with a child will yield different answers from talking publicly.
(g) Be a good listener (also see Carspecken, 1996).

In this section, I reviewed ways of data collection and emphasize the techniques of interviewing young children. I would like to use Graue and Walsh's (1998) insight as the conclusion for this section that best depicts the process of data collection:

> Learning how to observe and how to interview means beginning with the basics and learning them and then practicing them until one can do them without thinking, then just doing fieldwork. (p. 102)

# Data Analysis

Exploring identity construction is core to understanding a specific cultural milieu as well as different systems that constitute the society in which we live and coordinate our relationships with each other in the complex social network. Any research that explores cultural influences and formation cannot ignore identities people hold in a particular cultural site because these identities entail people's beliefs, values, and life experiences that are structured by a particular set of norms that consent, constrain, as well as support how people come to being. Carspecken's critical epistemology attempts to unpack issues of cultural oppression, power relations, and action motivations that are intrinsically linked to the issues of identity formation. In the following discussion, I explain the analytical tools and use a piece of data as an example to elaborate how each tool is used in data analysis. I divide the discussion of data analysis into two parts: first, the hermeneutic-reconstructive analysis; second, the system analysis. In this study, I minimize system analysis and concentrate on hermeneutic analysis because of the difficulties of full systems analysis in terms of time.

## Hermeneutic–Reconstructive Analysis

From many possible methods and concepts associated with hermeneutic-reconstructive analysis, I will focus on five: (1) meaning fields, (2) horizon analysis, (3) interactive power analysis, (4) body posture analysis, and (5) role analysis. I use the following excerpt in the study to demonstrate how each technique is carried out in reconstructing the meaning of an act:

**Kate**: Is this how "kasum" is supposed to be? (Kate asked me).
**Pat**: No. I know how to spell it (Pat was about to show her).
**Kate**: I am not asking you (Kate raised her voice, smacked the paper, and covered the word).
**Pat**: It is wrong.
**Kate**: So what? I know how to fix it.

1. *Meaning Fields*: The first step of meaning reconstruction is to articulate a range of possible meanings that an act may obtain. This is usually done mentally as an aid in coding, although it can be done explicitly. It is a stage of uncertainty as well as ambiguity in which researchers strive to familiarize themselves with their research site and differentiate the cultural typifications they employ to understand their participants and the participants' cultural typifications in the site. This is a hermeneutic process in which researchers position themselves with regard to their participants in understanding their meaningful acts. The process includes: (a) intersubjective understanding, (b) reflecting different norms applied by researchers and their participants and refining researchers' typifications to attain a more accurate understanding from the participants' position, (c) differentiating the highly individualized factors from the general cultural milieu in the site. Table 1-1 illustrates how meaning fields are constructed based on the above excerpt between two children, Kate and Pat.

---

Kate seems to express her anger and rejects Pat's help.
And she feels hurt by Pat.
And she doesn't want any help from other children.
And/or she rejects other's help because she refuses to be positioned as one who needs help.
Or she wants to show that she can handle the problems by herself.
Or she interprets Pat's action as if "You are making fun of me"
Or "You are showing off"

---

**Table 1-1 Example of Meaning Fields**

Using "and," "or," and "and/or" statements in constructing meaning fields is to show, on the one hand, the inconsistency between the researcher's interpretation and the participant's own meaning of the act, and to indicate, on the other hand, the ambiguity that all people, not just researchers, experience when understanding meanings, which always contain a range of possibilities. In exploring participants' identity formation, constructing meaning fields of their actions is important to the process of articulating all possible identities drawn by them, how their cultural typifications enable these identities, as well as how researchers revise their interpretive scheme in order to get the "insider's view." Moreover, reconstructing meanings by articulating a range of possible meanings will clarify researchers' biases, unfamiliar cultural typifications, and tacit assumptions applied by researchers and participants that are crucial to further data analysis. Understanding the "field" feature of meaning also enables the research to grasp how misunderstandings can occur between people, how intentional multiple meanings are sometimes conveyed, and many other aspects of everyday communicative practices.

*2. Horizon Analysis:* Horizon analysis is an intensive process and an effort of meaning reconstruction that brings the meaning of an act "into new levels of precision" (Carspecken, 1996, p. 103). Besides being intensive, it is an effort because it attempts to articulate the holistic experience as well as the implicit impressions of a meaning so deeply rooted in our everyday interactions that they are often taken for granted.

According to Carspecken (1996, 2001), the structure of the pragmatic horizon is constituted by two axes, the paradigmatic axis and the temporal axis. The temporal axis shows how the meaning of an act is carried out and how it might evolve based on our shared understanding and expectation. A single meaningful act results in an understanding of possible meanings only against assumptions about assumedly shared interpretations of events just past, and assumedly shared expectations of events just to come. The paradigmatic axis includes the semantic meaning structures (i.e., words, sentences, phrases) and pragmatic meaning structures (i.e., tone of voice, speech pace, facial expression, humor, registers, gestures). Moreover, the validity reconstruction attempts to make the implicit meanings of an act explicit through two dimensions of the interpretive scheme: (a) the vertical continuous axis from the highly backgrounded meaning to the most foregrounded, and (b) the horizontal discrete axis categorized into four types of validity claims (i.e., subjective, objective, normative, and identity).

As Carspecken (1996) explains, when we notice a certain object, we perceive it "against many other objects that are out of focus" (p. 103). We see the object through the contrast between that object and other objects in its background. Applying this notion metaphorically to the validity reconstruction, we understand a claim to be foregrounded and brought forth through contrasting it with our backgrounded experiences and knowledge that we assume to be common sense and expect other people to understand. Thus, a background is a deep set of assumptions taken for granted while a foreground is emphasized as the most immediate and explicit meaning put forth by actors in an act.

The horizontal axis attempts to apply the "intersubjective assumptions about how others in first, second, and third person positions could experience the act" (Carspecken, 1996, p. 103). Plus, based upon the reformulated praxis theory (Carspecken, 2002, 2003), the identity claim is the fourth dimension of the meaning horizon in understanding human praxis needs and motivations embedded in the act. Table 1-2 shows the horizon analysis of Kate's act.

---

**Possible Subjective Claims** (claims based on privileged access):
Foregrounded:
I am not happy about being told that I am wrong.
I am angry.

Less foregrounded:
I don't think that you are trying to help.
I don't want to be corrected.
I don't need your help.

Background:
I feel hurt and offended.
I know what I am doing.
I want to be in control.
I am sensitive when being corrected.

**Possible Objective Claims** (claims open to multiple access):
Foregrounded:
It is writing time in the classroom.
Children can ask for help when they need to.

Less foregrounded:
Some children work alone and some work together.

Background:
Children have different attitudes toward helping each other.

**Possible Normative Claims** (claims based on intersubjectivity):
Foregrounded:
One should not correct the other if one is not asked to.
It is rude to tell people that they are wrong.
Less foregrounded:
It is impolite to correct people in public.
It is important to ask people if they need help before doing so.

Backgrounded:
People should respect each other.
Helping others is not always appreciated.

**Possible Identity Claims:**
I am a capable writer who knows how to solve my problem.
I am the kind of person who is in charge of my learning.
I am a tough person who does not accept the other's help.

**Table 1-2 Example of Horizon Analysis**

3. *Interactive Power Analysis:* All actions, as Carspecken (1996) argues, are forms of power in that they "'intervene' in the stream of events and therefore 'make a difference,' no matter how large or small" (p. 128). However, acts of power differ in form and effect when fulfilling actors' goals. According to Carspecken (1996) and Weber (1978), there are four types of interactive power relations: (a) normative power, (b) coercive power, (c) contractual power, and (d) charismatic power. Each power relation is intrinsically tied with the cultural milieu that legitimates power as part of the norms functioning in a particular cultural site. Carspecken reinterprets Weber's categories of interactive power in terms of limit cases involved in blockages or shortcuts to fully attained consent on norms, statuses, rules and beliefs. Actual instances of power in human interaction are usually complex and involve a number of these limit-case types simultaneously.

In conducting data analysis, power analysis is important to understand the cultural norms that govern people's actions, support their belief systems, and condition their identity construction. Power functions as both means and ends, enabling as well as constraining one's action. It is enabling in motivating one's will to act and to make any necessary changes. It is constraining in that acts of power are monitored under a set of cultural rules, thus constraining forms and choices of power that one can have. Power analysis provides a useful framework in reconstructing different forms of power and structural components of culture and meaning.

To analyze the power relations between Kate and Pat following the previous example, Pat initiated the conversation by offering his help. Underlying his statement are two claims: (a) I am a nice person who likes to help people; (b) I am good at spelling and I should help those who need help in spelling. The first claim is a kind of charismatic power in terms of his personality and willingness to help the other; the second one is related to normative power under the rubric that the capable students should help the less capable ones. This is a major norm in this class during literacy team works (see more discussion in Chapter Three). However, Pat's help was completely rejected by Kate. For Kate, Pat's help is more like a threat to her. Her statements contain coercive and normative power claims to fight against the threat she felt. She forced Pat to step outside of her business. Eventually, Pat conceded to avoid further argument. Moreover, Kate also applied normative power to inform Pat that it was impolite to offer help without her consent. Plus, it is rude to correct people in public.

*4. Body Postures Analysis*: Body postures include the previously mentioned pragmatic meaning structures (i.e., tone of voice, speech pace, facial expression, body movement, gestures, register, etc.). Also, the interactive rhythm, setting shifts, and bidding a floor all contribute to the holistic meaning expressed through a body movement. People make claims not only through linguistic and sign systems, but also through gestures. Analyzing actors' body postures is another important clue in grasping the holistic meaning during interaction.

In Kate's reaction to Pat, we can see that her body postures changed when Pat persistently intended to "help" her: smacking the paper on the desk, pulling her paper away immediately, covering her spelling, raising her tone of voice, etc. All these postures help us understand Kate's act and reinforce the meaning she tried to communicate.

*5. Role Analysis*: Role analysis, according to Carspecken (1996), is a "secondary concept" because, in the case of studying human identity, it is applied to articulate actors' only very temporarily situated identities, which is "risky and will never fully capture what role is" (p. 136). Nonetheless, it is a useful tool in understanding roles that actors are playing from moment to moment during interaction and in different contexts.

Stryker's identity theory (1980/2002, 1994, 2000; Stryker & Burke, 2000; Stryker & Vryan, 2003) provides a useful concept in conceptualizing actors' social roles. He asserts that identity salience is the structural feature of one's role identities. The mechanism determining this hierarchy of identity salience is the degree of one's commitment to one's role identities: the higher the commitment to the role, the more salient the degree of one's role is in the hierarchy of one's role identities. Stryker (1994) uses an example to illustrate this concept:

> I have many relationships to many others important to me by virtue of being a professor; I am highly committed to that role. Because I am highly committed to the role, the salience of my professional identity is high, I behave like a professor in many

situations (depending on the salience level of alternative identities), even when the behavior is not especially appropriate. (p. 131)

In this class, many children are highly committed to the roles of being smart students or being capable writers and readers. These roles appear often in their narratives and social events in the classroom. In Kate's case, the roles she took on and reinforced include (a) a tough defender who tried to avoid any threat to her identity as a capable learner, and (b) an independent student who was in charge of her learning and made her own decision on the kind of help she needed.

## System Analysis

System analysis links the findings of a study to the other problems in the larger socio-cultural context and seeks to contribute to the current knowledge of social theories as well as improve our ways of thinking and living in the world. In this study, some children's sense of the self is threatened, challenged, and rejected in the complex school culture that intermingles with institutional standards and peer values. Their social identities are constructed under the rubric of fitting in, accepting what is given in school, and striving to be a good student. Some children try to stylize, produce, and perform their roles to maintain the "superior" status on the top of the social hierarchy in school official culture as well as in children's own peer culture. Moreover, there are also children who are, as Hall (1996b) suggests, in a constant "agonistic process of struggling with, resisting, negotiating and accommodating the normative or regulative rules with which they confront and regulate themselves" (p. 14).

These different forms of constructing identities reveal the complexity of children's school life and reflect the mainstream values and ideologies in the society. Schools serve as one kind of socializing agent for children, but they are also sites of cultural reproduction and contestation. Thus, the children's identity formation in school reflects the kind of educational institutions we have, the kind of society we create, and the kind of norms we live by. The system analysis in this study attempts to link the relations among the children's identity formation in school, educational institutions, and wide socio-cultural values; it then reveals the problems embedded within the relations that are faced by many children but are usually invisible to or ignored in school. More importantly, system analysis also directs our attention to new questions and solutions that will improve the quality of education. I discuss system analysis in Chapter Seven and bring up questions and suggestions based on the findings of the study. In this study, I did not perform an extensive system analysis because the amount of time and data required doing so.

# Discussion

I would like to conclude this chapter by discussing some ethical issues toward studying children. My attitude and respect toward each child is not different from that toward an adult. Nor do I consider children as subordinate or incapable in making their own decisions, which is an assumption prevalent in the adult world as well as in many institutions. Usually, in school, children have little control over their lives and most school activities are adult-constructed. In this study, however, I try to minimize the power that an adult has over a child. Even though I obtained parental consent to study the children's school life, this does not mean that every child is willing to or ready for sharing his or her life with me.

Especially during interviews, the children have the say about how they would like to proceed to be interviewed, such as choosing a comfortable place to talk, using different ways (i.e., drawing) to answer my questions, and refusing to respond to certain questions. For instance, when I asked Julia about her experience working with other classmates, she asked me, "Are you gonna tell anybody about this?" I honestly let her know that all the information collected would not be shared in class, and I also let her know that she did not have to answer the question if she did not want to.

My assumption is that children are intelligent, understandable, and capable of making decisions for themselves. This study is about children, their voices, their stories, and their lives. They have the right to choose what they want to do with it and to refuse it. My job is not to make children do things for my study. Rather, I ensure their right to decide whether to accept my invitation or not, how much they want to share, and in what way they would like to participate.

CHAPTER TWO

# Two Dominant Social Identities in School: Being Successful and Being Popular

There's a new ME this year,
An on-time ME,
A clean-desk ME,
A first-to-hand-in-assignment ME,
A listens-in-class-to-the-teacher ME,
An always-willing-to-be-good-and-help-out ME,
A dead-serious-get-the-work-done-and-hand-it-in-before-its-due ME,
The problem is
The new ME
Is not like ME
At all.

-Kalli Dakos (2003, p. 6)

This poem written in a child's voice seems to imply the mysterious difference between how we experience the self and how we are socially defined as who we are. As the poem suggests, the child seems to fulfill her responsibility projected in various kinds of "ME claims" as a good student in school. Yet, none of those MEs can really define who the child really is. It somehow sketches the paradoxical concept of identity debated by many philosophers and researchers from various disciplines. Is "identity" about a unified, integral whole of the self or a self that is always, in Derrida's term, "under erasure?" How about the postmodern performative self and the psychoanalytical sense of the conscious and unconscious processes of self-formation? In this chapter, I would like to explore (1) different kinds of "ME" the children identified with and/or differentiated in school, (2) the school norms that children tried to fight against, and (3) the implicit structure of identity claims embedded in the children's narratives. Several questions guided my inquiry: (a) What does it mean to be a successful student and a popular student? (b) How did the children position themselves against the school norms? (c) What sorts of problems were embedded in the children's narratives that inform us about their identity construction in school?

## The Meaning of Being Successful and Being Popular

To initiate my inquiry, let us hear some representative thoughts from the children about becoming successful in school:

> **Jeff**: Well, I would say um pay attention, and don't like—talk when the teacher's talking.

> **Ted**: Do the work they [the teachers] tell you. Try to do it without peeking at other people's work, and be quiet when they say.

> **Edward**: Um...making some friends first of all—

> **Mike**: Yeah.

> **Edward**: And then ask them what we are doing in the classroom and stuff. And then get to know how the class works, and then you'll build up stuff—

> **Mike**: Well, Maria (a new student in this class) came five months ago from Uganda and now she's a normal student like everybody else.

> *Ian*: *Um...I would say um a model of good listeners, somebody who has a lot of friends and somebody who is a nice guy, somebody who is fun to be around and likes lots of sports and follow the classroom rules... I would say uh no running out, no loud talking, uh no messing around, um being an active listener, sitting crisscross under your laps, um being a productive member in the class that kind of stuff.*

> *Winnie*: *...to be a successful student, you should listen to the teacher and usually um to be successful, what I would do is just do my best and listen when I am supposed to....Do what you are supposed to.*

All these basic principles and discourses are what the children had learned and become familiar with in school. Being successful, to some extent, refers to the sameness that each member of the classroom is committed to follow and maintain. It is a responsibility that everyone has to fulfill, a set of rules that everyone needs to follow, a network of relationships that connects everyone, and a collective goal that every successful student should try to achieve. Perhaps you may wonder how a seven or eight-year-old is able to fully comprehend and explain "success," such a complicated and broad concept. I purposely used the phrase "a successful student" during our conversations to see how each child was going to define it. Unfortunately, none of these definitions surprised me, but Mike and Edward's account caught my attention. As described, this new student from Uganda was an example of a successful student because she became "a normal student like everybody else." I wondered if every child comes to school to be just like everybody else. I also questioned whether the definition of success is constituted by a set of clichés listed above. I want to know more about how each child constructs a unique self that is beyond just a successful student. Thus, I shifted my inquiry to explore different kinds of success in school. Tammy's account provided me with a valuable clue:

> The people who aren't that popular are actually the good students. They behave a lot better.

Tammy suggested that another kind of success existed in school culture that caught my attention. When I discussed the issue of popularity with the children during interviews, the responses I got were dynamic, emotional, and full of examples. It took me a step further to understand children's identity construction through differentiating themselves from the popular students.

Before listening to the children's comments on being popular, it is important to keep in mind that while the children were telling their life stories, they were, at the same time, also showing how they feel toward the issue of popularity. In a way, these children may describe how popular students made them feel, but not how popular students *really* behaved. My purpose for mentioning the validity issue here is not to verify how "true" these children's narratives are, but rather to serve as reminders while interpreting and contemplating on what sorts of meaning are conveyed through their talks. After all, narratives are not confessions. My point for bringing up the feeling part of their narratives is to avoid giving the impression of overly identifying with these children's views and thus opening up more possible interpretations when exploring the children's school life.

Let us hear what Jeff said about the popular students he knew in school:

> **Jeff:** Well, I think the popular students just meet a lot of people. They just are like those personalities that some boys have and like, well, such as like they think that other boys think that's cool. Things that boys think are cool are like voices, actions, sports.

The popular students, according to Jeff, made an attempt to become popular and this attempt is for sure a semiotic one—I think "they think other boys think that's cool." It is thought about thought or a second order thinking

(Wiley, 1994) that constitutes an intersubjective web of thinking and meaning-making among social actors. Being popular also means to possess a kind of charismatic power that may not be available to everyone and this kind of power is intrinsically normative in its nature.

Tammy gave an example describing a popular student's privilege in school:

> For example Paula, she always talks to everyone and she's funny. She makes herself funnier than anyone else so she is popular... The popular people are always doing what they're doing and everyone is looking at them. They always raise their hands for everything and always get picked by the teachers. I don't think they are really that good. They do all of that so they can be popular so they can do everything and have more friends.

Acts are motivated by a will to power. Tammy's statement "they do all that so they can be popular" indicates popular students' intent to become popular. Among criminal charges, an attempt means that one had the intent to commit a crime, but for some reason, one did not complete it. However, no matter whether the crime is completed or not, one already takes a substantial step to commit the crime through premeditation and the punishment for an attempt could be as severe as for the completed crime. Perhaps the analogy between the concept of an "attempt" in criminal justice and Tammy's account of popular students can help us understand why popular students were considered "guilty."

One thing worth noticing is how Tammy positioned the teachers. She considered the teachers as the supporters of the popular students. The already popular students were even more popular and gained more public attention because they always "get picked by the teachers."

Ian's comments about popular students also brought up the teachers' involvement:

> The popular students um most of them I don't like to be with. They are kind of snotty because they are always so perfect and they like never get into trouble, but they are kind of mean. They um they like when they are doing their jobs, and then like when the teachers are around, they kind of act up a little bit. When the teachers are not around, they are mean and boss around.

Ian's remark regarded the teachers as naïve and easily tricked by popular students. Not only the teachers, but also the rest of the majority in the classroom, to a certain degree, were deceived by popular students. Questioning the credibility of popular students' "perfect" behaviors, a rhetorical question lay embedded in Ian's account: How can it be possible for people to be always "perfect" and "never get into trouble?"

Both Tammy and Ian seemed to implicitly question the normative binding power of the generalized other (Mead, 1934; Habermas, 1987) when the majority of the classroom ignored the "truth" about popular students and tolerated many of their "bad" behaviors. Disagreeing with the norms is a major step in defining who they are for these children, particularly when the norms misrepresent or threaten their sense of the self. Edward and Mike's comments suggested another threat from the popular students:

**Mike**: Popular students like to make fun of people.
**Edward**: They think they are popular for doing that.
**Mike**: They are just really good at things. It takes some people really long time to become smart and get their work done, but the popular students think it is obvious and easy.
**Edward**: They always behave like, "Dude, I am the most popular and smart student in school." It makes you really mad.
**Mike**: We successful students—you just get your work done, but the popular students would be—
**Edward**: They start to brag about it. It could really hurt someone's feeling a lot.

Popular students like to brag about their smartness, according Mike and Edward. Despite the bragging part, Mike seemed to be intimidated by the difference between him and the popular students. This difference defines who is smart and who is not. Children confront all kinds of differences among their peers. Some are smart and some need extra help in learning; some have lots of friends and some have trouble making one; some always get invited to join in a game and some are rejected. These popular folks, according to the children, possess power to be "smart," "cool," and "funny," and all these features of power grant them privileges to be "mean," "snotty," and "bragging." Through the differentiation of themselves from the popular students and the negation of the norms constraining their identity, the children's sense of self starts developing. Underlying the denial of the generalized other is the children's implicit identity claims that try to unfold *what is* through the peeling off of *what is not*.

Being popular is a complex social construct and identity involving discursive power relations and privileges that are available only for certain groups of people. Its complexity is also illustrated in the linguistic structure of the children's narratives in which a convoluted thinking process cuts across the normative culture, the self, the other, and the search for "truth." While explaining "being successful," the children regarded it as straight-forwardly following rules, doing "what the teachers say," and just doing what everybody else does. Being a successful student becomes a static and mechanically rule-governed identity that is regulated through sameness. Interestingly, it is while giving the meaning of being popular that the children gave more concrete experiences, expressed their feelings, denied the norms and challenged inequity in school, and thus shed light on the meaning of having a unique identity that is neither merely being successful nor being popular as defined by the school culture.

## Positioning the Self

Craib (1998) tries to conceptualize the notion of "I" that has been ignored by the Cartesian cognitive construct of the self. That is, before claiming "I think therefore I am," the "I" that does the thinking needs to be defined. In this section, I would like to focus on the "I" who distinguishes oneself from the other and challenges the normative power constraining the meaning of who one is.

> **Jeff:** I think I am sort of combined. I am successful and popular, but I like something that I don't think many boys do. I like something cute and I call almost everything cute (Giving a seemingly timid smile).

Like Jeff, many children choose to take a neutral position (both successful and popular in a positive sense) because they do not want to be unpopular in school. At the same time, they do not want to belong to the mean, snotty, popular group. Although it might be a safe bet to take a neutral position, Jeff still could not escape from the surveillance of gender discourses. He knew that he was not popular among boys because he liked and called everything "cute." "Cute" was considered a typical female expression in the boys' world, and Jeff knew what it meant when a boy used a girly word in school. I will discuss more about gender discourses in Chapter Six.

Ian also took a neutral position in defining who he was, but in a very different sense from Jeff:

> **Ian:** I am a successful student because I think I am very good at listening and I am very good at paying attention and I am very good at making friends. I think I am a nice guy to be around. And I have a lot of friends. I am the best at the writing workshop. I am also very good at reading. The popular students are hot-shot and mean. They could be good. This is just the average because I am the popular students, but I am not mean. Well, I am REALLY popular. I just have lots of friends. That's all I have. Around the girls, they think I am cute, hahahaha... (Laughing aloud), and around the boys, they think I am cool, but I really know me and my friends really know ourselves. And those popular students are just not nice.

Unlike Jeff, Ian took a more active role in presenting himself as a student who was both successful and popular because he worked hard for that (i.e., "I am the best in the writing workshop"; "I am also very good at reading"; "I am a nice guy to be with"; etc.). He also provided evidence from different gender perspectives to support his identity as both popular and successful in a positive sense. Furthermore, "having lots of friends" is probably the most important component in constructing his identity (i.e., "I just have lots of friends. That's all I have"). Through building up friendship, he formed a collective identity (i.e., the good popular group) as a kind of counter-force to fight against the "REALLY" popular group supported by or even constructed from, a generalized other in the classroom culture. In a way, Ian took a further step to change the normative structure in school by establishing a new group following a new set of rules and norms. Forming one's own group to differentiate oneself from the other is one major pattern in children's peer culture. I will discuss this in the subsequent chapters.

Despite the fact that most of the children considered being popular as negative and tried to differentiate themselves from the mean, snotty popular students, there was a contradictory feeling embedded in their narratives about not being identified as popular. Tammy pointed out that not everyone could be popular and that there were limited vacancies for those aspiring to the popular status:

> **Tammy**: I am good but I am not popular because everyone else already took over that.

She reluctantly admitted that she was not popular because the option of being popular was available only to certain people and not to her. Ted shared a personal experience about how he was prevented by popular students from joining in a game:

> **Ted**: For some reason they [the popular students] still don't play with me. I once asked something like this. Here is an example. I said I wanted to play with Peter, and Bill's like, "You can't play that. There's too much people already." But the other people do want me to play.

In a game situation, a child can immediately sense his social status within a group based on whether he is accepted or rejected. Ted realized right away that he did not belong in the group. Although he asserted that "the other people do want me to play," but nobody said or did anything for him. Ted's story unfolds a common phenomenon in peer culture: it is hierarchical in nature and sometimes arbitrary. His identity construction seems to dangle between his desire to belong and the rejection he experienced framed under the rules of peer culture. It a disturbing and confusing experience for him because "for some reason they still don't play with me." In the children's world, sometimes there is no particular reason why one person is more favored than the other. Children are usually straightforward in expressing their likes and dislikes. For those who are rejected by their peers as Ted was, usually the painful experience subsequently affects their confidence and identity formation.

In addition to setting themselves apart from the popular group, some children felt that becoming popular is nothing but a choice. However, it is still a difficult choice to make.

> **Mike**: I don't want to become popular. Everyone thinks Chris is very smart, but I don't think he is really really smart...We showed the dragon—you know the dragon in our class? (Pointing to the dragon, made out of construction paper, by the computers). We show that in the Life Skill Assembly, and it was me, Paul and a few other people's idea. And Chris was one of the people that got to hold it and I was, too. And I told Chris, "Did you know that it wasn't your idea?" And he said, "Yours, right?" I mean he is smart, but he made this bragging. He just brags of himself.

Perhaps you are as confused as I was when I first heard Mike's story. During the interview, Mike clarified his statement. Because Chris was one of the very smart students in school and everybody knew him, Mike suspected that most of the teachers and students would think that the dragon project was Chris's idea even though it was Mike and the other students'. Mike gave Chris a seemingly hostile reminder, "Did you know that it wasn't your idea?" Chris seemed to concur by replying, "Yours, right?" However, Chris's friendly reply did not relieve the threat Mike felt. He insisted that Chris bragged about himself even though Chris did not. Mike accusing Chris of bragging was intended to counter the threat that he perceived Chris to be. But if we examine Mike's fear carefully, it was not merely Chris's smartness or popularity that jeopardized his sense of self, but also, more importantly, the majority in school who dictate the norms and decide what "truth" is.

To conclude the discussion, several themes can be drawn from the children's statements for rationalizing and defending their identities. First, they all reference who they are by differentiating themselves from the popular students in school. Second, their identity claims reflect either the threat from or dissatisfaction with the generalized other in school. Whether they passively accept their identities as defined by the school norms or actively construct another new form of identity to challenge the school norms, the children implicitly or explicitly reveal the normative power, thus imposing on themselves and distorting the meaning of who they really are. Finally, their identity claims also revealed the privileged group in school that possesses resources and means to draw public attention and become "superior" to the other. It is also this privileged group that gives rise to discontent and self-doubt among children.

# Implicit Motivation for Constructing a Valid Self

So far, I have reviewed the school norms that form two crucial social identities dominating the children's school life. The exploration moves a step closer to the children's self-awareness or critical consciousness (Freire, 1973) in terms of who they are in school and whether or not they agree with their social identities that are given or constrained by the generalized other in school culture. In this section, I will examine the children's motivation for constructing a self that protests and challenges the status quo in school, uncover the embedded reasons for them to claim, defend, and justify who they really are, and explore the kinds of problems they encounter under the normative regulation in this classroom.

The motivation for the children to construct a valid self is intrinsically related to their identity claims embedded in their narratives. What motivates them to maintain and claim their identity, as Carspecken's (2002) praxis theory suggests, is the desire to be recognized by the other as a unique and valuable self. A motivation can also be a goal to be achieved in the future but that goal already exists or is assumed implicitly in one's present thought. As Mead (1934) suggests, in the process of an act, the final stage of the act is present in the earlier stages: the goal of an act is the presupposed outcome that manipulates and monitors the process of an act. When these children are motivated to construct a self that is free from the constraint of dominant generalized other positions in the school, they assume and believe that they already have a unique and valid self that is misinterpreted or repressed by the norms in school.

In the following analysis, I propose two ways of understanding the implicit motivations from the children's narratives by (1) eliciting the embedded identity claims in which the children try to clarify what kind of person they are, and (2) unpacking the underlying questions that confuse children's sense of the self and reveal the problems they confront in school.

## Eliciting the Embedded Identity Claims

According to Carspecken (2002), "Most action is praxis or praxis-relevant in that most action will include a motivating "identity claim" (p.65). I have already reviewed Carspecken's reformulation of praxis theory in Chapter One. To recap the main concepts involved in the embedded identity claims, the foundation of the theory of the self presupposes the social process in which the self is "longing for presence." Developed from Derrida's work, Carspecken relocates it in the notion of longing to know one's self and thus the desire for recognition. This "longing" is exemplified as a social desire or need to be recognized by the other that one is more than just a social product or an object, that one is empowered by being recognized, and that one is motivated by this praxis need presupposed in a given social context (Carspecken, 2003). The embedded identity claims are part of the complex of motivations and goals that presuppose motivations or goals that give crucial meaning to one's act.

Let us try to analyze a child's statement that "I am not popular." Apart from the surface-level meaning, the implicit motivation of the statement can be understood from three ontological (i.e., the subjective, objective, and normative) domains presupposed in one's claim:

(1)  Subjective: expressing her feelings or protesting certain norms in school that deprives her the right to be who she wants to be (i.e., "I feel hurt when I am positioned as not popular.")

(2)  Normative: disagreeing with a particular social status or defending her moral view (i.e., "Everyone is equal and nobody should be superior to the other.")

(3)  Objective: presenting facts and contexts of the social norms and cultural conditions in the classroom (i.e., "The other children and teachers respond to and act towards  in certain ways.")

The linguistic structure of the embedded identity claims is the first-person narrative (Carspecken, 1996). One's embedded identity claims show the motivations to defend one's sense of the self or to assert the kind of person one is: "I am a fair and moral person because I believe that everyone is equal"; "I am an honest person who is not afraid of revealing the fact that I am not popular in school." These identity claims are implicitly built into the meaning of the children's narratives that serve as a mode of motivation to carry on the conversation and convince the hearer that what they say is valid and true. Underlying the children's talk, there lies an essential need to be recognized as a real self, a self that is not willing to succumb to the normative constraint, a self that is eager to be free from being trapped in its social identity, and a self that is motivated to construct a unique whole through the dialogic interplay between the self and the other.

## Unpacking the Underlying Questions

To a certain degree, the embedded identity claims of the children's talk can be conceptualized as implicit problems they encounter in their school life. As their narratives indicate, these children are motivated to claim and defend their at-risk identity in school. Social struggles or conflicts are, to some extent, implicit in language use that implies a problem to be figured out, clarified, or debated. The implicit problems they encounter can be brought forth in the form of questions. These questions are part of the inner dialogues between one and oneself. Mead (1934) calls the dialogue between one and oneself an internal thinking. Bakhtin (1993) conceptualizes it as an "inner speech." This "inner speech" is monologic in form, but it is, as Bakhtin asserts, social in nature. Wittgenstein's (1953) theory of "language game" deconstructing the notion of "private language" is similar to Bakhtin's and Mead's social nature of internal dialogue in that being able to use language already presupposes social as well as intersubjective regulation.

To make it clear, the dialogue between one and oneself can be applied to the situation in which one tries to find possible answers or solutions to one's own questions or problems. It is this process of searching for possible answers to one's questions that motivates one to make all sorts of claims to defend one's identity. By unpacking the children's problems embedded in their claims, our understanding of identity issues expands to include what many children are directly confronting and other difficulties in the classroom culture that they are dealing with and reproducing unknowingly. Following the previous example, the motivation for making the statement that "I am not popular" can be reconceptualized as a set of questions that children themselves must cope with a various levels of awareness, such as: Why can't I be who I want to be in school? Why do I allow myself to be labeled as non-popular if I consider myself better than that? Why do I feel hurt by not being popular if I contest the social status of being popular?

Those implicit questions help us reframe children's identity construction as a set of problems implied in their narratives. Social actors are usually unaware of the potential damage done to their identity formation while coping with daily problems. An obvious consequence of the harm done to children's identity is when they are caught in the web of cultural reproduction, contesting the social norms constraining their sense

of the self and yet keep reproducing that discontentment unknowingly. By reconstructing the embedded questions in the children's narratives, we may expand our view when contemplating the problems existing in children's school life where they have little control over and thus must confront constant threats in their everyday school life, consciously or unconsciously.

Table 2-1 encapsulates (1) each child's embedded identity claims combined with their subjective experiences or feelings, and (2) the questions underlying their claims. As shown, many of these implicit questions are rhetorical in nature and thus reveal the tensions and contradictions in the process of children's identity construction. The primary purpose for digging out these questions buried under their narratives is not to provide any quick answers to them, but to sketch the structure of the classroom life that children are living in. Furthermore, these implicit questions are related to the core issue of forming a valid self, including why children prefer certain school activities, how they claim their uniqueness through text construction, why peer support is crucial for them, what the power structure is in peer culture, what sorts of official norms they try to fight against, how they produce and reproduce school culture unintentionally, how they develop at least partially counter-norms and partially articulated critiques of the dominant school cultures (both peer cultures and official cultures), and how they secure gender discourse as well as collective identity. All these issues will be explored in the subsequent chapters.

| Children's motivating identity claims | Underlying questions and problems |
|---|---|
| **Jeff**: I am not a macho type of boy like the other boys in this class. I know that I am considered unusual to use a girly word "cute." I know I am not popular, but I still think I am in-between being successful and being popular. | 1. Why can't a boy use the word "cute"? <br> 2. Who makes the distinction between boy words and girl words? <br> 3. Is school a place that allows students to be just themselves? |
| **Tammy**: I am a good student, but I am not popular because that choice is not available for me. I feel unfair that I am positioned as a plainly good student because I am more than that. I feel sad that I have no control of how I am positioned in school. | 1. What does it mean when one cannot be popular in school? <br> 2. Why does one passively accept her/his social identity if one disagrees with it? |
| **Ted**: I feel sad when I am not allowed to join in a game. I feel confused why I am rejected by the popular students. Even though I am rejected, I still want to become one of them. | 1. Why do some children want to be part of a social group when they know that they do not belong here? <br> 2. How does power operate in the children's world that makes some leaders and the others followers? |
| **Mike**: I am not a popular student because I choose not to. I don't like to become popular because popular students hurt people's feelings and make the other students look stupid. I am a smart student, but I am irritated that my smartness remains unnoticed in school simply because I am not popular. | 1. Why is one bothered by her/his own choice of not being popular? <br> 2. Is becoming popular the only way of being recognized in school? |
| **Ian**: I am confident that I am both successful and popular in a positive sense. I am a cute, cool, and fun guy to be with in school, so I have many friends. I am a smart student because I am one of the top students in reading and writing. I become popular because of who I am. | 1. If one can be popular because of who one is, then what does it mean for those who cannot be popular in school? <br> 2. Is it part of the process in children's identity construction to learn that not everyone is equal and treated equally in school? |

**Table 2-1 Routine Identity Claims and Their Implicated Questions**

# Discussion

I have investigated the children's identity formation by examining the two dominant social identities in their narratives as the crucial parts of the normative culture in school—being a successful student and being a popular student. They actively construct a valid self by (1) criticizing the meaning of the two norms defined by the generalized others in school, (2) constructing a fair ground for the meaning of who they are, and (3) struggling between the "me" who is socialized to fulfill the expectations and responsibilities as a member in this classroom and the "not me" whose self is beyond their social identities (that is, they are more than just being popular or successful).

Moreover, their action toward constructing their own identity projected in language use is through negation or saying "no" to the norms in school. In other words, they express who they are by telling us who they are not. Negation is intrinsic to their identity formation. They try to probe new ways of identifying themselves with and yet differentiating from the other. This negation, deriving from conflict or difference between the self and the other, is also what keeps these children actively deconstructing the old as well as reconstructing the new in the school culture.

Furthermore, children go to school where normative culture is already ideologically presupposed. What it means to be successful or popular is determined before they are aware of it. Children are simply expected to be successful in school. In a sense, the meaning of *success* is based on two major criteria: (a) how well they adapt to the school system (i.e. doing what one is supposed to, following what the teacher says, etc.) and (b) whether or not they get accepted by their peers with respect to teacher-criteria for success. *Success* then takes on different forms, including one that nuances it with "popularity" (see below). However, these two criteria fulfill only their social roles and obligations as a student in school. There is another subjective domain that they want to fully grasp, and they try to achieve it through actively constructing their own sense of a self. According to these children, they believe they are "good" and successful in their own way. However, there is an underlying problem in that they are thrown into the complex school culture where normative power is already in place and many of them must learn or struggle through the harsh lesson that their own version of success or being good is not necessarily valued or recognized by the normative standards. Thus, taking a "no" position toward the norms becomes a crucial social practice for constructing their identity in school.

In the simultaneous process of socialization and identity formation, the meaning of *success* develops, according to the children's narratives, into three forms:

(i)   It is simply reduced to following rules and fulfilling social expectations; particularly, following what the teachers say becomes the major official criterion in school.

(ii)  It becomes a normatively distorted version of success, an implicit standard as a "popular" type of success or the privileged social status that is only for those who are "smart," "bragging," "hurting people's feelings," seeking public attention, and obtaining the teacher's support (although it is arguable).

(iii) It is an unfulfilled identity project in which the tension between the self and the other, an individual and the socio-cultural structure, becomes the underlying force energizing the children to construct a desirable and valid self to be recognized and maintained.

(iv)

In summary, the three forms of success developed in this classroom explain why being a successful student does not seem to mean a lot to these children, while becoming a popular student is criticized and considered morally wrong. These forms of success contain asymmetrical power relations: the former is merely following rules and doing the same thing "just like everyone else" does; the latter is dictated by the normative consensus about who can possess the power and privilege to be recognized as a self and can do "whatever they want" in school. Thus many children's reaction to the school norms is to say "no" as well as to challenge the discourses operating in school. Through negation, they try to free themselves from the normative constraint that limits their autonomy and agency. In the subsequent chapters, doing whatever one wants, expressing oneself, and making one's own things all become important themes toward the children's self-determination as well as identity formation.

# CHAPTER THREE

# Structure of the Classroom Culture

Human identity is conditioned by its circumstances, including social classes, family backgrounds, race and ethnic histories, and gender discourses. As we have seen in the previous chapter, many children shape their identities as students by drawing norms and values from school as well as a broader socio-cultural totality in justifying their actions and choices. This broader socio-cultural totality is what we all belong to. As Appiah (2005) points out:

> Throughout our lives part of the material that we are responding to in shaping our selves is not within us but outside us, out there in the social world... To say that col-lective identities–that is, the collective dimensions of our individual identities—are re-sponses to something outside our selves is to say that they are the products of histories, and our engagement with them invokes capacities that are not under our control. (p. 21)

The "something outside our selves" is also something that constructs us as in-dividual social beings. The "something" that seems permissible both inside and outside of our selves is generally conceptualized by social theorists as "cul-ture" that we live through, draw upon, fight against, maintain, and transform on the way of shaping our identities.

By assembling a broader picture of how children's identity construction is conditioned in this class, I shift my focus to exploring the structure of the classroom culture. Research has provided macro-sociological accounts on how school culture reproduces social classes, maintains asymmetrical power rela-tions, and legitimates forms of knowledge (Bowles & Gintis, 1976; Willis, 1977; McLaren, 1986). Recent studies about curriculum and instruction cen-ter on issues of diversity and different cultural values and backgrounds that students have brought to school. These studies suggest that curriculum design should be closely related to students' life experiences, prioritize their voices, and provide space for meaningful learning (Warton, 2001; Valeski & Stipek, 2001; Sobieraj & Laube, 2001; Larson & Gatto, 2004). Peer culture and resis-tance culture in school (Adler & Adler, 1998; Corsaro, 1985, 1997; Corsaro & Emiliani, 1992; Dyson, 1989, 1993; Kyratzis, 2004; Dunn, Cutting, &

Fisher, 2002; McFarland 2001; Jordan, Cowan, & Roberts, 1995) are also popular aspects of school culture currently receiving attention.

Some of those themes related to students' identity formation, such as curriculum design, peer culture, power relations, and resistance culture, will be discussed in the subsequent analysis. In this chapter, I divide the exploration of the classroom culture into three major dimensions, and each of them is crucial to understand how the classroom culture is produced and reproduced through daily routines, regulations, and practices: (a) the official culture, (b) the unofficial culture, and (c) the discrepancies between the two. Framing under the theory of cultural production (Giddens, 1984) and the lifeworld-system relations (Habermas, 1987), there are three questions guiding the exploration of school culture that illustrates how social actors—mainly teachers and students—interact, conflict, and support each other through routine social practices and how the consequences of these social practices discursively reproduce system relations implicated in school that serve as trajectories for children's identity construction:

(1) What are the major features of the official agenda that operate in everyday routine activities in this classroom?
(2) What are some of the discrepancies between the official and unofficial school culture?
(3) How does the official culture constrain as well as enable children's identity construction?

## Theoretical Construct of Cultural Production and Reproduction

Applying several notions of Giddens's (1984) theory of structuration to understand school culture, I conceptualize schooling as a social system that involves "regularized relations of interdependence between individuals or groups" and which "can be best analyzed as recurrent social practices." These socially regularized relations and recurrent practices can be understood from the structure of the classroom culture. First of all, let us try to understand some key concepts in Giddens's theory that will be applied in this study to examine the structure of the classroom culture that affects children's identity formation.

### Structures and Systems

To study structures (or structuring properties) of school culture is "to study the ways in which that (school) system, via application of generative rules and resources, and in the context of unintended outcomes, is produced and reproduced in interaction" (Giddens, 1984, p. 119). According to Giddens, *systems* are sets of reproduced relations among actors, organized as recursive social practices, while *structures* are rules and resources implicitly and recursively implicated in the reproduction of social systems.

1. *Rules:* Rules are not a set of rigid regulations, but are, according to Giddens, both the medium and the outcome of the reproduction of social systems. According to Giddens (1984), "structure" (or the structural properties of a culture) develops not only as implicit rules used in the production/reproduction of social systems, but it also provides for "the vast bulk" of knowledge or actors' "practical consciousness" to interact with each other, carry out daily activities, and "respond to and influence an indeterminate range of social circumstances" (p. 22). The structural properties of rules implicitly operating in social interaction are often studied through discourse analysis in terms of turn-taking, opening, closing, and sustaining social encounters. "Rules," in Giddens's (1984) view, are tacit knowledgeability acquired in a culture to interact with each other in a socially "acceptable" manner, which implies a certain degree of sanction upon every aspect of social action.

2. *Resources:* Resources are considered by Giddens as the "bases or vehicles of power, comprising structures of domination, drawn upon by parties to interaction and reproduced through the duality of structure" (p. 122). For Giddens (1984), all acts are acts of power because "to be able to 'act otherwise' means being able to intervene in the world, or to refrain from such intervention, with the effect of influencing a specific process or state of affairs" (p. 14). Action presupposes an agent who is able to monitor him/herself as well as other's action (i.e., reflexive monitoring of action), who possesses the basic generalized competence to give reasons for his/her action (i.e., rationalization of action), and who acts with some sort of motivation consciously or unconsciously (i.e., motivation of action). Thus, to carry out an action is to exercise power in social practice. Power operates not only as the set of "rules" described above, but also as "resources" and "media through which power is exercised" (Giddens, 1984, p. 15).

3. *Maintenance and Transformation:* As Giddens argues, cultural production/reproduction is not only about social stability but, more importantly, also about social changes. The children in this study struggle to maintain their social identity through achieving authoritative standards, but their action also creates conflicts and distorts the official rules. Giddens sharply points out that

social reproduction is constituted by the continuous flow of purposive action with its unintended consequences. For example, social policies for improving the national economy are intended acts while the resulting social hierarchy is the unintended consequence. Following the official rule is an intended act, while conflict or distortion is unintended. Unintended consequences that result from an intended action are important aspects of social reproduction in that these unintended consequences, as Giddens (1984) suggests, "form unacknowledged conditions of action in a feedback fashion" to "reconstitute the initiating circumstances" (p. 27) of action. The reproductive loop (intended action—unintended consequences—reconstitution of action) is a crucial framework to explore how children in this study try to conform to the official rules (intended), and yet exercise power through applying these official rules in a distorted way (unintended) in their own unofficial culture. This power circulation both sustains as well as reproduces the official agenda and the unofficial culture in school. Figure 3-1 depicts this circular loop between the official and the unofficial.

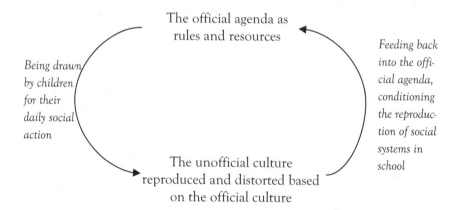

**Figure 3-1 Cultural Reproduction Cycle between the Official and the Unofficial**

Furthermore, action is not only to maintain but also, most of the time, to change the actors' current situation. Studies related to oppressive social groups reveal how changing current social circumstances is their primary concern (Appiah, 2005). In this study, making changes is one important and primary wish for many children about their daily school life. I will address this issue in the final chapter. For now, I want to emphasize how children are caught up in the cultural reproduction in school. That is, even though they try to change their daily routines in school, their action is still based on the rules of the official agenda as their "resources." An obvious example is how children attempt to change their social status in peer culture from the young to the mature, the incapable to the capable, and the subordinate to the dominant. These structural properties are criteria explicitly or implicitly implicated in the official agenda to frame every aspect of children's school life. Some of these structural properties are passed down and reproduced in children's unofficial culture. Later, I will discuss this part more.

## Corporeality, Sequences of Social Encounters, and Locale Reproducing Everyday Social Routines

The daily routines and institutional forms of social organization constitute each other as well as the acting individual bounded in time and space. Within different contexts, social reproduction of a cultural site is rooted in everyday co-presence of agents during social encounters. The major components constituting social encounters include (1) corporeality, (2) seriality or sequences of social encounters, and (3) locale bounded spatially and temporally.

1. *Corporeality*, according to Giddens (1984), refers to the body of acting individuals restricted within specific time and space in social encounters. School is an institution in which students and teachers are physically bounded and regulated in time and space corresponding to different social encounters. These social encounters are usually contextualized by various activities as well as different regions in the classroom.

2. *Social encounters* are constituted by series of "cueing devices" (Giddens, 1984, p. 73) for opening, continuing, closing and turn-taking during interaction. Sequences of a social encounter coupled with the agents' body postures evolved in the co-presence are engaged in an interactive rhythm determining when to talk, whose turn it is to talk, and how to pose one's body or make gestures corresponding to the shifting situations. All these seem to tie in naturally and intuitively in the process of social interaction. This seemingly intuitive knowledge of when, where, what, how, and with whom to act, according to Giddens (1984), represents interaction skills or "tact" anchoring in agents' "practical consciousness." These social skills function intuitively in a lifeworld as "latent conceptual agreement among participants in interaction contexts" (Giddens, 1984, p. 75). This also includes situations in which two or more agents engaged in a social encounter in a public place (e.g., in an elevator, in a hallway, in the park, on the bus) are able to enclose their interaction by filtering out those who are present but not participating. These agents involved in the social encounter are able to produce enclosure that is "a normatively sanctioned 'barrier' [separating] those engaged in the encounter from others who

are co-present" (Giddens, 1984, p. 75). This is particularly important in this study in understanding instances wherein children try to enclose themselves in their social encounters and prevent others who do not belong to their group from interfering. It is even more obvious when girls are co-present in the situation that boys filter or ignore girls' comments in their "male" encounters. As Giddens points out, this mechanism for sustaining one's ontological security also contributes to system reproduction—gender division in this case. I will discuss gender issues in Chapter Six.

3. *Locale* is "the use of space to provide the setting of interaction, the setting of interaction in turn being essential to specifying its contextuality...[and] provide for a good deal of the 'fixity' underlying institutions" (Giddens 1984, p. 118). Here lie two major dimensions of locale: (a) contexts and (b) regions. The context is a situation or, in Habermas (1987) terms, a segment of a lifeworld in which a particular theme is the focal point in a social encounter among actors, such as two or three people discussing the weather or watching a basketball game together. "For those involved, the action situation is the center of their lifeworld; it has a movable horizon because it points to the complexity of the lifeworld" (Habermas, 1987, p. 123). This concept of a lifeworld is similar to what Giddens (1984) calls the actors' knowledgeability or "practical consciousness" as their cultural reservoir in which "rules" and "resources" are drawn from for their daily routines.

However, "themes" in a context may shift, for instance, from talking about the weather to an upcoming plan for a trip, or from watching a ball game to having some beer or arguing about game strategies. No matter what sort of themes arise in everyday communicative practices, as Habermas (1987) points out, "there are no completely unfamiliar situations. Every new situation appears in a lifeworld composed of a cultural stock of knowledge that is 'always already' familiar" (p. 125). Actors carry out action by drawing from their lifeworld knowledge; by drawing from it, they also continue as well as reproduce it, which echoes Giddens's structural duality that a lifeworld is both the medium and the outcome of social practices. The context highlights a specific segment of lifeworld, while the lifeworld reservoir is backgrounded as well as taken for granted in the context of daily social practices.

Regions are not just localization in space but "the zoning of time-space in relation to routinized social practices" (Giddens, 1984, p. 119). Regionalization, closely related to corporeality, is particularly important in exploring school culture because children's body movements and behaviors are rigidly organized and regulated by the temporal schedule as well as by spatial arrangement in the classroom. Moreover, based on Goffman's (1961, 1963,

1974) dramaturgical viewpoint, Giddens divides space-time zoning into the front region and the back region in co-presence. The front region is like the "façade" of the co-presence, implying its inauthenticity and yet making disclosure for authoritative surveillance. The back region is, on the contrary, authentic and yet enclosed for the actors themselves in which they try to protect and avoid surveillance or intrusion. Applying the regional concept to school settings, generally speaking, the front region is related to the official agendas as well as authoritative standards in which children's body movements and behaviors are under intensive observation. Children must reveal what they are doing, show teachers that they follow rules, and do a good job in every activity in school. Most classroom rules are front-regional in nature for maintaining the order of co-presence between teachers and students in public spheres.

The back region, however, is where children disclose their "real" self as well as recover "forms of autonomy which are compromised or treated in frontal contexts" (Giddens, 1984, p. 127). The back region is intimately linked to the children's unofficial culture in terms of (a) how they coordinate between the front region and the back region during co-presence in the classroom and (b) how they develop their own peer rules in terms of doing their own "private" stuff without getting caught. In this study, retreating from the front to the back region is an obvious tendency in children's school routines. Back regions also contain rich and "interesting" data. They are areas in which children negotiate autonomy and privacy. However, there is no clear-cut boundary between the back regions and the front regions of co-presence in school routines. In fact, the back and front regions often co-exist and intersect with each other in a complex way. For instance, even in the front-regional setting of the formal class instruction in which children are under intensive surveillance, they somehow manage to find a way to "communicate" back-regionally, such as making faces, winking, kicking each other under the table, passing notes to each other, whispering, and so forth. Thus, the division between front and back regions is more accurately determined by the degree of children's autonomy and how intensive the official surveillance is in a situated context. For instance, in the official class meeting, the official rules operating in the front region of the co-presence are maximal while individual autonomy is minimal. The individual or group work time after formal instruction is more like a back-regional setting in which the official rules or surveillance is not as intensive as in the formal settings and thus allows children more freedom to carry out their task or to do other things besides school-work. This is the case also when children have more opportunities to interact with each other with minimal official control.

However, every aspect of school life is more or less under official regulation, although during certain periods of time, children have more control of themselves. This official regulation is somehow implicit in daily routines, and it becomes obvious when children's autonomy is out of control; that is, when the whole class is too loud. At this juncture, the authoritative sanction comes in by re-initiating the official co-presence between teachers and students to remind everyone about the rules and the rewards and punishments. In the following sections, I discuss the official agenda in this classroom: how children react to them and what sorts of tensions appear, and how these official rules are reproduced in children's unofficial culture.

## The Official Agenda

The official culture represents, in a sense, the more visible pattern of children's classroom life. It shows regularized relations between teachers and students exemplified through daily routines and social practices. The following discussion is about some of the challenges many teachers confront in classroom management and instructional decisions, but not to blame or identify whose fault or responsibility it should be.

### Predictability

It is important for routines to become established in the classroom so that children feel comfortable, safe, and have a sense of belonging to learn from and interact with each other. These routines bring a certain sense of security and help children to familiarize with the when, where, what, and how of doing different activities and for different purposes. However, when routines become a solidified set of rules or repetitive patterns in school, issues of boredom appear. I will discuss the issue of boredom later.

Remember the newspaper article written by the children about "A Day in the Classroom" in the introduction:

> First we have D.O.D. Then we have song time. Then we have morning meeting. Next we have team reading. Then we have a story web to work on. Then we have morning work time, and then writing workshop or invitations. Next we have recess and lunch. Then we have D.E.A.R. time. Next we have read aloud. Then we do some activities.

These are routines that each child follows every day in this class. Different activities are carried out in different regions of the classroom. For instance, the big rug area is where formal meetings take place and when the teachers make official announcements, read stories aloud, and demonstrate instructions to the whole class. The children's seating area is where they finish their work and discuss with their neighbor friends. During reading and project time, children are allowed to stay anywhere in the classroom. These classroom routines bounded in time and space are recurrent social practices situated in various activities in the classroom.

## Curriculum Design

There are always many activities carried out simultaneously in the classroom, including writing pen pal letters or thank-you letters, making classroom books, attending the writing workshop, organizing community visitor journals, enjoying math stories, reading books, working on school projects and invitations, writing the classroom newspaper (columnists working on their own columns), practicing spelling, and so on. As one of the parents once commented, "This is a very busy classroom. A lot of busy beavers." The teachers also encourage the "busy" and hardworking spirit seen in children's everyday routines. As the teachers told me once, it was good to keep children busy so that they did not waste time talking to each other.

Despite the intensive literacy activities occupying a major part of the routines, the second feature of the curriculum is its partner-up system. As in many classrooms, working with partners is a major way of carrying out different school activities. The purpose of partner-up is for children to help and learn from each other in school. The pattern of partner system is to pair the more capable writers or readers with the less capable ones, which may somehow correspond to Vygotsky's (1978) theory of zone of proximity.

Furthermore, different literacy activities in this class contain internal standards built into them. These standards prescribe who can be involved and what sorts of literacy capacities are expected from the children. For instance, in order to join the "cursive club," as Oscar, a child, told me, "you have to write well and try to get into the cursive club." Writing well could be challenging for many children at this age, which means that not every child is able or suited to learn cursive. Another example is writing articles for the classroom newspaper. There are two parts to the classroom newspaper: (i) reporters working as a team to report classroom news (e.g., our cubbies, fieldtrips, our pets, our play, etc.), and (ii) columnists, each writing an individual column about different subjects. Writing a column is particularly only for those who sign up for the job. Every child can sign up for writing a column in the newspaper, but being a columnist means that one needs certain skills and "knowledge" to write a column. As Linda pointed out:

> They [the teachers] want to make sure that you do not spend an hour working on
> your column. And they want to make sure that you know how to use computers, um
> because if you don't, then uh, like you are going to be ... you need to know what your
> column is going to be and you need to know like quite a bit about it, and you need to
> know that it's going to be a good column. Say, like if someone is going to write a col-
> umn about Captain Underpants, then that would not be allowed. You need to do like
> a good column that would give information, not just silly stuff... So like science um,
> math, nature, weather, sports, you know, stuff like that.

Such demands for writing a column also indicate that not every child is able to sign up for the task.

Finally, the curriculum design attempts to place more responsibility on children's own learning and being productive members in the classroom. Every week, children need to write the "math contract" and the "weekly goal sheet" as a way of reflecting on what they have done or learned during the week and then planning on what they will achieve in the following week. In a sense, it is an official way of asking children to reveal what they have done not only to the teacher but also to themselves and to the whole class. The official agendas have a lot to do with asking children to *reveal* themselves in public for the purpose of either sharing or demonstrating their responsibility and capability, which becomes another form of surveillance through self-reflection.

## Directions, Punishment, and Rewards

*1. Directions*: "Following directions" is a major part of children's school life. "Directions" that children need to follow include the routine jobs mentioned above, approved regions for different activities in the classroom, permission to go out of the classroom, and general rules of how to behave properly during class. Bringing or playing with toys is not allowed in the classroom. Even though a child asks the teacher's permission to go to the bathroom, the teacher may reject the request particularly at certain moments when the teacher is announcing an important event or demonstrating a new activity. Moreover, the teacher seems to somehow tacitly know who "really" needs to go to the bathroom and who simply uses it as an excuse to go out of the class-room, which is another interesting aspect of the teacher's "knowledge" that is worth exploring.

*2. Procedures*: Different kinds of "procedures" in this classroom are decided and agreed upon by the students. These procedures are made during the "community circle" time in which all children and teachers sit together on the rug and form a big circle to discuss classroom matters. Once, the teacher an-nounced that the whole class was getting very noisy during work time and asked the class, "What can we do about it?" Children made suggestions for how to improve the discipline in class and the teacher wrote their suggestions down on posters (Table 3-1) as the official procedures and reminders for the whole class. All these posters were hung on the classroom wall.

In addition to the written form of rules, music is another crucial instrument to control the flow of the official agenda, divide one activity from another, give warnings before making an official announcement, and raise children's attention when the class is too loud. Whenever children hear the music, they are supposed to freeze, stop talking, and listen to the teachers. Sometimes, the teachers would ask the children to practice freeze: "Do I get a good freeze? I spy someone is still talking. Let's practice again." The music was turned on and then was turned off again. The class practiced freeze again and the teacher said, "Much better this time."

| *Work time Procedures* | *Rug Procedures* |
|---|---|
| 1. We should be silent or whisper and we should hear the cricket chirping. | 1. Keep your hands to yourself |
| 2. We should listen to the teachers. | 2. Sit on your bottom |
| 3. On the rug, don't sit by a friend. | 3. Do not lie down |
| | 4. Raise your hand to talk |

| *Getting Ready to Go Home Procedures* |
|---|
| 1. Clean up quietly |
| 2. Put chair up with your backpack on it |
| 3. Check your mailbox |
| 4. Line up quietly by groups to go home |
| 5. Help others |

**Table 3-1 Official Procedures**

*3. Punishment and Rewards:* Very often, punishment and rewards share the same medium. An obvious example is the action that was once taken to punish the class when discipline deteriorated—the rug was removed. For several months, children had to sit on the floor without the rug during class meetings. In order to get the rug back, the children had to behave cooperatively to earn 25 points from the teachers. The teachers added points if the whole class put effort into maintaining class order. Taking the rug away is punishment while giving it back becomes a reward. Adding points is a reward while subtracting points is punishment. That rewards and punishments share the same instrument also applies to other rules. For instance, writing children's names on the board is both a warning as well as punishment to remind them to behave, and erasing their names becomes a reward or acknowledgment of their improvement. Writing names on the board is also a kind of reward when these names on the board are of those who are good models for the whole class. For instance, there is a list of names on the board titled "The clean cubbies."

After the class won the rug back, the class still kept the punishment-rewarding system by adding/subtracting points. The points could earn them what is called "bonus recess," that is, children will have extra recess if they behave. However, the system of earning bonus recess is more like an instrument that keeps reminding children to follow rules they made and agreed upon. When the class does not reach the official standard for maintaining the classroom order, the teachers subtract from the bonus recess points as punishment for the whole class. Whenever this occurs, children blame those who talk too loud or do not pay attention.

Of course, there are also many cases of individual punishment. For instance, Oscar was asked to leave the rug area during the Read Aloud time and sit on his own seat: "Oscar, go back to your seat. You are not ready to join us yet," said the teacher. Kate's name was written on the board to remind her to behave. Don was asked to copy the rug procedures, take it home, and have it signed by his parents. Sometimes, when children, particularly boys, do not stop talking, the teachers would ask them to sit next to those who are quiet, usually girls, which, for most boys, is considered a punishment. This has a significant implication for understanding the gender issues that I will discuss in the next chapter.

Individual rewards vary in form: winning free drinks from the teachers, helping teachers, receiving praise in public, writing names on the board as "good models" for the class, being a line leader when the class lines up, and so forth. Generally speaking, more girls get individual rewards than boys in this class. When helping the teachers, girls seem to gain more trust from the teachers to carry out more detailed or challenging tasks. For instance, Gina was asked to help the teachers to check and write down the pizza flavors each child wanted for a forthcoming pizza party. Julia was in charge of helping out a new student from Uganda and checked her reading and writing. Winnie was constantly asked to help the teachers check if everyone handed in their work. The boys, on the other hand, seem to help with the heavy-duty tasks, such as carrying chairs, planting vegetables in the garden, cleaning or moving tables. Moreover, I observed that boys have a stronger tendency to challenge or violate the rules than girls do in this class. I will also explore this issue in Chapter Six.

## Teacher's Talks

Teacher's talks are crucial cueing devices that remind children of regulations, give warnings, and control the class order. Roughly speaking, there are four types of teacher's talks for maintaining the classroom discipline:

*1. Reminding*: The teachers usually send out this kind of warning to raise children's attention levels. For instance, Mr. Smith reminded children during DEAR time, "It's reading inside your head," which implies that it is silent reading with no talking allowed. Also, while children were gathering in the rug area for Read Aloud, Mr. Smith told Oscar, "Make a good seating choice," which reminded him about one of the Rug Procedures that children are not supposed to sit with their friends. Not sitting with friends reduces the chance for children to talk to each other. Furthermore, Mrs. Jones once made an announcement in the morning time, "We're going to have A LOT of practice for the pin-dropped quiet time," suggesting that children have not reached the official standard of "pin-dropped" quiet yet.

*2. Compromising*: This kind of talk is a contract between the teachers and the students in which the teachers allow some flexibility or freedom in the class in exchange for students' promises to maintain classroom order. This is used particularly when children move from highly active to more passive tasks. Usually, after lunch and recess or after cleaning up the classroom, the teachers would allow a short period of time for the children to settle down:

> **Mrs. Jones**: You will have one minute to settle down (After one minute, Mrs. Jones played the music and made an announcement). The one-minute settle-down is officially over.

Another example is to play the music during the work time:

> **Mrs. Jones**: If you promise to work quietly, we will play the music during work time.

Compromising the rules within a limiting range is usually effective to maintain the flow of classroom order. This is sometimes used as a reward for the whole class.

*3. Warning*: This is another effective way of getting children's immediate attention to not only examine their own actions but also monitor each other in a situated context. The actions of some activate the public sanction. The following are two examples showing how the teacher's talks generate the effect of public sanction and achieve an immediate improvement of the classroom order.

During Read Aloud, Mr. Smith suddenly stopped reading the story because some children were talking and playing:

> **Mr. Smith**: Oh, I might just stop here.
> **Children**: Why?

**Mr. Smith:** It's a bit violent I guess. Maybe we should wait until tomorrow (Closing the book).
**Children:** No, no, no, continue...
**Mr. Smith:** Oh, my Gosh! (Indicating that children were too loud again; the class suddenly became very quiet). We'll see what we can do here (Pausing for a while until the class was completely quiet and then continuing reading).

Another example is when Mrs. Jones was about to announce an incoming event, but the class was still noisy.

**Mrs. Jones:** I guess we are not going to tell you about the fieldtrip.
**Children:** Shhh, shhh, shhh... (The children warned each other to be quiet).

4. *Immediate rewards:* This is a way of triggering the mechanism of surveillance within children themselves to monitor their own actions and check with each other to meet the official standard. The reward can be the acknowledgment of the whole class's cooperative effort in maintaining order in their shared environment and the fulfillment of their responsibility as a productive member of the class community. There are two examples of this.

The music was on, indicating Team Reading was over. Mrs. Jones announced, "This was the best Team Reading this year." Then, she added 10 points to the bonus recess on the board. The whole class was excited and behaved extraordinarily well the whole day.

Another way of encouraging discipline is to reward those who behave the best. This is also an indirect way of telling the rest of the class to keep working on the discipline problem by following these good models.

**Mr. Smith:** Ding! (Making a bell-ringing sound to draw the whole class's attention). We are now in a quiet silent mode. Since Fred behaved so well this afternoon, I will erase his name on the board. Linda, do you want your name on the board?
**Linda:** No.
**Mr. Smith:** Man oh man! I got a good table. Greg's table gets free drinks.
**Greg:** Thanks, Mr. Smith.
**Max:** Thanks, Mr. Smith (Greg and Max sat on the same table. They were excited about the reward. The whole class was quiet at the moment, seemingly waiting for the teacher to pick their table for rewards).

To summarize the official agenda in this classroom, the most intensive structural principle implicated in the three aspects (regular routines, curriculum, and classroom rules) of the official standard is the notion of *cooperation*. This cooperation is between teachers and students and among the students themselves. The official agenda is rooted in enacting children's collaboration and in becoming a social member in the classroom community. Following the classroom rules is to cooperate with each other to maintain order in the class-room. Working with partners is to learn cooperatively and assist each other to accomplish school work.

The ultimate goal of cooperation is to develop as well as constantly enact this self-governing mechanism within every child so that each can work inde-pendently as well as cooperatively. Mead (1934) considers this self-monitoring mechanism (the "Me") as an organized set of social rules internalized by each social member in a society. Almost every structural principle in school is more or less related to this apparatus of self-regulation and most of the social identi-ties developed in school also evolve around it. For instance, being a good stu-dent, a productive member, a responsible partner, a good friend, and so forth are simply different aspects of this social monitoring mechanism, ideologically forming various social identities to remind and regulate children's action in school.

Whenever this cooperative boundary between teachers and students is broken (e.g., violating rules), official and/or public sanction enters to restore that cooperation, thus reinforcing as well as activating the children's self-monitoring mechanism. However, the cooperative relationships between teachers and students and among students are more complex than just follow-ing or breaking rules. Under the surface of cooperation, there are many prob-lems and difficulties that children face and deal with every day in school in situations that are beyond official control or surveillance. Following rules is one thing, but really agreeing is another. Cooperation may solve immediate discipline problems in school, but there are also embedded conflicts and ten-sions creating "unintended" consequences within the school culture. Let us explore this issue further by looking at the general discrepancies between the official agendas and the practices of those who live by these agendas.

## The Discrepancies

The discrepancies reveal tensions in this classroom between the official culture and the children's experiences and reactions to the official agenda.

### Boredom

**Andy:** Borrrrrrrrrrrrring (Elongating). Everything is boring. My favorite part is lunch, recess and gym...

**Jeff:** Usually in school I am so bored that I just draw on my books. That's one of the reasons I like drawing so much.

> **Kate**: I just feel bored because um there are so many things to do in school, and when you do all them, you have nothing else to do. When it gets boring, you can't do it anymore, and you have to something different, like playing in the playground, reading books in the library or visiting other classes.

Being bored seems like a feeling many students have from time to time in school. That is also the most challenging aspect of teaching. Recess, lunch, gym, and drawing are part of the routines in school, but these are usually favorite parts of school life for many children perhaps because these are moments when they have more control over their activity and are subject to less official constraints.

At the same time, we need to be careful when interpreting children's boredom toward school life. First, feeling bored does not necessarily mean that children do not value the official standard. Nor do they attempt to resist the official agenda. Quite the contrary, children such as Andy, Jeff, and Kate tried very hard to adapt to school routines and achieve the official standard as much as they could. Second, children's boredom somehow reflects their problems in learning and thus their frustration. Those who constantly feel bored in this class are usually the ones who are identified as "struggling" learners. Thus, how to design a curriculum that would engage every child and fulfill her/his needs is a constant struggle for every teacher. Third, children's boredom can suggest a periodic pattern and serve as an important reminder for teachers to reflect on the curriculum and make any necessary adjustments. Teachers may think about how to bring the joy of outside activities to the curriculum inside the classroom.

## Work—Too Much or Not Enough?

This is somehow related to the intensive nature of the curriculum. As many visitors and parents suggest, the first impression of the classroom is that this is a *busy* classroom where children are busy doing their work almost all the time. Keeping children busy is different from engaging them in doing their work. Moreover, keeping children busy sometimes also creates boredom toward schoolwork. The following interviews are the children's reaction toward the intensive agenda in school:

> **Ted**: Annoying. THE CLASS (emphasizing by raising his tone with his eyes wide open) is annoying. They are like, always doing uh math a hundred times.
> **Mike**: Um-I don't-I usually like pen pal letters, but if you have three jobs, I kind of—
> **Edward**: And the three jobs are all writing—
> **Mike**: Yeah, so I kind of get bored of writing. In the first job, it's ok, but the third job—

**Edward:** Oh, man (Indicating that he agreed with Mike's feeling about too much writing).
**Mike:** Um, well, sometimes we get three jobs, and they are all writing. And the third job is the hardest for me because I've done so much writing. And-um it's really hard for me, so I get bored.

As Mike pointed out, the last job of writing was the most difficult part to handle. It is hard not because he does not know how to do it, but because he loses interest and energy in writing if he does too much of it. Ted considered it "annoying" to constantly practice math, which is a common official way to brush up on math skills. Of course, one may argue that all these are just common complaints children have about school, but I consider them crucial information for educators to achieve a balance between maintaining children's learning motivation and practicing enough to learn. "Enough" is a vague and individually variant concept. How much is "enough" and how much is "too much" differs from person to person. To make the matter more complex, Bill's perception about the lack of intensive schoolwork presents an opposing view:

**Bill:** ...most of the time on weekend, since this class doesn't do a lot of writing, my mom has me write like the last story I can think of. I-my mom had me write what I thought the 5th Harry Potter book would be like (According to Bill, the 5th Harry Potter book was not out yet at the time I interviewed him)... Well, I think do more writing and math... because if the 2nd graders aren't doing that much, they won't be prepared for the ISTEP in 3rd grade.

For Bill (and perhaps his mother), this class did not practice enough in writing and he regarded it necessary to have a more intensive agenda and to practice more for the state test in third grade. This, again, points out various curriculum demands from teachers. How to provide a curriculum that is challenging enough for some children and yet not overly taxing for others is a difficult task teachers continue to confront. Thus, the discrepancy seems unavoidable due to the individual variance in the classroom.

## Questionable Official Standards

1. *The Seemingly Untrustworthy Official Standards:* The "official standards" here specifically mean the criteria of rewards for those who follow rules. Many children, particularly boys, strongly oppose the idea of obeying rules all the time. Edward confessed bluntly, "I hate following directions." Andy wanted to reverse all the official rules (see the next chapter). Probably, the controversial part related to rules is how the teacher determines who behaves and who does not. Tammy shared her experience about this confusion:

> The one thing I don't understand is that all the popular people get free drinks and
> the good people Mr. Smith is looking right ahead of and behave real good he doesn't
> call on... And I don't know why. That happened to me yesterday.

Tammy questioned the credibility and fairness of the authoritative judgment of rewards. First, she felt she behaved as well as those who got free
drinks, but she did not understand why she was not picked by the teacher.
Second, Tammy considered that the teacher did not treat everyone equally
and that those who were chosen to get rewards were "the popular people"
while those who were ignored but "behave real good" were "the good people."
I have discussed the issue of popularity more completely in Chapter Four.
Third, her typification for interpreting body gestures during student-teacher
interactions proved her wrong and thus confused her. Her meaning-making of
the teacher's eye contact with her seemed to make her feel betrayed by the
teacher. The mismatch between her typified understanding of the teacher's eye
contact with her and the teacher's final decision to reward someone else
seemed devastating for Tammy in that she was confused about the official
standard of rewarding. Nor could she stop wondering whether the teacher was
fair about this matter.

2. *The Paradox of Not Talking to Friends in School*: The rule of not talking to
friends is to reduce the chance for children to talk to each other during class.
As Bill indicated:

> If you don't pay attention on the rug to know what you're going to do, you don't
> know what you need to do and you'll ask the teachers and they'll say, "Well, that's
> your problem. You didn't listen." So just-just so you heard but you weren't paying at-
> tention to it [because] they were talking to their friends.

Since this is a big class with 45 children, the discipline issue is extraordinarily important for this class. It is challenging to make sure every child pays
attention and listens carefully to what the teachers say. That is why the teachers sometimes purposely refuse to answer the children's questions after the
official announcement because they want to set up a pattern wherein children
pay attention each time it is expected during class. It is the children's responsibility to listen carefully when a teacher is talking to them. However, Tammy
had a different view about it:

> One rule is "Don't talk to your neighbors," but sometimes you have to... Like when
> you don't understand something, the teacher says "hands down" and won't let you
> ask because she is still talking. And you are really confused. Or you need to go back
> and ask, but she just doesn't answer it.

Tammy did not think that it was reasonable to be expected to refrain from talking to a neighbor all the time. There are some situations in which children need to consult with each other or clarify what the teacher says. From the official point of view, however, if children ask questions while teachers are talking, it would be chaotic, the message would be fragmented, and the lesson might be even more confusing for most of the children. Thus, the issue here is not to make a judgment on who is right or who is wrong; rather the focus is to point out the tension between the rule maker and the rule follower. This adds another issue to the teacher's challenging list of concerns.

Furthermore, many children consider "talking to friends" important in their school life. As Bill reflected, "In this great class, we are doing sort of other works all day and all that. You didn't have a chance to talk to people and get to know people further." This, again, points out the intensive nature of the curriculum that prevents children from talking to each other in class. It may also be one reason why children tend to form the same groups, because they do not have time to make other new friends. Linda also commented that there should be a block of free time to talk to friends in school:

> I hope that we can have time to talk with our friends about things happened in school or at home because you only meet friends at school and if you want to talk to them, you have to talk to them at school, but you are usually not allowed to talk with friends in school.... Well, I think that we should have free — one [block of] free time in the classroom where you can talk to your friends for a while. And like if you have a problem that you got, then you can just spell that out ... Yeah, just speak out. You could speak out like 15 minutes in one day. You can talk to your friends for 15 minutes a day.

Interacting with each other is how children build up friendships in school. Linda seems to suggest that "talking to friends" should be included as a part of the official agendas and that the official agendas should consider not only what the teacher wants but also what the children want.

As already mentioned, discipline is a critical issue in this classroom. There are 45 young children in the classroom, which makes maintaining discipline a formidable task and requires a lot of effort from both teachers and students. The rewarding standard and children's understanding of that standard, the maintaining of the class order, and the building up of friendships are all equally important for children as well as teachers. Unfortunately, these issues somehow oppose each other and are a source of conflict in the classroom culture.

3. *The Hidden Agenda:* The "hidden" agenda means a set of implicit system values that are unintentionally and unknowingly reproduced to support or mar-

ginalize certain groups of students in school. Although every child is encouraged to be a columnist of the classroom newspaper, not every child signs up for the task as discussed previously. Nor is every child, as a matter of fact, able to handle the job. Being a columnist already pre-supposes certain standards as Linda pointed out: knowing quite a bit about a particular subject, finishing writing within limited amount of time, and making sure the column is about "valid knowledge" instead of "silly stuff." Even though the purpose of writing columns in the classroom newspaper is to create a space for children to share information with each other, "columnists" implicitly become synonymous with the "smart" and "popular" group in this class.

## Collaboration or Domination-Submission

Before starting our discussion, let us hear some of the common problems many children confront when working under the partner-up system. The following quotations are from children who have the subordinate position in partnerships in class:

> **Tammy:** She [My reporter partner] always does all the writing...So I just sit and watch. It's just boring... um usually whenever she is gone, I try and write the rest of it, and she just erases it... because that's not what she likes and she wants everything to be her way...I want to go with mine (my way) but I have to go with hers because she always erases mine.

> **Julia:** That's hard to work with my partner Michelle. Probably, probably um because Michelle (lowering her voice) is kind of um... Michelle is kind of annoying because she like ~ always wants to do everything by herself. She never ~ she always wants to do everything her own way and then she always thinks that she is, she is, she is ~ She always thinks that she is right. And then it ~ but she takes so long to write her part. It takes like an hour to write this much (using her fingers to show how little Michelle wrote).

> **Jeff:** I like all the writing activities except the spelling test and reporters. I don't really like being with Edward, doing everything with him because he usually like ~ takes over and seems mean.

> **Mike:** I don't like it [working with my partner]. Well, my partner is Don.
> **Edward:** Oh, he is REALLY mean sometimes.
> **Mike:** And he he's kind of selfish sometimes, and he said, "No, I don't want to write," and um—
> **Edward:** You just have to go along with him, or sometimes he would like punch you.
> **Mike:** Well, not really punch but get really mad at you.
> **Edward:** And yell at you and stuff.
> **Mike:** Yeah, and so ~ I ~ It's really hard for me because he just thinks of ~ Whatever my idea is, he says no...
> **Edward:** I have a partner and his name is Jeff. Sometimes Jeff is pretty hard to get along with.

**Andy**: I just let him [my partner] do what he wants... I like my idea. I don't like his that much, but I just don't want him to yell at me... I'll just let him do what he wants.

Although the curriculum design is geared toward promoting cooperative learning among children, the disagreements that most children, according to the interviews, experience in the partner-up system show that the real working situation functions more like submission-dominance rather than cooperation. In order to understand this, we must examine the partner-up system in terms of how it works and why it creates rather than solves problems.

When pairing up children, the teachers either assign or sometimes let children choose their partners. Whether the choice is made by the teachers or by the children, the teachers encourage children to work with different partners and make sure that each team has a capable student to help the other if need be. The 1st graders (Jeff, Tammy, and Andy) think their 2nd grade partners always "take over" during writing and are mean and bossy. The 2nd graders (Julia, Edward, and Mike) regard their 1st grade partners as incapable, selfish, and difficult to get along with. The disparity between the official agendas (collaboration) and the situations most children are confronted with (submission and dominance) reproduces itself as a form of a constant tension between 1st and 2nd graders or between the capable and the less capable.

Table 3-2 summarizes the five main discrepancies between the official agenda and the children's perceptions.

| Aspects of the official agenda | Discrepancies derived under the official agenda |
| --- | --- |
| 1. Predictable routines | 1. Boredom |
| 2. Intensive curriculum | 2. Decreasing sense of fun and motivation in learning |
| 3. Authoritative standards of rewards, punishment, inclusion, and exclusion | 3. Questioning the credibility as well as fairness of the authoritative judgment |
| 4. Partner-up system for promoting cooperative learning | 4. Formation of tensions within relations of domination and subordination |
| 5. High standards and expectations embedded in column writing | 5. Hidden agenda creating an elite group in school |

Table 3-2 Summary of the Five Main Discrepancies
Between the Official Agenda and the Children's Perceptions

# The Unofficial Culture and Peer Rules

Here I focus on how the official agenda and the discrepancies noted above become "resources" for children to develop their own unofficial culture and peer rules. Following Giddens's (1984) theory of structuration, children's unofficial culture is not simply constrained but also "enabled" by the official agenda, while the (unintended) consequences of the authoritative standard "feed back" into the life cycle of the classroom culture, producing and reproducing as a circular loop. "Enabling" is Giddens's important notion to help us understand the coordination between the official and the unofficial culture in school but does not reduce it to a mere binary opposition between the two.

## Literacy as Media for Constructing Collective Identities among Peers

*1. Grouping and Friendship:* As just mentioned, being a columnist implies following a hidden curriculum of creating an elite group and a system of grouping based on one's literacy capacity or interest. Children group and are grouped into various categories when building up friendship. This kind of grouping or categorization is a constant phenomenon during working time in which most children tend to habitually gravitate toward their own. The following are some examples of how columnists work and get together as an elite group in this classroom.

> **Paul:** I do a pre-historic life column. Mike and I partnered up and did Megalodon. Mike is about the one who knows the second most about dinosaurs, but I know the most about dinosaurs than anyone in the other 45 kids in the class.

Paul, a dinosaur and pre-historic "expert" in this class, constantly works with Mike, who also knows quite a lot about prehistoric life. The one who knows "the most about dinosaurs" partners up only with "the one who knows the second most about dinosaurs." This is how columnists get together, become good friends with each other, and, in a sense, exclude the others from joining them. An elite group is formed in this way, but there are sometimes hierarchical relations also *within* the elite group.

Literacy capacity is one of the major components for making friends in the unofficial culture. As Oscar told me, "Eric is my good friend because he reads a book about this thick," with his finger pointing to an encyclopedia on the bookshelf. Bill also pointed out the fact that most children like to be friends with smart students:

> "If you are smart and you can show them stuff about what to do, it will be easier to make friends because you will help them and then you will become friends with them. They will trust you because you're helping them and they want to be your friends." Peter and Ian's friendship provides another example:
>
> **Ian:** We wrote a chapter book together.
> **Peter:** It's super long.
> **Ian:** Well, um I think our ideas are kind of the same.

**Peter:** And we're good friends.
**Ian:** Yeah, we write many things together. I don't like my other writing partners. I only like to work with Peter.

Writing together happens particularly among capable writers in this class and they seem to form the popular dominant groups among their peers. This phenomenon often extends beyond literacy activities into recesses. Gina observed this during recess:

> Um, well, I kind of notice Peter is the most popular because everybody is like trying to play with him... He is always like when we play the game, he always gets pick his best friends. And lots of people just hang out with him. There are just like 10 or 5 people that he normally plays with, but there's a bunch of other people just kind of look up to him.

The smart students want to be with smart students; capable writers only write with the capable writers; most of the students want to play with popular students. This is how most children group themselves and gravitate toward those who are smarter and more capable in various aspects. The dominant popular groups, thus, are derived from the classroom culture in which literacy is used as media to reinforce the social hierarchy in the children's world.

   2. *Tensions between the Capable (the 2nd graders) and the Less Capable (the 1st graders)*: As mentioned before, working with partners is the major pattern of how literacy activities are done in this class. I also pointed out that the real working situation with partners that many children have experienced is more like domination-submission rather than collaboration. Thus, in the children's unofficial culture, tensions often appear among children between the capable and the less capable, particularly between 1st and 2nd graders:

> **Andy:** My reading partner is the kind of 1st grader that I have to live with pain. He can't read a lot of stuff.
> **Kate:** My reporter partner is a 1st grader. She learns a lot from me because she can't even spell the word "my." She can only spell her name. She can't spell many words and she has swampy hand-writing. I have better hand-writing than her when I was a 1st grader.
> **Tammy:** Usually, 2nd graders are kind of mean to the 1st graders. And 2nd graders have accomplished a lot, lot, lot more than 1st graders. I think 1st graders should try to get along with 2nd graders.

Being able to read more, write better, and accomplish more seems to be how 2nd graders assert their "superior" identity under the partner-up system of the official agenda. Many fights or disagreements between 1st and 2nd graders in unofficial settings are seemingly rooted in grade difference, in which

2nd graders position themselves as more knowledgeable and mature than 1st graders, while 1st graders consider themselves "victims" because they are younger, less capable and physically smaller than 2nd graders. Perhaps, this is why "growing up" is important for many young children as growing up is equated with becoming more capable and in control in school.

Older or more capable children tend to consider it as their "right" and, perhaps, as their obligation to point out the younger children's mistakes during literacy activities. While the class was writing letters to the U.S. soldiers before Thanksgiving, two 2nd graders, Ted and Vivian, were commenting on 1st grader Leo's writing:

> **Ted:** ti-sf-bla-h... (Reading Leo's writing and shaking his head) Leo, your letter to the soldiers doesn't make any sense.
> **Leo:** Sop peaking (Yelling and covering his letter with his elbow).
> **Vivian:** Leo, we are not making fun of you. We are just telling you that the soldiers won't understand your writing.

In the unofficial classroom culture, age difference and literacy capacity are implicit instruments for claiming power among children.

## Ritual-Like Rules and Power Claims for Fairness

In the children's world, the idea of being fair is crucial. Many arguments and complaints in school result from issues over fairness. As discussed in the previous chapter, many children's discontentment about normative regulations in school arises from issues of unfairness, in that not everyone is treated equally and the school norms favor certain groups of people. Many children also felt that some rules of the official agenda are not fair, such as having no time to talk to their friends, questioning the authoritative standards, working with difficult partners, and the like. Thus, children develop their own ways to resolve issues of fairness in their peer culture. These problem-solving rules have two features: first, they are ritual in form; second, they function as a negotiating mechanism. Especially during a game situation, the ritual-like rules (i.e., nursery rhymes) are applied to initiate the game and resolve tensions during the game. In order to sustain the game, there needs to be a strategic mechanism that allows parties involved to negotiate when issues of fairness appear.

The following long episode is an I-Spy game involving five children, Ted, Vivian, Tammy, Nick, and Linda. Nick invited the other four to play the game. Each one took turns to spy an object in the book and the rest of them had to find out where the object was based on one's description of the object. Whoever got the turn to play could also pick the next person to play. The argument had been revolving around whose turn it was to play during the game. Nick thought that it was fair for him to decide who played next because he initiated the game. Ted claimed fairness by chanting nursery rhymes to decide whose turn it should be. When the conflict between Nick and Ted was about to end the game, Vivian and Linda brought in the negotiating mechanism to sustain the game:

> [1] **Ted**: It goes Tammy, Nick, Linda, Vivian and then I just have this one turn. And then, Nick said it's Vivian's turn (Ted seemed unhappy and tried to get his turn of playing).
>
> [2] **Linda**: I'll say it's your turn (Linda supported that it should be Ted's turn).
>
> [3] **Ted**: I know but Nick said it's Vivian's turn. (Raising his voice)
>
> [4] **Nick**: I said it's Vivian's turn (Yelling).
>
> [5] **Vivian**: Ok, it's Ted's turn. No one's doing anything. It's just a reading game and we are not supposed to argue.
>
> [6] **Nick**: I say it's not Ted's turn. You know that I was the one that got this book! (Yelling madly)
>
> [7] **Vivian**: Ok, then you need to choose who goes next. But after whoever you choose, it would be Ted's turn.
>
> [8] **Ted**: Yeah.
>
> [9] **Nick**: I choose Tammy.
>
> ............
>
> (After Tammy's turn, they argued again whose turn it should be).
>
> [32] **Vivian**: Now it's my turn to ~
>
> [33] **Ted**: No, it's my turn to go (Raising his voice).
>
> [34] **Nick**: I spy with my little eye ~ (Ignoring Ted's claim)
>
> [35] **Linda**: Shhh, be quiet (Reminding the boys to lower their voices).
>
> [36] **Ted**: Can I get my turn now? (Seeming irritated)
>
> [37] **Vivian**: Oh, yeah, it's Ted's turn. Right after Tammy, it's Ted's turn.
>
> [38] **Ted**: I spy a balloon.
>
> .......
>
> [43] **Linda**: Right there? (Pointing in the book)
>
> [44] **Ted**: No.
>
> [45] **Tammy**: Right there?
>
> [46] **Ted**: Yes.
>
> [47] **Nick**: It's my turn.
>
> [48] **Vivian**: No, Ted gets to pick now.
>
> [49] **Nick**: No! Not Ted (Shouting).
>
> (Nick was yelling and trying to stop Ted, but Ted ignored Nick and started chanting the nursery rhymes to pick the next person to play. Whoever was being pointed at during the last word was eliminated.)
>
> [50] **Ted**: Eenie, Meenie, Miney, Mo,
> Catch a tiger by the toe,
> If he hollers, let him go.
> Eenie, Meenie, Miney, Mo.
> My- mother- said- to- pick- the- very- best- one- and- you- are- not- it (Pointing at Nick).
>
> [51] **Tammy**: Nick's turn? (Tammy was not sure.)
>
> [52] **Ted**: No, he's out.

[53] **Nick**: Hey! It's unfair (Shouting with his face turning red).
[54] **Ted**: (Ted still ignored Nick). Eenie, Meenie, Miney, Mo,
Catch a tiger by the toe.
If he hollers, let him go.
Eenie, Meenie, Miney, Mo.
My- mother- said- to- pick- the- very- best- one- and- you- are- not- it (Pointing at Vivian, meaning Vivian was out).
Inky, pinky, ponky,
Daddy bought a donkey.
Donkey died.
Daddy cried. Inky, pinky, ponky (Pointing at Tammy, meaning Tammy was out and Linda was chosen).
[55] **Nick**: Hey, that wasn't FAIR. He knew that would point at me first. It wasn't fair 'cause he knew it would point at me first (Keep shouting). I don't want to play with you (Taking the book away).
[56] **Vivian**: Nick, don't (Vivian tried to persuade Nick to stay and play).
[57] **Linda**: Ted got to pick and it's my turn (Linda argued by sticking to the rules of the game).
[58] **Ted**: Nick, they are not gonna play with you any more if you keep being like that to everyone. You will NOT have a friend.
[59] **Nick**: Everybody is choosing ~ everybody is choosing me ~ (Keeping yelling; the music was on, indicating the reading time was over).

Let us take a closer look at the sequences of interaction as well as power shift among these children. Ted argued that everyone should take turns to play and accused Nick of violating the game rule. Linda sided with Ted and agreed that it should be Ted's turn to play. Nick disagreed and the argument became the quarrel between Ted and Nick. The girls were somehow on the periphery of tension and took on the role of negotiators during the argument.

Vivian tried to ease the tension between the boys by taking on a big-sister role and reminded them that it was just a game and that they should not argue. Nick claimed his leadership role by pointing out that he was the one to initiate the game and invite everyone to play. Vivian recognized Nick's claim and strategically negotiated contractual power by letting him decide whose turn it should be this time, but in return, he had to promise to follow the game rules by letting Ted take his turn to play.

When the contract between Nick and Vivian was about to collapse, Ted started chanting the nursery rhymes as a tactic to negotiate fairness and try to stop Nick's yelling. Chanting nursery rhymes (i.e., Eenie, Meenie, Miney, Mo; Inky, Pinky, Ponky; etc.) is a common ritual to initiate a game and a "fair" way to settle down arguments, which is a kind of normative rule acknowledged by every child participating in a game. Although Nick acknowledged the normative rule of the nursery rhymes, it did not keep him quiet for very long. The tension continued between Nick and Ted. Ted's nursery rhyme chanting eliminated Nick from taking a turn to play. He accused Ted of a "conspiracy" to purposely eliminate him, believing that Ted already knew the last word of the rhymes would fall on him.

Applying coercive power, Nick threatened to terminate the game. The negotiating mechanism was initiated again by Vivian to sustain the game and seemed to ask Nick to continue the game. Ted warned Nick that his unreasonable reaction in the game would have serious consequences—he would have no friends to play with. Nick felt threatened and treated unfairly because everyone, except Tammy, seemed to pick on him and argue against him.

This is one example of how the children get into arguments and resolve conflicts about issues of fairness that they have been fighting over in school. The children practice carrying out rules and sanctions in a game situation in which different value judgments and norms are mediated through various power claims (Carspecken, 1996; Weber, 1978). The rituals developed and the negotiating strategies used in a game are a set of communicative actions among children to test out, bargain for, and create ways of upholding the game and reaching the agreement of fairness in the children's unofficial world.

## Negotiating Private Time and Space

According to Goffman's (1963, 1974) dramaturgic theory, the regional section in which actors perform their action is divided into the front and the back region, as I have discussed previously. This part of analysis focuses specifically on the back-regional settings in which private time and space is crucial for many children in school. Most of them enjoy the temporary enclosure of getting together with their friends and doing all sorts of "fun" things, which may not be allowed according to the official rules. Nevertheless, I argue that the primary motivation for creating private space and time in school is not to "resist" the official rules, but to recover autonomy as well as to have fun. Moreover, even though most activities in the back regions may be considered "mischief," it is, I argue, the (unintended) consequence of the rigid official agendas on framing every aspect of children's school life. In order to adapt to the official regulations of school life and maintain autonomy, children are conditioned to produce the kind of tactics that could coordinate between the two. The more intensive the official surveillance is, the more "advanced" the tactics are in the children's unofficial culture to preserve autonomy. Usually, children's way of following rules is to not get caught by teachers, which is different from actively "resisting" the adult rules as many studies suggest.

Doing all sorts of fun things covertly is how children try to balance between preserving autonomy and obeying official rules. The children's unofficial culture accommodates their own needs and conforms to the official standard. Both the official and unofficial reinforce each other to reproduce the causal coordination between them—the official regulation controls children's action in time and space while children try to regain their control by doing all sorts of things back-regionally in which their own unofficial culture is enabled and conditioned by the official agenda.

The following episodes represent the typical back-regional activities happening in the classroom where children try to regain control and to strategically protect their temporary social gatherings from being sanctioned or intruded upon.

1. *Manipulating between the Official and the Unofficial:* During work time, children were reading and writing their pen pal letters. The teachers gave each child copies of the local newspapers and encouraged them to find interesting topics to write to their pen pals. Ian was fumbling around in the pile of newspapers in which many advertisement pamphlets were attached. He found an advertisement about Valentine's Day where a man and a woman were holding each other on a couch. He showed it to his friends and whispered something in their ears. They giggled and seemed excited. Unfortunately, I was not able to hear what they said.

After whispering to each other and giggling for a while, Ian suddenly commented aloud, "This is so nasty." When other children came to Ian and whispered something to him, Ian giggled with them but then seriously told his classmates aloud, "Stop talking about it. It's very inappropriate." Ian said it aloud as if he would like to draw the teacher's attention and show that he wanted to stop this "inappropriate" whispering from the other children and that he was not part of this mischief. But, in fact, Ian was the one who initiated the "nasty" whispering. His action of spreading the "nasty" joke through *whispering* and then saying *aloud* to the other classmates to stop it is how he manipulated the official and the unofficial, the front region and the back region in a playful way. It is his way of both having fun and preventing himself from getting into trouble with official sanction.

2. *Fun of Mischief:* The following is a short excerpt from a long episode of work time. All are columnists. Ian invited his friend Edward to write his game column with him; Peter wrote his food column. The three of them sat at the same table working and talking. I placed the tape recorder on the shelf next to their table. They were talking about their favorite games and movies and joking around until they could not stop laughing.

**Edward:** Should I punch a hole in that [eraser]?
**Peter:** Yeah, hehehehe... (Laughing at how Edward poked the eraser and buried the pencil in the eraser).
**Edward:** (Laughing) It's like—
**Peter:** Put the pencil in it.
**Edward:** It's like, "Lights out, pencil," tsss (indicating the light was out), waaaaaaaa (making crying sounds as if the pencil was crying because the light was out).
**Ian:** "Lights out, penis." (Giggling)
**Edward:** "Lights out, penis" (Laughing aloud while repeating Ian's words).
**Peter:** "Lights out, penis" (Laughing, repeating, but trying to lower his voice).
(The three of them laughed as if they could not control themselves).
**Ian:** "Lights out, my penis."
**Edward:** "Lights out, my penis."
**Peter:** "Lights out, my penis" (The three of them laughed left and right).

It is another way of having fun by enclosing the social gatherings among friends to talk about something considered inappropriate from the official point of view. Ian took the play a step further by changing "pencil" into "penis" and the three of them burst out laughing in an uncontrollable way. The linguistic strategies they use to create alignment and inclusion in the peer group include (a) narrating through role-playing to engage peers into a playful imaginative world (i.e., the pencil's talk), (b) repeating each other's sentences to build solidarity among peers, and (c) communicating and constructing collective gender identities (i.e., "penis") (Kyratzis, 2004; also see Corsaro, 1997 and Cook-Gumperz & Kyratzis, 2001).

Observing them laughing in such an uncontrollable way made me wonder whether the official surveillance reinforces the fun of conducting some "mischief." They know that such jokes are inappropriate in school, but enjoy the risk-taking. The fun comes not only from its inappropriateness but also from the challenge of watching out for official surveillance. However, in this case, they were so out of control that it did not escape the teacher's attention. The teacher gave all three a warning.

3. *Secret Spots:* In Chapter One, I discussed children's "secret spots" in the classroom and what they do in those areas. Interesting data can come from these areas, but it is challenging to collect those data because these are the very places where children want privacy and freedom without any intrusion.

Oscar and Max threw the ball inside the closet and yelled "touch down" as if the closet is the goal of the football field. In the closet, children also share their toys with their friends. Toys are not allowed in school, but leaving them inside the closet seems still within the "legal" boundary.

During reading time, some children like to move around between different places. "Let's go to another place" is a code for initiating the team reading between partners. For instance, Zach and Fred hid in the gap between the couch and the book shelf during reading time, but their "secret spot" caught Mrs. Jones's eyes and she warned them, "This is not a good seating choice." Then they moved to another place under the table where the fish tank was located. After a while, Mrs. Jones caught them again and asked them to sit at their table. It is sort of like the game of "hide and seek" between children and teachers. The teachers make sure that every child is within the scope of official surveillance; if one is out of this guarding range, the teachers would either pull children back into this range or expand the scope of supervision. Children would have to come up with more tactics to negotiate their autonomy and freedom in the classroom.

## Discussion

Applying Giddens's cultural theory in terms of structures, systems, corporeality, social encounters, and locales, I have mapped the classroom culture with the three structural components: the official culture, the unofficial culture, and the discrepancies between the two. In the official culture, I laid out four major aspects of the classroom regulation: (1) the predictable routines, (2) the curriculum design, (3) the directions, punishment, and rewards, and (4) the teacher's talks. Each aspect reveals how the authoritative standards and curriculum objectives constitute a set of recurrent social practices in this class. Undergirding the recurrent social practices are the discrepancies between the official and the unofficial school culture that many children try to adapt to their constant conflicts and negotiate discontentment in school. These discrepancies include: (1) boredom toward predictable daily routines, (2) exhaustion of intensive curriculum, (3) unfairness of authoritative standards, (4) tensions derived from teamwork, and (5) hidden agenda of creating elite culture.

Unintentionally evolved from the official regulations, some normative values and standards of the curriculum design pass down to the children's unofficial culture. The authoritative standards of literacy learning and curriculum design produced in the official culture are reproduced in the children's unofficial culture as a set of discursive criteria in positioning each other and in defining who they are. Friendship, peer groups, and teamwork are implicitly defined, regulated and stratified as system relations in which literacy is the primary medium of power assertion and the criterion of inclusion and exclusion in children's social networks. These reproduced themes in the unofficial culture, in return, "feed back" into the official culture, reinforcing the official standards and rules, and thus reconstituting the reproduction loop coordinating between the official and the unofficial as well as sustaining the reproduction of the system relations operating in school (i.e., social hierarchy and categorization among children, literacy as the medium of power assertion, popularity as the major cultural capital).

However, some features of the children's unofficial culture do not feed back directly into the official culture. Rather, they exist parallel to the official culture as a set of strategies to negotiate dissatisfaction and to restore individual control of learning in school. As mentioned before, exploring the issue of fairness and negotiating autonomy are elements of the recurrent social practices in the children's unofficial culture that are usually carried out in a game situation or in a playful way.

Furthermore, the reproduction loop coordinated between the official and the unofficial school culture is also the social condition of the children's identity construction in school. This can be seen from the following aspects of children's identity construction:

- Being smart and capable in reading and writing
- Enclosing one's peer group
- Enhancing group solidarity as well as collective identity
- Constructing a positive sense of the self (see Chapter Two)
- Preferring activities that recover one's autonomy and control of learning (see Chapter Four)
- Adapting the normative standards and yet negotiating as well as transforming the cultural milieu

Figure 3-2 summarizes this production/reproduction loop in this classroom.

In addition, I would also like to clarify the notion of "resistance" prevalently discussed by researchers in early childhood, critical pedagogy, and cultural studies (Bowles & Gintis, 1976; Willis, 1977; McLaren, 1986; Adler & Adler, 1998; Corsaro, 1985, 1997; Corsaro & Emiliani, 1992; Dyson, 1989, 1993; Kyratzis, 2004; Dunn, Cutting, & Fisher, 2002; McFarland, 2001; Jordan, Cowan, & Roberts, 1995). I argue that most children in this study are not motivated to produce "resistance" culture just for the sake of challenging the teacher's authority. Rather, some try or even struggle to conform to official standards. What some call "resistance" is merely a way of recovering and negotiating autonomy that has been repressed or rigidly regulated in the front-regional official settings.

Dewey (1934) defines children's resistance as a creative way of living and bridging the gap between the self and the environment. This is why creating private spots for doing their own things is crucial and considered the fun part for many children in school. Even though there are many studies about adolescents who defy school rules or teachers' authority, the real motivation underlying their purposive action is not to resist but, more importantly, to change their oppressed social status, to fulfill the desire of constructing a positive sense of the self (Willis, 1977), and to create opportunities to express themselves freely without fear of sanction (McFarland, 2001).

Finally, the discrepancies that I have pointed out between the teacher's official agenda and the children's experiences are not to criticize or make any judgmental remarks on the teacher's professional knowledge and instructional decisions. Quite the contrary, I want to emphasize the challenges of teaching with respect to satisfying students' individual needs, trying to be as fair as possible in maintaining classroom order, and providing an engaging curriculum for every student. I would like to also emphasize that it is necessary and helpful for every teacher to step outside of their curriculum from time to time and look at it from the students' perspectives.

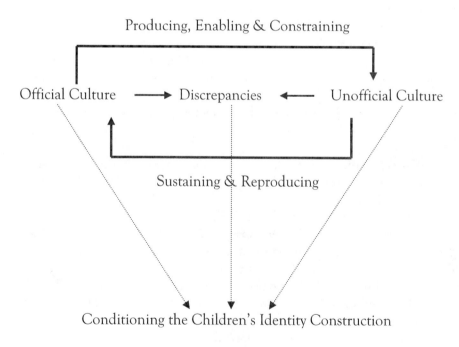

Figure 3-2 Production/Reproduction Loop

CHAPTER FOUR

# Creating "MY OWN" Thing: Being an Author

*Ted: My favorite is – I would have to say this (pointing to the book he wrote)... Because I get to write "MY OWN" (emphasizing) book ... it's just fun.*

*Jeff: It's – it's just so fun and I just just just love it so much, just like the best thing in the world.*

*Winnie: Well, what I like to do the most is um writing my own story because then I get to choose what I really want to write about.*

*Paul: Oh, I like to share information... you can choose anything in the whole world to write in your story.*

*Ian: Well, I like the writing workshop because more people get to share my story and that's really fun writing books because they last longer than just a piece of paper.*

*Peter: Well, we write a story for us. It's our story and we write it and stuff. And it's not for the classroom newspaper. They have to put others' writing in it.. Our story is stuff like we are writing our OWN anything we want and create like we can write God, demon and something.*

Writing is not simply putting words on the paper for these young authors. It is creating, making their own story, expressing themselves through written language, showing who they are as authors by fabricating pieces of their life into a particular genre, and assuring their readers that they know what an author can do and do well. As Ted suggested, writing "my OWN book" is "fun" as well as serious. Moreover, it is about the freedom to try out various possibilities of text construction like an author usually does in writing a story. Peter is specific about how special and different it is to create one's "OWN" story compared to other types of writing (e.g., the newspaper writing), and he emphasizes the luxury of being able to choose any topic—from "God" to "demon"—to write on. An author can do anything she wants because she can control and manipulate language, construct the particular genre, decide what details would be included, and invite readers to appreciate the imagination and creativity of her work.

There is more to being an author that these children are excited about. As Jeff suggests, creating something by oneself is "the best thing in the world." It is not just about creating something by oneself but also about oneself. That is, there is some sort of a magical power about being an author that is so wonderful that it is beyond even what language can describe and Jeff cannot help but to "just, just, just love it so much." Paul asserts his authority as a dinosaur expert through sharing his writing about dinosaurs. It is not only what he writes, but also who he is, as expressed through his writing, that is important. Furthermore, an author creates something called books that, as Ian points out, "last longer than just a piece of paper"—just like Rowling's *Harry Potter*, Dickens's *Christmas Stories*, or Stevenson's *Treasure Island*.

I was fascinated by these young authors' passion, energy, and confidence when they told me about the story they wrote and their personal literacy history of becoming an author. For them, it is more than just being an author. It is about who they are, what they want to do, and how they enjoy their accomplishment through being an author. Their talks convince me that they are authors and further inspire me to explore how wonderful it is to be an author for these children and what this particular identity means to them in their school life.

I divide my inquiry into three parts corresponding to three guiding questions: (1) What does it mean to be an author for the children? (2) What do these young authors do in their books that makes it such a wonderful experience for them to be an author? (3) What can we learn from these young authors about literacy? The first question ties into the identity of being an author at both the individual as well as the social level. The second question focuses on the young authors' stories and tries to probe the dialogic, in Bakhtin's sense, between the self as an "author" creating works and the other as a "hero" created in these works. The third question elicits some pedagogical implications from these young authors by paying attention to what they can achieve through language.

The first section of this chapter introduces Bakhtin's (1990, 1993) early philosophical concept of the author-hero relationships—and his later essays of novelistic discourses as part of the conceptual framework guiding the exploration of understanding children's authorship—and links it to recent research about children's writing. The second section unpacks the first two queries listed above by focusing on six children's narratives showing their passion, will, and joy at being an author. Each of their works, which represents its writer as an author and/or a character in the stories, serves as a link to investigate the identity issues involved, bringing forth the meaning of being an author as something wonderful, powerful, playful, and truthful. Finally, section three will discuss the possible implications drawn from these young authors and attempt to understand their perceptions about what it means to write and to create through language.

# Bakhtin's Novelistic Discourse

## The Author-Hero Relationship and Dialogism

In his early essay *Art and Answerability*, Bakhtin (1990) depicts the aesthetic relationships between authors and their heroes (or their fictional characters) as he explores the dialogic nature of authorial discourses constructed between the self and the other. For Bakhtin, there is a parallel between the author-hero relation and the self/other relation: the author creates a hero as an independent whole who is segregated from the author's domination. As Bakhtin (1990) indicates, a hero in a novel is "an aesthetically consummated phenomenon" (p. 17), a consciousness of the author's consciousness and a "being" existing in the author's "excess of seeing" (p. 22), and yet a separate individual entirely outside the author as another living organism. Creating a work of verbal art is, for Bakhtin, a construction of social relationships between the self (author) and the other (hero). This creation of verbal art is based on the author's position outside himself, that is, the author's intersubjective, third person perspective: "the author...must experience himself on a plane that is different from the one on which we actually experience our own life... He must become another in relation to himself, must look at himself through the eyes of another" (Bakhtin, 1990, p. 15).

Because of this "otherness," the author is able to create a hero, another living being possessing its own value and moral views, existing in an already complex world, facing and dealing with situations during various moments of life. This aesthetic wholeness of a hero is possible because of the author's "surplus" (Holquist, 2002) seeing and knowing in relation to his hero. The author's excess of knowing and seeing is rendered from social relationships between the self and the other. This concept of "otherness" becomes fundamental in Bakhtin's later essays (1981) on novelistic genres and discourses. Several crucial concepts constituting Bakhtin's philosophy of dialogism (e.g., Heteroglossia, dialogic discourses, speech genres, polyphonic novel, etc.) are intrinsically tied to this "otherness" in relation to the self.

One important epistemological question that Bakhtin (1990) wrestles with in the author-hero relationship is the elaboration of the self/other relationship through an aesthetic lens. Bakhtin (1990) argues that in order to understand the profound meaning of the author-hero relationship, one should not approach it from psychological or sociological methods because these "scientific" methods "lack a sufficiently deepened formal-aesthetic understanding of the fundamental creative principle in the author-hero relationship, situating for it various psychological and social relations and factors that are passive and transgredient to the creating consciousness: the hero and the author cease to be constituents of a work as an artistic whole, and instead become constituents of a prosaically conceived unity of psychological and social life" (p. 9). For this part, Bakhtin shares a similar view with Heidegger's (1962) skepticism about various "scientific" approaches toward the meaning of human existence.

For Bakhtin (1990), a hero is an aesthetic constitutive whole of particular self-manifestations and this unitary whole is the author's reaction or relation to his hero; it is "a reaction that assembles all of the cognitive-ethical determinations and valuations of the hero and consummates them in the form of a unitary and unique whole that is a concrete, intuitable whole, but also a whole of meaning" (p. 5); it is "the whole of the hero and the whole of the author" (p. 9). Bakhtin's aesthetic author-hero relationship is constituted by two consciousnesses: "what is constitutive for such [aesthetic] events is the relationship of one consciousness to another consciousness precisely as an other" (p. 86). This dialogic relationship also grounds Bakhtin's view of human existence— that is, the self or the event of being a self is a dialogic process and that in dialogism, consciousness gives rise to otherness. Holiquist (2002) interprets that "[consciousness] is the differential relation between a center and all that is not that center" (p. 18).

The two active consciousnesses develop a reciprocal relationship in which an author is "the uniquely active form-giving energy that is manifested not in a psychologically conceived consciousness, but in a durable valid cultural product, and his active, productive reaction is manifested in the structures it generates—in the structure of the active vision of a hero as a definite whole, in the structure of his image, in the rhythm of disclosing him, in the structure of intonating, and in the selection of meaning-bearing features" (Bakhtin, 1990, p. 8). The hero is an "incarnation of meaning in existence rather than a validation and demonstration of the truth of an idea" (p. 10). Thus, for Bakhtin, the real understanding of the author-hero relationship is to unpack the creative structure of the work of verbal art—a novel.

Bakhtin's dialogic interaction between an author and a hero—and later on, his idea of dialogic relationship between the self and the other—bears resemblance to Mead's (1934) theory of the self. Bakhtin searches for the answer of the self through everyday dialogues among individuals and regards the dialogic interaction between the self and the other as a dynamic, vibrant, coming-alive clash between the centripetal and centrifugal forces (Bakhtin, 1981). This unconsummation or conflict in our everyday dialogues is what keeps us living and acting. Mead, similarly, theorizes a concept of the self through everyday human action in which the profound meaning of the self resides in the whole process of every meaningful act. The emergence of the self in Mead's pragmatism presupposes and deals with an individual actor's social routine of encountering and solving problems. Mead's otherness is internalized as a generalized other that monitors, interacts with, and gives rise to the self. This also echoes Bakhtin's novelistic discourse in that even utterances voiced by a single author or individual are internally as well as externally in dialogue with the other's voices or words.

In summary of Bakhtin's view of the author-hero relationship, an author is an active agent who "[enriches] the self-activity of the subject or hero, in a fashion that could only occur because [the author] is external to it" (Hicks, 2000, p. 234). The structure of the author-hero relationship is the author's aesthetic response to the world and is possible only through the social dialogic relation with others in the world.

## Heteroglossia as Meaning-Making Repertoire

If we agree with Bakhtin (1986) that all the diverse areas of human activity involve the use of language and discourses, and that individual utterances are possible only through the co-existence of the other's voice, then how one recreates and appropriates the other's language and discourses into one's own becomes significant for understanding the meaning one tries to convey through one's work of verbal art. More importantly, the meaning inherent in an author's work is intrinsically related to his authorial identity. It is particularly obvious in the young authors' writing in this study. First of all, let us briefly review what Bakhtin's language philosophy informs us about language use and how it relates to an author's identity as an author-creator.

As Bakhtin's (1981) novelistic discourse indicates, novels are a powerful and artistic way of shaping perceptions and transforming another's discourse into an aesthetic unity. The "speaking person," along with his/her discourse in a novel, is a crucial concept for Bakhtin in defining the genre of a novel. As Bakhtin (1981) points out, the speaking person and his/her discourse in a novel is: (1) an object of verbal artistic representation, (2) a confluence of potential languages that strive for certain social significance among the heteroglossia of language use, and (3) an experiment in trying out one's ideological positions, discourses, or a particular way of viewing the world. Thus, Bakhtin's concern is not so much about the person who speaks but rather about what has been spoken through that speaking person: "Characteristic for the novel as a genre is not the image of a man in his own right, but precisely the image of language" (Bakhtin, 1981, p. 336). Other people's words or utterances become the resource for our daily communication, interpretation, discussion, evaluation, and argumentation. Bakhtin (1981) continues,

In real life people talk most of all about what others talk about—they transmit, recall, weigh and pass judgment on other people's words, opinions, assertions, information; people are upset by others' words, or agree with them, contest them, refer to them and so forth....in conversational hurly-burly of people in a crowd, everything often fuses into one big "he says...you say...I say..." reflect how enormous is the weight of "everyone says" and "it is said" in public opinion, public rumor, gossip, slander and so forth... Every conversation is full of transmissions and interpretations of other people's words. (p. 338)

Creating a novel, to a great extent, is to transform these everyday *hurly-burly* conversations, the "primary" (or simple) daily speech genres (Bakhtin, 1986), into the "secondary" (or complex) ones (e.g., novels, dramas, research papers, all sorts of documents). This metamorphosis from the primary every-dayness to the complex novelistic genres is an artistic, sociopolitical, or ideological transformation appearing in various human activities or social events.

According to Bakhtin, there are three general aspects grounding the meaning of a novel in terms of its genres, its novelistic discourses, or the reformulation of everyday dialogues and another's utterances: (1) the situated context of a novel (i.e., the concept of "chronotope"—time and space); (2) the emergence of new meanings as well as semantic changes derived from a novel; and (3) a novel as "the zone of contact" (Bakhtin, 1981, p. 345) where various discourses meet and mix. These three aspects of a novel carry significant implications for understanding the children's authorial as well as artistic discourse in their works.

The concept of "chronotope" is the spatial and temporal relationships expressed in a novel that relatively ground the meaning of the texts throughout the story. An author's unique novelistic discourse is to re-formulate the everyday dialogues and another's voices into an aesthetic whole under a particular context. This unique novelistic discourse is the product of "interanimating relationships with new contexts" (Bakhtin, 1981, p. 346) through constant interaction with the other. This ceaseless interactive mixture between the self and the other creates new meanings as well as changes the old meanings of utterances: "[T]he speech of another, once enclosed in a context, is—no matter how accurately transmitted—always subject to certain semantic changes" (Bakhtin, 1981, p. 340).

Moreover, as Bakhtin asserts, authorial discourses contain various competing contents in which different discourses are pushing boundaries between one another. These competing forces of discourses awaken individual consciousness as well as activate one's dormant semiotic potential for heteroglot ways of meaning-making. Creating a novel or a work of verbal art is to draw various persuasive discourses of another into this artistic "contact zone" where these diverse discourses are contested, synthesized, recreated, and hybridized into a unique authorial and novelistic discourse. This "contact zone," as Bakhtin (1981) suggests, "creates fertile soil for experimentally objectifying another's discourse" (p. 348), gradually frees one's self from the authority of the others' discourses, and creates one's own distinctive, dialogically hybridized discourse.

For Bakhtin, dialogism and heteroglossia are the constituting conditions for the emergence of independent consciousness, the active transformation of language use, and meaning-making. How do all these relate to an author's identity for creating his story? Why do many children in this class love to be an author? I will now turn to the framework of this study.

## The Identity of Being an Author

The parallels between the author-hero relationships and the self/other relationships drawn from Bakhtin's theory serve as the main conceptual framework guiding the inquiry of this chapter: the relationships between the children's authorial identity and their work of verbal art. The author's "speech will" determines the "speech genre" she has chosen for shaping her work. The purpose of studying language use in terms of recreating the other's words into one's own is to understand the meaning conveyed through one's artistic reformulation as well as through the appropriation of the other's voices.

Through the boundless heteroglossia of manipulating and testing out various genres and utterances, being an author becomes many children's favorite literacy activity in school, as shown at the beginning of the chapter. It provides authors with unlimited semiotic possibilities of inclusion, exclusion, hybridization, addressivity, and answerability that the creative force of the self is emancipated from complex social relationships, discourses, conventional speech genres, and voices of the other. What I mean by emancipation of the creative self from the other is not in the sense of detaching the self from the other. Quite the contrary, this emancipating force is derived by throwing the self into a constant dialogic interaction as well as an unlimited interplay with the other that creates infinite possibilities in the immense universe of heteroglossia. It is particularly obvious in language use when an author tries to rework another's voice into his own and create his speech genre or authorial discourse by moving intersubjectively inside and outside of the story.

The relationship between an author and the speaking person(s) in the story reveals an author's different ways of claiming his identity through dialoging explicitly and implicitly with the other and remaking this "otherness" into his own discourse. An author's unique discourse or genre is expressed through his language use in a particular writing style. That is, an author more or less chooses to foreground a particular structural component through writing to highlight the meaning he tries to convey through his work. Thus, the inquiry of this chapter is mainly to reconstruct three aspects:

(1) the authors' identity conveyed through their conversation during inter-views about their experiences and goals as an author,
(2) the dialogic interaction between the self and the other expressed in the authors' works; that is, how multiple discourses are involved and reshaped in their works, and
(3) the authors' intentionality achieved through their work.

In the next section, I will analyze six young authors' narratives about being an author and how they express their authorial discourses in their works. The six authors' works represent the most typical genres of stories (e.g., autobiog-raphy, information books, fiction, adventures, etc.) created by the children in this class.

## The Young Authors and Their Works

### The Favorite Literacy Activity

The writing workshop is many children's favorite literacy activity in school. Research about the process of writing (Graves, 1983) and writing workshops (Ray, 1999; Ray & Cleaveland, 2004; Atwell, 1998; Calkins, 1994; Lensimire, 1994, 2000) explore the power of writing through student ownership, control of texts, and goals achieved through writing. Freedom of choice and the flexi-ble nature of the writing curriculum are two additional reasons why children are so engaged and determined to be an author. It allows more time and space for them to maneuver their agency and autonomy through the use of lan-guage. As indicated in the beginning of the chapter, one strong desire articu-lated by these young authors is to make writing their "own," because they know that ownership is the privilege of an author. Being an author is serious business for these children (Harste, Woodward, & Burke, 1984). As Ray and Cleaveland (2004) suggest, "during writing workshops, they [children] are makers of books and we build all our teaching around that identity...being a maker of books is a very big part of a child's identity" (pp. 16–17).

There are eight procedures serving as guidance in the writing workshop in this class: (1) brainstorming, (2) story web, (3) rough draft, (4) edit with a friend, (5) edit with an adult, (6) publishing center, (7) illustration, (8) author celebration. These eight procedures were written on a large poster containing plastic pockets for each procedure and hung at the entrance of the classroom. Next to each procedure are the children's name cards, indicating the writing stage of each child.

The class holds an official writing workshop every Friday morning, but the children are allowed to work on their own story anytime any day as soon as they finish their main tasks in school. The children could choose their own topic, work with their friends, and finish at their own pace. They can also take it home and work with their parents. Mrs. Jones and Mr. Smith are flexible about the writing workshop, for their main purpose during the writing workshop is to provide children space and time to work on their own stories and explore writing on their own as well as with each other. The writing workshop values the students' autonomy, control, and ownership (Calkins, 1994; Graves, 1983; Lensimire, 2000). There is no deadline for publishing their books; publishing and sharing their work is encouraged but not forced. So, those who work fast could have more than one book published and those who work slowly or who still have trouble writing would have only one or no books published in a semester. The school has a publishing center where young authors send in their handwritten draft and have it typed up and bound into a book.

## The Young Authors' Stories

The self projected in these young authors' works is intrinsically related to (a) the genre of their writing, (b) the inclusion of the content, and (c) their personal beliefs conveyed throughout the work. Most of the children's self-created stories are constituted by these three basic components with varying emphasis on each. According to their emphasis, we can roughly divide the children's stories into three types: (1) the emphasis on one's own beliefs or personal experiences—the "who," (2) the emphasis on the representation of the structural content—the "how," and (3) the emphasis on a particular genre—the "what." Each foregrounding component in the books reveals the writer's identity as an author dialoging with the other, exploring different possibilities of meanings, reformulating the other's languages, bathing in the web of endless heteroglossia of discourses, and finally achieving their unique authorial discourses in their works.

### *Ted*

My book is about my life. Actually I am also the reader of my book. The most interesting part of my book uh I'll have to say page seven because it has all my pets' names. I have eight pets: dogs, fish, and a tarantula.

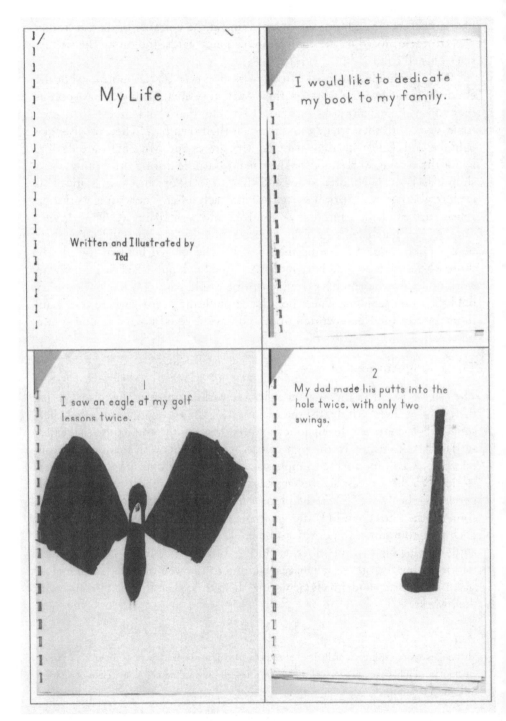

My Life

Written and Illustrated by
Ted

I would like to dedicate
my book to my family.

1
I saw an eagle at my golf
lessons twice.

2
My dad made his putts into the
hole twice, with only two
swings.

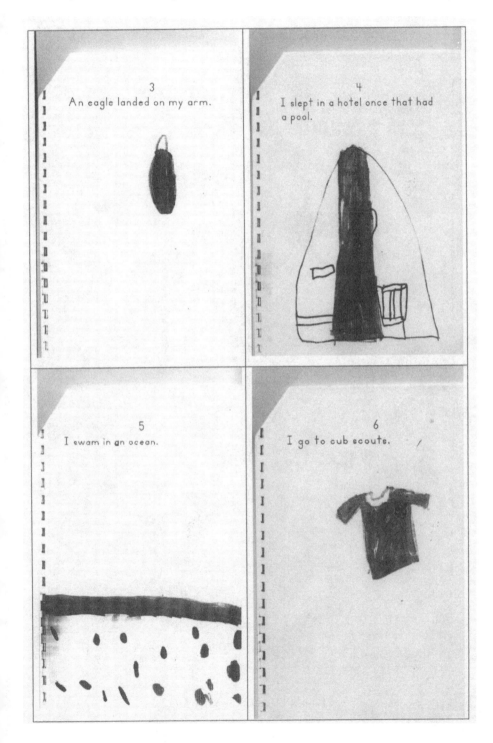

**Table 4-1 Ted's Story:** *My Life*

Like many young children, Ted's memoir is the primary source for his writing. It is also the most direct way that an author communicates with his audiences by sharing his own life. Ted's book (Table 4-1) is about his life, different moments of it: playing golf with his father, seeing an eagle landing on his arm, living in a hotel with a pool, swimming in the ocean, and having eight pets. It is strung with his memories chosen as his authorial discourse in his writing that directly communicates with the other through the first-person narrative. It is Ted's autobiographical "truth" over which he has absolute ownership as well as subjective experience. This type of personal memoir is probably the most popular story that many children have created in this class. They like to write something they are familiar with, such as my dog, my cat, my mom, my family, my trip, and the like.

One interesting point Ted made is that he is also "the reader" of his own book. Bakhtin considers that creating a novel is a struggle between an author and himself. When writing a story, an author is the first reader of his own book; and as the first reader, he needs to be convinced, that is, he must experience the process that involves the dialogic interaction between the self and the other in that the self is able to take the role of a reader while also being the author. Moreover, each author is taking multiple roles simultaneously when constructing his own story. Multiple roles and discourses are organized and orchestrated by an author who dialogues intersubjectively between the self and the other through his work.

### Winnie

> Usually I would just write my story because when I write, I really don't care about what others think. If I think it's a good book, it's a good book.

This is Winnie's absolute power claim as an author. Her story is about her belief in "fairies," an area of knowledge that she has read from in another author's book: "I have a series called Elves. And it's my favorite story. It's about an elf's adventure." Reading and writing are inseparable as the dialogical interplay between the self and the other. Reading other authors' books opens Winnie's view toward the meaning of creating book:

> I've heard different three kinds of The Three Little Pigs that are totally different from each other. Like one they [the three little pigs] can come out of their own story book, and they kind of jump out of the pictures...But then in the other book, they are just being chased by the wolf in their houses. And it gives like ~ the one the first one that I've ever heard really maybe ~ with them just their straw, brick, and stick houses. But then once I heard the book while they can come out of the story and go to different pictures, it just ~ it gives me a whole different impression on the book 'cause I used to think that that's the only way I could hear it.

# Fairies

Written and
Illustrated by
**Winnie**

I would like to
dedicate my
book to my
little sister Lily.

## Introduction

I chose to write
about fairies
because I like them.
I did a beginning,
middle, and end for
my story like all good
authors do. And I
did it all on my own!

## 1

There are all
different kinds of
fairies. Some *people*
believe they're real
and some people
don't.

They're not
real!   Yes they are.

**Table 4-2 Winnie's Story: *Fairies***

The different versions of *The Three Little Pigs* make Winnie realize that an author is privileged to create her story based on her beliefs. As the other authors do in their versions of *The Three Little Pigs*, the little pigs do not need to be chased by the wolf and an author can decide and manipulate these fictional characters to achieve the meaning the author wishes to convey. Winnie was amazed by what authors can do to create multiple versions of a story through re-writing, reinterpreting and reformulating. It is the fun part about writing to create multiple versions and test out different perspectives through creating a story.

As her book (Table 4-2) indicates, "fairies" might be imaginative and some people believe in them and some don't. However, "most important of all...I believe!" This is Winnie's definition of being an author embedded in her statement that she has full control of what to write and how to mean.

Both Ted and Winnie impress their identity claims upon readers as the speaking person in their stories. Ted's subjective experiences in his life and Winnie's personal beliefs about what an author can do are what they choose to foreground in their stories, and this, in turn, leads us to understand how they construct their authorial discourse as well as identity through creating a book.

### Jeff

> Well, my story is called *Or Else*. It's about two boys Ed and Ted. And Ed just keeps running into trouble when he does what Ted says that he shouldn't do. It's called *Or Else* because um well um whenever — like um Ted says ~ like ~ for instance, like "Don't go in my bedroom or else," and Ed says "Or else what?" and then Ted says "Or else or else."

Applying a playfully reiterative writing style in his story (Table 4-3, pp.102-103), Jeff seems to build up the tension between the two characters by repeating the same sentence structure throughout the story and then ending it dramatically by breaking up the repetitive flow of the story. This kind of repetitive genre is popular in young children's literature. Thus, repeating the same sentence pattern throughout the whole story is how young children start constructing written texts. Jeff told me about his literacy history and how "young" he started to read:

> You know how young I started getting into books. I pretty much like a lot of books and uh when I was smaller, I was just like three years old and that's when I started to get into books...When I write, I just sort of open my mind I think. My ideas are from the pictures and the comic type of books that I am familiar with.

Table 4-3 Jeff's Story: *Or Else*

"Open my mind" is Jeff's way of brainstorming because his mind is filled up with the other authors' books, ideas, and voices.

When asked what the most important thing is in a story, Jeff provided an insightful view:

> Well, probably the most important thing is what it means 'cause just um like hearing the sounds of the words and like looking at the pictures and it's about uh it just means something and so you can understand it. And pictures are also very important parts so people that cannot read might get it. But words are also extremely important so that you can know complete what happened because sometimes the pictures just show part of something that was on the page... So words are extremely important.

For Jeff, words, pictures, and purposes of texts constitute the meaning of a book. When children write, drawing is also part of their text construction. We can see how drawing has constituted part of Winnie's and Ted's stories as well. Any sign (words or graphics) is dialogic in nature, for "a sign can be a sign only if it appears as something other than itself, only in dialogue with another sign of the contextual relations" (Mladenov, 2001, p. 443). This is similar to Peirce's semiotic theory of the trichotomy (i.e., sign, object, and interpretant) in that "a sign exists only if it is mediated by its interpretant: i.e., there is no sign without the other sign which interprets it. Each time this occurs, the interpretant in its turn becomes another sign. The identity of the sign (i.e., its meaning) lies in the field of mediation between the sign and its interpretant" (Mladenov, 2001, p. 443). I will discuss more about children's drawing in Chapter Five.

In addition to drawing, what Jeff chose to foreground in his story is a repetitive and rhetorical pattern of utterances (i.e., "Or else...or else what...") that draws the reader's attention until the dramatic change at the end of the story. It surprises readers with a fun, humorous ending remark, "WANT TO ASK [FOR] A SPANKING?" Capitalizing the letters, as Jeff explained, meant "screaming."

### Paul

> My book is actually based on *Dinotopia*. It's called *Chomper's Return*. It's got a big picture, a picture I draw for my book cover... a big mouth of like an allosaurus or T-rex with the jaws open wide.

Paul's story is based on a book he read (*Dinotopia–Chomper* by Donald F. Glut), and he creates his own version of the story about a giganotosaurus named Chomper. This kind of "literacy borrowing" (Lancia, 1997), borrowing from or dialoging with the other authors, is a strategy often used in children's creative writing. When introducing his book, Paul gave thorough background "knowledge" about his story:

> Chomper is a giganotosaurus. And it is the second biggest carnivore ever existed on earth...he grows up in the town from a hatchery. And then he has to travel to the most dangerous part in the ~ well maybe the second most dangerous part of Dinotopia, the rainy basin where huge carnivores live and [there are] dangerous swamps, quick sand... Chomper is only a teenage giganotosaurus ~ uh probably about this height of this ceiling (Pointing to the ceiling of the room)...An adult giganotosaurus is actually getting a little over three stories... My story is about how they live, how they how dinosaurs hunt and how they grow up.

Paul is the dinosaur *expert* in this classroom. His talk shows his knowledge of prehistoric life and he would reference the size of a particular dinosaur with the dimensions of concrete objects such as the "height of this ceiling" or "three stories." He pointed out the size difference between a teenage giganotosaurus and an adult one. Not only that, he also knows the size difference among different kinds of carnivore dinosaurs: "[giganotosaurus] is the second biggest carnivore ever existed on earth." He knows so much about dinosaurs that I sometimes could not quite catch the complicated, long polysyllabic dinosaur names that he had no trouble pronouncing. Not only does he know each dinosaur's name, Paul is also familiar with each dinosaur's size, shape of the skull, habitat, how it hunts, and what it eats. I once asked Paul if he ever did his dinosaur research on the Internet. He responded even before I finished my question: "No, I didn't. I know so much about dinosaurs that I really don't have to go on to the Internet."

He enjoyed asking questions about dinosaurs and then answering them by himself during our conversation:

> What is the dinosaur with the flattest head? Monolophosaurus. Its head is about only a centimeter thick. I've seen the two skeletons. It was a Chinese dinosaur.

Paul's statement reveals his strong identity as a prehistoric expert and an author. For him, being an author is equal to being an expert about something written in the book. Different from the previous authors' creations, Paul's story is a long chapter book without any pictures except for the cover of the book. I quote only part of his book in Table 4-4.

Paul's story is about the friendship between a boy named Perry and Chomper, a giganotosaurus. Perry used to take care of Chomper when Chomper was a baby. In this story, when Perry revisits Chomper, Chomper already has his own family—a wife and four little giganotosaurus. The story

The last time Perry had seen Chomper, Chomper was only 23 feet long. He had probably doubled in size. Was he still alive? Perry hoped that there would be some baby Giganotosaurus...

When he got over to the other side of the bridge, he found out that the little Giganotosaurus was actually Chomper's son, and that his name was Carlon. Chomper led them back to the Giganotosaurus Olympic Field...

There, Perry saw the entire Giganotosaurus clan... Above them was a Giganotosaurus that had been beside Chomper. Perry had not seen her before. Her name was Lightbow. She and Chomper were the parents of all those little Giganotosaurus... Chomper now was 50 feet long. Lightbow was 47 feet long.

...A huge Tyrannosaurus rex crashed through the brush. Suddenly, Chomper jumped from where he was. The two got into a big fight. Luckily, Chomper had been scale wrestling, and Chomper won.

There, all the males in the park were fighting for some reason. Perry asked Chomper what was happening. Chomper told him that is was mating season and all the males would fight for females. When Perry looked at Carlon, he was imitating his elders!

Chomper came up to Perry and said that Perry could take one of his kids home as a gift for taking care of him when he was little.

**Table 4-4 Paul's Story:** *Dinotopia—Chomper's Return*

reflects a mixture of Paul's prehistoric knowledge (i.e., how dinosaurs live, mate, fight, hunt) and his human culture as well as social relationships (i.e., friendship, family structures, male/female viewpoints, language use). It is through this aesthetic lens, in Bakhtin's (1990) sense, that human sociocultural relationships are able to merge with dinosaurs' life and behavior and thus make the conversations between human beings and dinosaurs possible through Paul's work of verbal art. The personification of dinosaurs in Paul's story is the result of a dialogic hybrid between human discourse and animal discourse whereby animal life can be interpreted through human perspective, and human sociocultural relationships can find common ground and connection with animal life.

Both Jeff and Paul create their fictional characters (or "heroes" in Bakhtin's term) as the speaking persons in the story. Unlike Ted and Winnie who are themselves the "I" in the first-person narrative of the speaking person in their stories, Jeff and Paul speak through "he" or "they," a third person narrative. More importantly, they try to convey meanings through using everyday conversations, spoken by different characters in their stories, such as how Ed and Ted get into arguments in Jeff's story and how Perry, Chomper, and Chomper's family talk about things that happened in their life.

### Peter and Ian

> Ian: I like to write because I think I like adventurous stories and I mean it's ten times better than the movies because ~
> Peter: You are doing your own thing.
> Ian: Because you're doing it and the adventures are really exciting and stuff. It's basically like you are in another world....Our ideas are kind of the same.
> Peter: And we're good friends...I like to write my own stuff sometimes with people and sometimes by myself. And I just like to write my creative stuff.

Peter and Ian love to create their adventurous stories, fantasize about different kinds of monsters, create hypothetical dangerous situations, and work out the solutions in the process of developing the story. Their devotion to create their adventurous stories is a projection of their social relationships and identities. In the previous chapter, I discussed how children use literacy to group themselves and build up collective identities among peers. Peter and Ian's friendship is one example. They also differentiate themselves from the other authors in this class by emphasizing the type of the story they create:

> Peter: We have done a long uh ~
> Ian: Well, last year, we were making a um ~ we're publishing a story. It's called uh ~
> Peter: The Vanishing of the Dragon Boat and it's got um 26 chapters.
> Ian: Super long...we wrote it together the whole last year.

> Peter: It took us the whole year and we had to edit it this year 'cause it's real hard and we couldn't read aloud to the class.

Like every author, Peter and Ian shape their stories by using various cultural materials they are familiar with (e.g., books, comics, TV, movies, video games):

> Ian: The book I really like is the mummy book because there are a lot of interesting things in it. My favorite [type of] book is probably mythology.
> Peter: I like mythology, too....
> Ian: I like mythology because um I just like um monsters and I like um medieval things and I study um I like fossils a lot. Oh, movies, yes, movies.
> Peter: Crush the Titans. I have that one and um ~
> Ian: One of my favorite monster movies is um I like the old-fashioned one, the original Mummy. My dad used to see that. And the original Wolfman is pretty cool.
> Peter: Oh, I have seen those and I have seen original um Dracula and other movies.
> Ian: Sssssss-rrrurrrrr-ooowaaaaa-rrrow... (Making Dracula's growling voices) Oh, oh, oh, yeah, The Lord of the Rings is one of my favorite.
> Peter: I have that....
> Ian: It's awesome.
> Peter: And I've seen Star Trek—Nemesis.
> Ian: Oh, yeah, Star Trek—Nemesis...

Pop culture, media power, and super hero shows or stories and the like are an important part of the multimodality (Kress, 1997, 2003) of children's world. These cultural resources provide heteroglossia and endless semiosis for children to master living in the world. It explains why it is exciting for Peter and Ian to try out various discourses in their books: through creating their own books, they experience what it is like to be "in another world" and the dynamic and complex world that they are living in and awaiting to explore. While Peter was telling me what his book was about, he and Ian had an argument:

> Peter: I have my own story that I wrote and it's getting published. It's called "The Ancient Pyramid and Dragons. It's about um these scientists who have a potion and this guy dropped the potion and then it was all smoke and stuff ~
> Ian: Because it's full of smoke ~ (Ian seemed to know Peter's story well).
> Peter: And then um he um looked at the mirror, and he saw they become dragons. And to survive, they had to defeat um ~
> Ian: To defeat themselves (Ian interrupted Peter).
> Peter: NO! (Raising his voice and seeming angry) Stay away from it! This is MY story, Ian.

This kind of argument usually happened when the author's ownership was invaded during conversations. Even though Peter and Ian are good friends, the author's ownership seems a more serious business than friendship—particularly when ownership is under threat.

Since Peter's (Table 4-5) and Ian's (Table 4-6) chapter books are "super long," I shorten them for the purpose of the study.

The Ancient Pyramid and the Dragons

**Chapter 1: The Spill**
Once there live four men. So it started when they were working in their lab. They were creating a poison called "Dragon Juice." It could turn people into dragons! One of them was drinking a vanilla soda. He walked past the poison and a little drop fell inside the poison! Smoke started coming out, and when all the smoke cleared, they were dragons! They thought it was amazing but they did not know that it poisoned their brains.

**Chapter 2: Pain**
... Then their started having a lot of pain. They started getting really strong and they grew arms, huge wings, and big muscles... So, they flew to Egypt... They liked to explore for gold!

**Chapter 3 (no subject)**
The four dragons ran away from the Cyclops. Soon an evil angle flew down it. It had amazing power. It had blue electric fire balls and an electric slime fire water lava shield. They tried and tried to defeat it, but they couldn't... a knight made out of fire flew down on a Pegasus, and it melted the evil angel to wax! "Wow!" the dragons said...

**Chapter 5: The Search for the Ancient Pyramid**
...This was their best journey to the pyramid. If they found it, they had to fight Lord Dreadson, the most powerful and evil in the universe... they heard a big rumble. A giant serpent came out of the ground. They fought for almost a year and a half... They went down and there was Lord Dreadson. They fought for 17 years. They won the battle and got all the gold...

**Chapter 6: The Serpent Rage**
...A skeleton was rolling the boat. The skeleton could not talk... They saw giant scorpions. They fought and fought until they defeated the queen and all the scorpions, but the king wasn't dead. He was behind them... but they melted the king with fire!

**Chapter 7: The Two-headed Blind Ninjas**
...When they got into the cave, they saw two-headed blind ninjas. They fought until they wounded all the ninjas. The ninjas tried to tell the dragons that they were good. They stayed for a while and then left.

**Chapter 9: Life and Death**
... There were billion-year-old houses and skeletons. There was a red stream of dead rats, skeleton eyeballs, and other dead things and body parts. Then when they looked on the ground, there were bugs of all types; millions! ...

**Chapter 10: Then End of Dreadson**
They flew home and there was Lord Dreadson. They blew fire at him but it just went through him. He had done a transformation. One of the dragons said it's impossible. "We can't beat him; he's just too powerful." Then suddenly, the fire knight jumped out and sliced Lord Dreadson's arm off and they lived happily ever after.

**Table 4-5 Peter's Story:** *The Ancient Pyramid and the Dragons*

Peter's novelistic discourses can be detected from several aspects. First, he adopted the conventional structure of the book composed of several chapters and a predictable ending that everyone (except the enemies) lives happily ever after. Second, power is another interesting concept explored in Peter's story. The four scientists were accidentally turned into four powerful dragons. However, the transformation was painful. Peter created different kinds of enemies, crises, dangers, and battles to test the dragons' power, courage, resilience, and perseverance in the story.

Third, to make the whole adventure exciting, Peter manipulated the spatiotemporal dimensions in his story. The space started from a lab where the great transformation happened and then moved to Egypt where they fought a series of battles and finally came back home after defeating "Lord Dreadson." During the process of the adventure, the dragons flew to different places to fight with different monsters, such as a ghost town, different caves, and the pyramid. Some settings in the story also produce the iconic effects through descriptive words, such as "a red stream of dead rats, skeleton eyeballs, other dead things and body parts, bugs of all types; millions!" These words create eerie images and a frightening atmosphere when reading the story. Temporally, the "billion-year-old" houses and "skeletons" situate the context of the time in an ancient setting. The names of the wars—the "year and half"-long battle between the dragons and the giant serpent, and the 17-year-long battle between the dragons and "Lord Dreadson"~ show how Peter references the difficulty of the battle by the length of time.

Finally, Peter seemed to touch on a complex moral issue that was not fully developed in his story. Nevertheless, I think it is worth noticing and could potentially become a curricular topic to cultivate children's critical thinking. In his story, Peter mentioned about the ninjas who were enemies of the dragons at the beginning, and then they somehow became friends when after communicating with each other the dragon realized that they were actually not bad guys. There are some questions we could invite children to think about when they construct an adventure story: What does it mean when you consider someone as your enemy? What can be done to resolve the tension with your enemy? Peter's story introduced a strategic action that a hero can take to solve a problem, an action that is different from the stereotypical story plot, that is, a hero does not always have to fight in order to win; a hero can resolve tensions and threats through negotiation and make peace with enemies.

Ian also wrote an adventurous story:

> My story is called The Golden Pendant. It's about um these four boys, me, Ian and Peter, him, and two of my other friends. And we were scientists. And we went on this adventure to an island. And we had to fight this like ~ native people and stuff, but we have this secret power and we can flee together.

Instead of creating fictional characters, Ian used people in real life, including himself, as heroes in his fictional world. One serious issue appeared in Ian's story—death. It seems that death has to be part of the story and that death happens not only to enemies but also to heroes. Whenever there is a war, there will be casualties on both sides. Ian seemed to balance out the issue of casualty between the scientists and the natives in his story.

Moreover, the moral discourse between the good and the bad, justice and evil, is ideologically divided into two camps: the gun-firing scientists representing modern civilization versus the arrow-shooting natives living in a savage tribal type of society. Also, another ideological assumption is how Ian positions the scientists as those who explore "the unknown places" and are thus excused for the righteous mission to invade the natives' land while the natives are blamed for shooting some arrows at the intruders for protecting their homeland.

Finally, because there are only three scientists (one died during the mission) fighting against the "whole city" of natives, the scientists need to have "special powers" to win the battle. Power is an important issue in both Peter's and Ian's stories. As a matter of fact, the purpose of the adventure or fantasy type of stories is to manipulate, try out, and explore different kinds of power that one can generate, endure, or resist. Gerard Jones (2002) argues that fantasy or superhero type of stories help children deal with frustration, create venues to express their feeling and thoughts, and empower them to control their life.

He further asserts that for decades many psychologists have tried to prove that media violence makes children more aggressive, desensitizes them, or distorts their views of reality, but only very few studies pay attention to why children are attracted to it or what possible positive effects it might have on them. What really attracts children toward media culture is not just the action part of it, but also the complex moral and ethical issues, feelings, desires, constraints, and all sorts of rules confronting them in their real life:

> Mastering a world, finding the hero's proper place in that world, learning rules and limitations, integrating various powers and functions, completing collections, understanding the connections among the good, the bad, and the in-between can be more important to young fans than the simple excitement of the action. As the real world that our children have to master becomes more complicated, so do the fantasy worlds they're attracted to. (Jones, 2002, p. 223)

My argument, similar to Jones's, is that children want the power to control their own lives. Being an author who is privileged to create anything one wants becomes a critical part of a child's life to try out inventive as well as imaginative literacy power through language use.

Both Peter and Ian foreground the genre of adventure and fantasy by diversifying the interplay between space and time as the fundamental structure of their stories. Complex moral dimensions, power struggle and the issue of life and death are also important parts of their novelistic discourses. These are everyday issues that children try to understand in their social worlds. As Bakhtin (1981) suggests, an author's work is "the contact zone" where various discourses mix, conflict, integrate, and reshape with each other, it is also like a gigantic conversation where all participants and perspectives inside and outside of the story bring their desires, fears, pains, experiences, knowledge, and challenges to negotiate, contest, and compromise.

---

*The Golden Pendant/The Time Machine to the Dragon World, The Series*

### Chapter 1: The Two Men

...The scientists, Joe and Evan, went on a plane to an island called Matenewie... Joe said he would go and explore. He got out and went into the woods. He walked for about 15 minutes. He saw something he could not believe!

### Chapter 2: The Discovery

There were natives. A whole city of them! He ran off to get Evan, but then a panther came out and Joe immediately got his gun and fired it by him...When he found Evan he was surrounded by all these natives with arrows pointed right at him!

### Chapter 3: Evan Dies

One native saw him and fired the arrow right at him. Luckily it missed. But another native killed Evan. Joe ran away. He found a cave and hid in it...When he looked out in the distance, he saw a huge mountain. It looked like a huge skull!

### Chapter 4: Repeating of Bad Things

He decided to check it out...When he finally got there, a bunch of arrows started coming right at him. Luckily, they all missed. Then, someone came running down the mountain, and he realized it was his friend Ian!

### Chapter 5: Another Friend Comes

They ran into the woods and found a camp site... In the middle of the night, somebody woke Joe. It was another friend, Peter, and he was Ian's best friend....

### Chapter 6: The Native King

....Ian was surprised to see Peter. They agreed to go up to the top of the mountain and see what is up there.... When they were about 100 feet in the air, a giant boulder came crashing down at them! Luckily, it did not hit anyone..... At the top there was a native. It looked like he was the leader of the tribe. He had a sword and a bow and arrow!

### Chapter 7: Powers

Ian reminded Peter and Joe that a long time ago they discovered that they had special powers. Ian's power was telekinesis. Peter's was that he could read minds. Joe's power was that he could run at the speed of light. Ian remembered that he also could make anything come out of his hands.

### Chapter 8: The Defeat

.....The native king stood by two of his best warriors. Peter and Joe agreed to fight the warriors and Ian would fight the native king...Finally Peter destroyed the warrior...Then he helped fight the native king. Joe got stabbed in the arm, but he was ok. The battle continued for a long time. Then Ian destroyed the native king!

### Chapter 9: End of the Mission

Joe, Ian and Peter were glad to see that Joe's plane was still there. They flew off, and when they finally arrived at their city, they were glad to be home!

## Table 4-6 Ian's Story: *The Golden Pendant*

# Discussion

The questions I have been trying to answer are: Why is being an author the children's favorite literacy activity in school? What do they actually achieve through being an author in their works? There are three conclusions we can draw from the analysis. First, the children empower themselves by becoming authors who make most of the decisions in the process of accomplishing their works. Their identity as authors is embedded in their unique as well as artistic discourses foregrounded in their work. Table 4-7 summarizes their novelistic discourses in their works and the meaning of being authors:

| Authors | Novelistic Discourses | Identity as an author |
|---------|----------------------|----------------------|
| Ted | Narrating his objective (e.g., the events he took part in and the pets he has) and subjective experiences in his life | Empowerment Control Creation (through mixture, |
| Winnie | Impressing readers with her beliefs | hybrid and reformulation of |
| Jeff | Applying a repetitive and rhetorical pattern of utterances | different discourses) Imagination |
| Paul | Emphasizing his expertise in a particular knowledge domain | Experiment Surprise |
| Peter | Fantasizing an adventure, manipulating spatio-temporal dimensions in the story, and presenting power under different situations | Humor Freedom Ownership |
| Ian | Creating a series of action scenes on an adventurous mission accompanied by some ideological assumptions and power issues during a war | |

**Table 4-7 The Authors' Novelistic Discourses and Identities**

Empowerment is essentially related to ownership: doing their "OWN" thing, creating their "OWN" stuff, and making their "OWN" book. It is also reflected in the children's novelistic discourses of exploring power through their life experiences, beliefs, skillful ways of language use, knowledge, and imagination. Moreover, making a book is another powerful medium that motivates children to create and achieve their goals through text construction. Putting words on paper has some sort of magical power that seems to make the creative part of the self actualize in reality. As Ray and Cleaveland (2004) point out, "Stapling the paper together and calling it a book makes a big difference in what children actually produce when they write... The book medium is a whole different suggestion entirely, and it causes them to do a very different thing with writing" (pp. 8–9).

Second, being an author frees the self to try out different ways of making sense of the world. The curriculum goal in the writing workshop provides

guidance but not authoritative rules to facilitate children on their way to cultivating their potential as authors. Lensimire (2000) uses Bakhtin's (1981, 1984)
concept of "carnival" as a metaphor to argue that writing workshops "embody
important carnival characteristic. Workshops create unofficial spaces in
school, loosen the grip of traditional roles and tasks in classrooms through
increased student control of their own literate activities" (p. 8). It is through
this unofficial space that the teacher and students find a common ground or
"the unscripted third space" (Gutierrez, Rymes, & Larson, 1995, p. 459), a
space where the students' interests merge with instructional goals.

Third, freedom or the emancipated power of being an author sets the self
free in the act of writing out and making something one's own. Smith (1994)
argues that we cannot directly observe ourselves thinking nor have direct access to our consciousness. As discussed before, Mead (1934) and Bakhtin
(1981, 1986, 1993) also propose that in order to develop or be aware of the
self, the social or dialogic is the presupposed condition. However, as Smith
(1994) adds, we can observe the products of our thought in our writing.
Through the act of writing, we encounter the other; recreate the other's voices,
utterances, or discourses; and develop the consciousness of the self through
this dialogic process. When we write, we make use of the old (e.g., conventions) to create the new. Writing leads these young authors to experience and
explore their unlimited potential that is constantly expanding through the
process of action:

> By writing what I think I know, I develop what I potentially knew. Writing does more
> than reflect underlying thought; it liberates and develops it. (Smith, 1994, p. 35)

By exploring one's potential through writing, one experiences the strength of
being oneself and understands the profound meaning of the self.

Harste, Woodward, and Burke (1984), Dyson (1989, 1997), and Wells
(1986) have done major studies about how children strive to make meanings
through talking, drawing, and writing. This meaning-making process is what
Short, Harste, and Burke (1996) call *authoring*, a form of learning and the
process where children outgrow themselves through reading and writing. I
want to argue further that the motivation of authoring, learning, and outgrow-
ing oneself is to make something one's own. Meaning-making contains not
only making sense of the world but also, more importantly, creating one's own
way to mean and live in the world. This is why being an author is such a wonderful experience as well as a significant literacy event in the children's school
life.

# CHAPTER FIVE

# Expressing the Self

**Kate:** There are two masks, Happy and Sad, and they want to plant a flower. They put the seed inside the soil, but it never grows. So they water it and water it. And then the flower starts growing, growing, and growing. It grows so big that it becomes a big flower monster. And one day it attacked the baby.

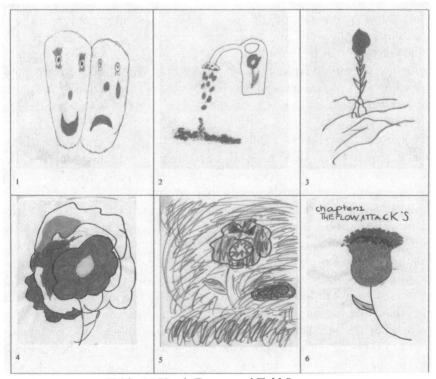

Table 5-1 Kate's Drawn and Told Story

In the previous chapter, I have discussed how significant the writing workshop is for many children to construct their identity as an author. However, there are also some authors in the classroom who use different sign systems to compose their stories. Thus, we need to broaden our scope to include different sign systems in meaning-making. As Dyson (1993) suggests, children write primarily by drawing and talking: "With those tools, they not only represented their imagined worlds but also connected with their friends, as they talked about and at times playfully dramatized each other's drawn and told stories. Their actual writing was but a small part of their multi-media productions" (p. 12).

Kate narrates her story with her drawings. Its structural content is filled with lines and colors of different intensities. As a complex medium, it demands a different kind of intelligence from that of linguistics. The drawn story also shows Kate's thinking process, which differs from what children usually are taught when constructing a story. Most teachers demonstrate the process of writing by deciding a title first and then brainstorming the content (see the eight procedures of the writing workshop in this class in Chapter Four). What Kate shows here is just the opposite. She lets her imagination take the lead and develops the story anywhere her imagination takes her. There is no specific title to restrict her creativity. Giving the story a title is her last step in constructing the story. Thus, children follow different orders of thinking and different ways of constructing texts. However, looking at Kate's story, is she considered an author in this classroom? Let us keep this question in mind until later.

For now, I would like to focus on the kind of meaning-making that is self-made, spontaneously and creatively, by many young children: drawing. There are several reasons that have motivated me to explore children's drawing. First, as I mentioned in the methodology chapter, drawing with children helps me build up a pleasant rapport naturally with them and channels a way to enter their world. Because of drawing, they get to know more about me and I get to know more about them. Checking what I drew on my sketch pad became a routine interaction between the children and me. Because of drawing, they moved their things to the corner where I usually sat in the classroom and *drew* with me even when I was taking notes instead of drawing. Interested in drawing, they used my markers and also offered me their crayons so we could do something together. They drew in their self-made books and also on my sketch pad or field notes. "Let me show you" is their friendly warning before drawing on my sketch pad. If drawing helps me to establish closer relationships with children and pave the way to enter their world, then drawing must, I believe, carry great significance in children's school life.

Second, without any instruction, most children are capable of drawing and love to draw to make meanings. Unfolding what they actually accomplish through applying their self-selected media in meaning-making will help us know more about why drawing seems to be such a natural and spontaneous way to create meanings on their own. If one sign system is applied effortlessly in making meaning, it will provide pedagogical implications for understanding how children learn and how we can create a curriculum that takes advantage of this natural flow of learning.

Third, I want to challenge the ideological views that consider children's drawing in simplistic ways: "They just love to draw," or "Children draw more when they are young," or "It is normal that children's interest in drawing wanes as they age." These taken-for-granted assumptions ignore the significance of children's creative potential as well as simplify the complexity in their meaning-making. I want to resist these developmental ideologies and question why it is regarded as *normal* if such rich, innovative, and natural semiotic power dwindles or is replaced by another sign system as children advance in school.

For decades, many researchers have been trying to answer these questions: Why do most children love to draw and make meaning effortlessly in one sign system while taking pains in learning another? Why is one literacy event more meaningful or significant for them while the other is simply a piece of school-work? Educational researchers, psychologists, pediatricians, art therapists, and early childhood scholars raise similar questions and take different approaches to answer their queries. Malchiodi (1998) believes that art expression is a complex process in which children bring together diverse elements from their environment to create a unique whole of meaning. He also emphasizes that the complexities of children's visual communication and their creative potential and capacities should not be sacrificed or reduced to an explanation or interpretation by a therapeutic test generated from one single graphic or by quantifying certain characteristics of drawings.

Criticizing the rigid stages of Piaget's developmental theory that demonstrates weak correlation between a child's age and her cognitive development in artistic talents, Gardner (1980, 1990) urges researchers and educators to continue exploring diverse facets of the various meanings of children's drawing, such as "the reasons that children's art follows its characteristic course (as well as the reasons behind any deviations); the precise relations between the child's drawing and other aspects of his mental, social, and emotional development; and the aesthetic status of the work that he produces" (Gardner, 1980, p. 13).

Klepsch and Logie's (1982) and DiLeo's (1983) studies focus on psycho-therapeutic cases and try to elicit from children's drawings material buried in the unconsciousness and understand their psychological problems. Their accounts are based on the metaphorical assumption that the human mind is an entity containing the *inner* and *outer* aspects and that through a child's drawing, the inner portion of her thoughts becomes visible in graphic forms and thus conveys profound meaning that linguistic forms cannot express.

Goodnow (1977) proposes an epistemological orientation containing three analytic aspects for understanding children's drawings: spatial patterns (i.e., arrangement, pictorial units, boundaries), sequence (i.e., direction, inclusion, omission), and equivalents (i.e., signs that stand for or represent objects or concepts). It directs our attention toward children's drawings on: (a) how children apply elements in everyday environments in their drawings, (b) how the increasing demand of visual communication in the world affects children's meaning-making, and (c) how children transform "knowing that" (their sociocultural resources) to "knowing how" (their active construction of meanings).

Sharing similar views with Goodnow, Kress (1997, 2003) asserts that meaning-making is more a social rather than a psychological construct and argues that the Piagetian predictions of the cognitive development or Chomskian preexisting schema of language acquisition cannot explain the finding of children's active meaning-making. Opposing this autonomous view of meaning-making that underplays the social, cultural, and historical dynamics in language use and meaning-making, Kress wants to propose a literacy theory that examines what is really going on when children make meanings: "My account is the story of the active engagement of bodily humans with all aspects of their cultural environment, which constantly transforms language, individuals, and their cultural world" (Kress, 1997, p. 113). I will return to Kress's theory in the following section.

Arguing against the Vygotskian view that narrowly defines human thoughts in verbal forms and questioning works in discourse analysis that emphasize merely the linguistic aspect of meaning-making, Harste et al. (1984) assert that "thought is never totally linguistic" (p. 171) and thus they propose a literacy model that takes into account different sign systems in defining children's learning (Short, Harste, & Burke, 1996). Winterbourne (1996) and Cornett (1998) explore the creative connection between images and prints in children's literacy development and try to integrate writing with drawing throughout the curriculum.

Despite different views among scholars from different disciplines, the shared assumptions toward children's drawings are that (1) drawing is a special kind of symbolization as well as representation that can express what other sign systems cannot in meaning-making; (2) children are active and creative meaning-makers who make great attempts to understand and communicate in the world; and (3) it is important for researchers and educators to keep exploring children's drawings in order to unfold the underlying principles at work. Siding with these assumptions, my inquiry in this chapter not only explores what and how children achieve meaning-making with drawings, but also tries to perceive the action of drawing from the children's perspective and examines the significance of drawing in the process of children's identity construction. If drawing for most children in this study is considered fun and enjoyable, what it achieves is not simply meaning-making but also, more importantly, satisfaction in the process. This kind of satisfaction makes drawing a special kind of meaning-making that differs from the other school literacy activities. I want to emphasize this satisfaction in meaning-making that children achieve in their own way without much help from adults and try to conceptualize literacy through the children's accounts.

Kress (1997) tries to reconcile the two polemic views in education toward human action: individuality and sociality. That is, human action in meaning-making cannot be fully explained by either view alone because meaning-making is, on the one hand, a social action in which people draw from what is available in their socio-cultural repertoire, and on the other hand, it is an individual action in that people are also capable of creating new meanings and inventing new signs to mean. My argument is that the seemingly opposite views—individuality and sociality—are the two sides of the same coin, that meaning-making is the process of an interplay between these two phases and that it is a "both-and" rather than an "either-or" relationship.

In the following discussion, I will review the theoretical constructs that explore children's creative action, elaboration, and self-expression in meaning-making and explain how children's identity construction is implicitly related to their pleasure of using markers or crayons to create a set of meaningful lines on paper. Moreover, through analyzing children's text design, I want to reexamine the following questions:

(1) What sort of meanings do they try to convey in their multimodel texts?

(2) How do they express their ideas through graphic design and how does it support or differ from written words?

(3) How can we conceptualize literacy in children's terms?

## Making Meaning Through Drawing

### Representation

Nelson Goodman (1976) considers representation through a picture as involving a complex organization that "classifies, is classified, may make or mark connections, analyze objects, and organize the world" (p. 32). For him, representation is how the sign maker, an artist or a writer, "grasps fresh and significant relationships and devises means for making them manifest" (pp. 32–33). In a sense, an important aspect of understanding children's meaning-making is to see how they create the new from remaking the old and how they experiment with different kinds of elements drawn from their environment and build up new relationships among them.

Kress (1997) points out four major dimensions in understanding the representation of children's drawings: (1) interests of the meaning-maker, (2) motivated signs for the purpose of communication, (3) multiple modes, means, and materials applied in texts, and (4) transformative action that generates new forms of meaning. Interest in meaning-making is what one tries to achieve, which is usually mixed with cultural discourse and personal creativity. Children's active meaning-making, Kress (1997) argues, is not only that they are capable of using "what they have to hand" (p. 91) but also that "what they have to hand" are usually objects and materials that are not conventionally "considered materials for making signs and messages by their parents, teachers, or carers" (p. 91).

"Motivated signs," such as sizes, shapes, colors, directionality, sequence, and the like, are deliberately selected by the sign-maker to best represent the meaning she wants to convey in her text. As Lakoff and Johnson (2003) indicate, the human conceptual system is metaphorical in structure as well as in nature. Motivated signs are intentional, communicational, and functional for the purpose of getting meaning understood by the audience. In this case, as Kress asserts, motivated signs are also determined by the sign-maker's interest.

"Multimodality" in meaning-making is, according to Kress (1997), the evidence of "how children make their own paths into literacy" (p. 97). Multimodality of children's meaning-making also reflects the landscape of modern media culture (Kress, 2003), which permeates our environment and the way we communicate with each other. As visual communication becomes more popular and greatly changes our life and view of the world, the traditional idea about literacy as dominantly verbal is seriously questioned and challenged by more and more researchers and educators. Multimodality becomes an important feature of children's meaning-making, including the media used, means applied, and various possibilities offered in our media culture.

Transformation is the process of sign re-creation. Many semioticians agree that meanings or signs are never copied or imitated but created and transformed. Peirce's famous trichotomous cycle also depicts a transformative relationship among an object, sign, and interpretant. For Peirce, sign is a generic concept that comes into being only through development out of other signs (Peirce, 1985). Sign-making is a process of unlimited semiosis.

Furthermore, Peirce theorizes sign-making as a process of hypothesis formation (Peirce, 1958–1960; Borgaard, 1999) and calls it a theory of abduction that is previous to the process of deduction or induction. This preexisting hypothetical process is the process of meaning-making that, according to Peirce, follows some sort of rational control by the sign-maker. Thus, for Peirce, the action of meaning-making is both the formation of the range of permissible hypotheses and the limitation of this range (Borgaard, 1999).

Pierce's account preserves the Kantian view about rational explanation as well as about the reason for human existence and action. Sebeok (1999) paraphrases Kant's principles about signs: "'raw experience' is unattainable; experience, to be apprehended, must first be steeped in, strained through, and seasoned by a soup of signs" (pp. 14–15). Inferring from Peirce's theory of abduction, we may say that children's meaning-making is a process of transformation as well as hypothesis formation that has its rational structure, with proper adoption, rejection, inclusion, and exclusion. In the subsequent analysis, the transformative dimension of children's drawings focuses particularly on what as well as how new meanings are generated and what sorts of imaginative or hypothetical semiosis are at work.

## Expression

The following theories of expression provide useful frameworks to understand the implicit process when one really expresses oneself and how this particular kind of meaning-making becomes precious experience for one's own being.

1. *Nelson Goodman:* While *representation* shows the explicit textual design, organization, and relationships of signs in meaning-making, *expression* reveals the more implicit, unpredictable, and creative process underlying meaning-making that is significant for exploring the meaning-maker's identity construction. This part is also an important aspect of children's drawing that is usually left untreated in literacy research. Although Kress (1997) tries to go beyond the view that "they [children] were just expressing their feelings" (p. 90) in their drawings, the meaning of *expression* needs further clarification. We should define it from the children's own accounts. I would like to argue that, first, what they express is not simply feeling and, second, that meaning, action, and feeling are together one inseparable process of meaning-making.

Goodman (1976) protests the notion that the primary function of art is to express feelings or emotions. What a sign-maker (e.g., an artist, a poet, a writer) expresses, he argues, may be something other than a feeling or emotion:

> An actor's facial expression need neither result from nor result in his feeling the corresponding emotions. A painter or composer does not have to have the emotions he expresses in his work. And obviously works of art themselves do not feel what they express, even when what they express is a feeling. Some of these cases suggest that what is expressed is, rather, the feeling or emotion excited in the viewer...The actor need not feel sad, but succeeds in expressing sadness just to the extent that he makes me feel sad. (p. 47)

Then what is expressed by the sign-maker other than merely feelings or emotions? Before answering this question, I should try to define what an "expression" means. In my view, an expression is a complex process of achievement involving one's feelings or emotions but not dominating the process. This partially explains Goodman's belief that an artist does not have to have a certain emotion in order to express it through her performance because what she achieves is an action of expression that she successfully communicates through a complex process of sign-making, be it body movements, painting on canvas, or music from a score.

Furthermore, what makes an artist or a child achieve an expression cannot be fully explained by her intentions. Rather, it is her continuous action and active engagement that leads her toward achieving that satisfaction. What she achieves is rather an unexpected encountering or surprise in the process of meaning-making in her work that makes her realize and experience something new about herself, something that she never thought that she could accomplish. She comprehends her achievement through reflection that is monitored from her sociocultural repertoire, previous experiences, or responses from the audience. In other words, an *expression* is achieved in the process of meaning-making and this achievement is not—and cannot be—a planned-ahead result but rather an unexpected outcome.

Following Goodman's example, when an actor successfully achieves an expression, she may not be able to articulate what really happened to her at the moment and how she did it. It just happened in the process of action and was a unique achievement in a particular moment of action that she cannot go back to or duplicate. That is why every human action is unique in its own way. Hence, children's drawings are not imitations of objects, but instead their one-of-a-kind expression.

2. *Herder*: Herder's (1793-7/2002) expressivist anthropology, which considers the human conduct of life as a whole, is the expression of the self that is a creative, vigorous, and continuous process of action. For him, human action is a process of unfolding the individual unique core and potential—a process in which human beings come to realize the self through action and utterances.

Contrary to the Kantian view that places rules or teleological reasons in the center of understanding human action, Herder considers that human action carries a natural capacity to transform the "spontaneous urge into authentic self-expression" (Joas, 1995, p. 85) and "allows the imagination to craft metaphors where understanding and reason should struggle to elaborate concepts and ideas" (Swift, 2005, p. 224). Although Herder asserts that expressing the self is a natural innate genius within each individual, not every human action, as Joas (1995) argues, is an expression:

> [W]e speak of expression only in connection with animate beings and their deeds. Yet not everything about these beings and their deeds can be considered an expression, and we know intuitively whether a sentence or a gesture has expressed something well or less well. We often look for a better expression and we can help others in their search. (p. 75)

Herder's view of human spontaneity and creativity in action is one of the important aspects in understanding children's meaning-making. An expression is constituted within the triad of the self, the other, and the action of meaning-making. Besides, Joas (1995) calls our attention to the fact that there are different kinds of meaning-making, but not every one of them is considered as an *expression*. Thus, the focus of this chapter is particularly on the kinds of meaning-making that children create spontaneously in the classroom, to express themselves fully and to engage themselves in constantly.

3. *Marx*: Marx's theory of action accentuates the problem arising from the notion of production. Marx considers human action as material production that creates something useful for maintaining a living as well as for fulfilling the self in its aesthetic sense. However, the power of production achieves self-positing only through creating something new rather than merely reproducing the old. Considering this notion of production in our capitalist society, the action of production becomes simply labor power in which human expressive needs and the sense of the self are alienated from the process of production. The bondage between the creator and her product is broken and replaced by labor wages. "Alienated labor," as Giddens (1971) interprets, "reduces human productive activity to the level of adaptation to, rather than active mastery of, nature" (p. 13).

To limit our discussion to children's meaning-making drawn from Marx's accounts, expression happens when one (a) creates something new, (b) feels satisfactory about the self through one's work, and (c) learns as well as outgrows oneself in a rounded cycle of expression. Marx's theory also raises another important issue related to what I mentioned at the beginning of this chapter: that is, children's rich and diverse ways of meaning-making seem to dwindle and are gradually replaced by verbal forms. This stirs some problems and raises questions: Has an important part of children's identity been taken away or alienated in the process of transferring their natural and creative semiotic power, focusing only on one particular sign system? Is this a "normal" process every child has to go through as he/she learns and uses more verbal forms to mean? Are we, as teachers, parents and researchers, simply considering it as a "developmental" passage when children use more words and less drawing? Or, are the children involuntarily abandoning drawing for other ways to expressing meaning as they grow? I will address these issues when analyzing children's literacy artifacts.

4. *Dewey:* Dewey's (1934, 1952/1989) notion of expression is holistic and functional in viewing human action that tries to unify and overcome the epistemological dualism in activity theory. Dewey provides a long list of dualisms:

> The material and spiritual, the physical and the mental or psychological; body and mind; experience and reason; sense and intellect, appetitive desire and will, subjectivity and objectivity, individual and social; inner and outer. (Dewey 1952/1989, p. 408, cited in Garrison, 2001, p. 276)

This long list of dualisms is, for Dewey, only a practical epistemological distinction, not an ontological one. Human existence is a process of transaction and one fulfills a completed, rounded experience in meaning-making when there is a balance between what one is doing and what is undergone in one's action: that is, when doing and undergoing are one inseparable whole. This occurs when one is completely absorbed and engaged in action, just as children continue drawing and keep doing what they like whenever they can. This is also, according to Dewey, how action is transformed into precious and *real* experience:

> [W]e have an experience when the material experienced runs its course to fulfillment. ....A piece of work is finished in a way that is satisfactory; a problem receives its solution; a game is played through; a situation, whether that of eating a meal, playing a game of chess, carrying on a conversation, writing a book, or taking part in a political campaign, is so rounded out that its close is a consummation and not a cessation....In such experiences, every successive part flows freely, without seam and without unfilled blanks, into what ensues. At the same time there is no sacrifice of the self-identity of the parts. (Dewey, 1934, pp. 35–36)

For Dewey, expression is a need, but this "need" is not limited to the Marxian view of material production. Expression is the clarification of one's feeling and impulsion. It transforms one's blind surge "into thoughtful action through assimilation of meanings from the background of past experiences" (Dewey, 1934, p. 60). There are also three major aspects in Dewey's definition of "expression" constituting part of the conceptual framework in understanding children's actions in drawing: (a) creativity, (b) spontaneity, and (c) unpredictability.

(a) Creativity: Expression is an intellectual juncture of the new and the old as well as a "re-creation in which the present impulse gets form and solidity while the old, the 'stored,' material is literally revived, given new life and soul through having to meet a new situation" (Dewey, 1934, p. 60). This "re-creation" or remaking of the old and giving it new forms are the basic structures of human semiotic activity.

(b) Spontaneity: Dewey (1934) distinguishes spontaneous action from an act of emotional discharge: "Emotional discharge is a necessary but not a sufficient condition of expression...To discharge is to get rid of, to dismiss; to express is to stay by, to carry forward in development, to work out to completion" (p. 62). Arguing that spontaneous expression is not simply letting go of one's emotion, Dewey (1934) emphasizes that spontaneity is neither a sudden nor a random mode of action. It is the outcome of a long period of activity and cultivation. As Eisner (2002) purports, children, like the rest of us, stay with things they like as long as possible. Drawing is such a spontaneous act that it serves like a magnet to which children attach themselves and linger over whenever possible in school.

(c) Unpredictability: Both Dewey and Mead bring up the concept of unpredictability in the process of action that challenges the notion of "intentionality." This also expands our view about children's meaning-making from acts of situated identity (Gee, 1996, 1999) to acts of one's situated creativity rendered spontaneously and unexpectedly from one's expression in the process of identity construction. Dewey (1934) uses an everyday example of how we act toward a friend to explain that we act organically but not always intentionally:

> The act that expresses welcome uses the smile, the outreached hand, the lighting up of the face as media, not consciously but because they have become organic means of communicating delight upon meeting a valued friend. Acts that were primitively spontaneous are converted into means that make human intercourse more rich and gracious—just as a painter converts pigment into means of expressing an imaginative experience. (Dewey, 1934, p. 63).

For Dewey (1922/1983), purposes, goals, or motives in action are not predetermined but rather are developed, altered, or redefined in the process of action.

To sum up Dewey's view of human action, we can say that acts of meaning-making in the process of identity construction are mostly unintentional rather than a pure means-ends schema. Moreover, meaning-making in terms of expression starts from an impulse and takes its shape in the process of action through experimenting and creating a horizon of possibilities for different situations in life. It is a process of transformation by remaking materials and entering into new relationships with the environment.

5. *Mead*: Sharing a similar view with Dewey, Mead's theory of the self also tries to conceptualize human action as a unifying whole with the interplay between

the social and the individual, the conventional and the creative, the normative and the active, or, in Mead's terms, the "me" and the "I." Simply put, Mead considers the self to be constituted by the "me" and the "I." The "me" is the socio-cultural aspect of the self produced by discourses and norms that one acquires to function as a social member in a society. The "I," on the other hand, is one's innovative, creative, and active part of the self that is able to find solutions to a problem, create new experiences, and make changes in one's life. But exactly how does the "I" (creativity) and the "me" (sociality) work in the process of meaning-making when children draw? Perhaps it is better understood from how an artist creates a piece of her work.

Let us imagine what happens when an artist moves her paintbrush to canvas. An artist knows the techniques of painting and applies her cultural repertoire (the "me") as her resources for creation. She starts out her work with a rough plan or goal. However, her goal is changed or refined in the process of painting because the more she acts, the more determined she becomes in what she is trying to achieve. By moving the paintbrush to canvas (the "I"), she discovers something new about each stroke she makes and gains new experiences accumulated from a series of creative movements and exciting moments. These experiences attract her to stay the course and keep on exploring through drawing. It is a joyful engagement through which she is able to release her impulsion and transform it into the essence of meaning-making. It is the kind of action that gives rise to one's expression when the social convention one internalizes (the "me") does not constrain or obstruct her creativity and spontaneity (the "I").

Applying Mead's "I"-"me" concept, we understand that one's active, immediate impulsion and individual creativity are coherent and in harmony with one's social environment as well as normative boundaries: it is when the individual and the social, the "I" and the "me," are unifying as a rounded whole of action. Put into a graphic form (Figure 5-1A), children love the activity when it generates a positive feeling toward themselves or when the gap between the "I" and the "me" in the structure of the self is reduced and bridged through an act of expression.

However, there are also activities that work the opposite; the "I" and the "me" work against each other or one's spontaneity and creativity get pushed far away from or suppressed by the normative power (Figure 5-1B). This occurs when one's identity becomes a problem in which one needs to act out or rebel against the conflict or oppression toward one's unifying sense of the self. Teachers may reflect on the kinds of literacy activities implemented in their classroom: the kinds that promote unity for children's sense of the self or the kinds that dissect it.

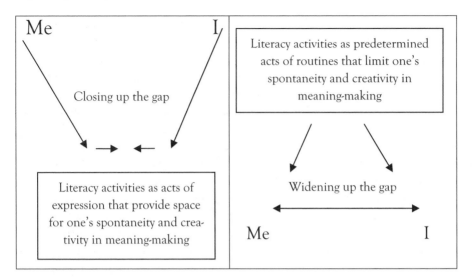

Figure 5-1A                                                    Figure 5-1B

**The I-Me Structure of the Self in Relation to Literacy Activities**

Drawing is the kind of activity shown in the first graphic that has generated expression in a creative, spontaneous, vibrant, and joyful manner. It maximizes one's semiotic power under the balance between one's creativity and sociality. It is the sort of intelligence that many young children possess. When you give them a box of markers or crayons, they know what to do. It is the way they use their semiotic power to put meaningful dots, shapes, colors, and lines on paper. It is the type of consummation and satisfactory experience they crave in their school life.

## Children's Drawings and Other Literacy Artifacts

Following the above framework constituted by "representation" and "expression," I would like to reconstruct the meaning of children's drawings and other literacy artifacts that they create along with written texts.

### Drawings in Pen Pal Letters

Eight pictures have been chosen from a pile of similar drawings in children's pen pal letters. As illustrated in Figures 5-2 (by four boys) and 5-3 (by four girls), these pictures provide extra information about who they are in the pen pal letters with a sign such as "P.S. Look on back" or a big arrow pointing to the back of the letter.

Edward showed a battle scene to his pen pal because he loves jets and battles. Around the time he drew the picture, he was in the process of creating his story of the war between Japan and America. Ian loves mythology and fantasy and, therefore, considers himself very capable of writing and drawing about monsters. Kevin is an expert in creating robot types of monsters. His sketch pad is full of imaginative robot monsters. Ted has created a very complex monster for his pen pal and claimed that "it has sharp teeth and its tail can shoot out bullets." The girls are prone to show  images of themselves. Gina and Michelle portray even imaginative images of their pen pals and depict how they go hand in hand or pick flowers together. Michelle clearly indicates "you" and "me" with arrows pointing to the pictures as the essential constituents of their friendship. Vivian's self-portrait, which occupies most of the space on the back of the letter, seems to emphasize that "this is me." Tammy reinforces who she is by outlining her self-image with the subtitle "a picture of me."

There are some interesting differences between the boys' and the girls' drawings. First, the four boys draw fiction characters or situations while girls draw images of humans. Second, the boys' pictures portray scenes of action while the girls' depict their perspectives of their relationships with their pen pals. Third, they both mark the ending of the letter with drawings, which seems to impress their pen pals with what they can do through drawing—to draw something for them, or to build up the relationship with them.

All the above are the foregrounded representations of the text constructed in their pictures. Why do the boys draw imaginary and active scenarios while the girls draw real human images? If drawing is one way of expressing themselves while communicating with their pen pals, what do these boys and girls try to show their pen pals about what they are in their drawings? Perhaps it has something to do with their gender interest for pursuing friendship.

For the boys, their way of building up friendship is to "do" something together or "share" what they can "do" with their friends. For the girls, friendship has a lot to do with telling who they are in a *real*, *truthful*, or *faithful* manner rather than what they are capable of doing. This gender difference of building up friendship is supported by how they comment on their friendships in the classroom. Ted regarded Ian and Peter as his good friends because he considered them cool and fun to play with. Oscar claimed that Andy was his "buddy" because they both were really good at playing basketball. The case is different for the girls. Julia said that her friendship with Rose was history because "she wants to become popular and I don't think it's right to make yourself popular... And we are not friends anymore." Tammy complained that

"Paula is very good at making friends and she just makes herself funnier than anybody else in this class...She just did that so that she could be popular." Thus, the boys consider being capable of doing something together as the fundamental way of building up friendship, while for the girls being who one really is is essential, while trying to become someone else will threaten friendship.

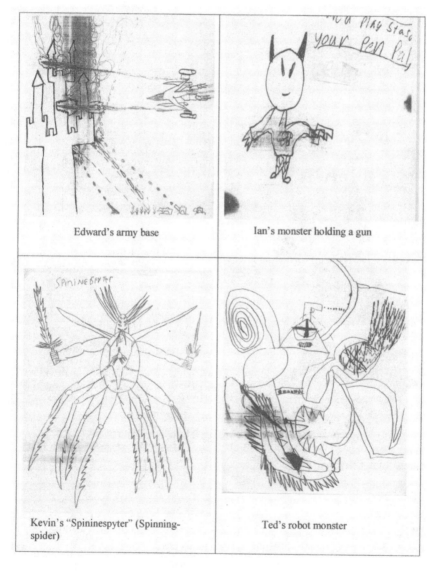

Edward's army base

Ian's monster holding a gun

Kevin's "Spininespyter" (Spinning-spider)

Ted's robot monster

**Figure 5-2 Boys' Drawings in Their Pen Pal Letters**

Figure 5-3 Girls' Drawings in Their Pen Pal Letters

## Pirates and Dinosaurs

*1. Jeff's Pirate*

By looking at Jeff's design, we understand that the conventional meanings about pirates that he is familiar with from books or movies include: (a) a stereotypical image of Captain Hook with one arm replaced by a hook and one leg by a stick, (b) the symbol of Jolly Roger (the skull and crossbones), and

(c) how pirates behave and live (i.e., bare feet, a pet on the shoulder, a gun or weapon in hand, pirate talk such as "Aaarrgh" and "Man overboard"). The new elements that Jeff brings in to redefine the meaning of pirates are (i) the "free jelly beans," (ii) a "welcome" sign on the ship, (iii) an angel (left) and a devil (right) side by side with the pirate. How Jeff expresses and redefines pirates can be interpreted from several aspects of his drawing.

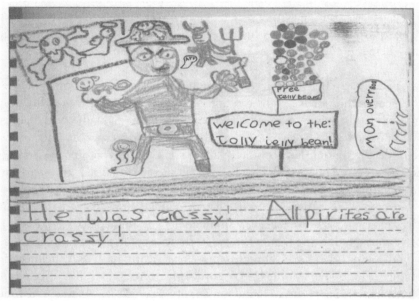

**Figure 5-4 Jeff's Pirate: "He was crassy [crazy]! All pirites [pirates] are crassy [crazy]!"**

First of all, being greedy is how pirates are traditionally defined because they fight for gold and hunt for treasures from the other ships. However, Jeff's "crazy" pirate is generous to "welcome" people to the ship and offer them "free jelly beans." Second, the images of the angel and the devil side by side with the pirate is how Jeff interprets the complex features of pirates who could be fighting in a heroic battle and helping others and, at the same time, carrying out a raid on another ship. Perhaps this is one of the fascinating characteristics of pirates who could be good and evil, heroic and cowardly, noble and selfish simultaneously. Third, this conflicting feature of pirates becomes Jeff's new technique of constructing his text through contrasting: the seemingly wicked image of the pirate (i.e., the raised eye brows, the popping eyes, twisted lips, black teeth) versus his generosity of welcoming and giving out free jelly beans. Moreover, by showing the images of the angel and the devil, Jeff tries to show the abstract and conflicting moral conscience of pirates. This is how drawing is a better and a handy medium for Jeff to express this difficult conceptual dilemma. Finally, Jeff draws several wavy lines to concretize as well as represent the invisible odor coming from the pirate's bare foot.

All of the above demonstrate how Jeff recreates the meaning of pirates either by adding new components to or by reordering the conventional ideas about pirates. One crucial element that Jeff brings to redefine pirates is that he creates a contrasting sense within the meaning of pirates, such as greed versus generosity, the angel/good versus the devil/bad, the dirty filthy setting versus the cheerful welcoming sign and free candy. Even though these are the conflicting features highlighted in his drawing, Jeff seems to harmonize these opposing elements and unify them into a new form of meaning about pirates.

*2. Ian's Dinosaur*: The war in Iraq was the headline news at that time, and Ian made a connection between the war and dinosaurs. He thought that dinosaurs would be good soldiers if they helped the country to fight the war. Because most dinosaurs have a gigantic body, sharp teeth and claws, pointed spines and/or deadly venom, Ian considered them good soldiers who possessed great destructive power in battles. That is how he reconceptualized dinosaurs and their function in the modern world.

Ian creates an active war scene where many actions happen simultaneously. This vigorous as well as lively simultaneity and immediacy seem easier to achieve through drawing than writing. Ian shows a soldier on a tank holding a gun and yelling, "Let's go," and a dryptosaurus wearing a U.S.A. helmet and shouting, "Thet's kike but [Let's kick butt]!" Meanwhile, a jet flies through the sky and a paratrooper, gun in hand, jumps with a parachute. At the same time, the two tanks marked with "usa" and the American flag approach toward the left while the dryptosaurus is following behind. The words "usa" or the American flag appearing on the tanks, parachute, and helmet reinforce that this is the U.S. troop moving from the right to the left, marching toward the enemy base even though the enemy is not shown on the scene. For Ian, showing the enemy is neither his primary interest nor his motivated sign because his primary concern is that the U.S. soldiers are going to war and that the dryptosaurus is part of the U. S. army. Moreover, Ian's drawing reflects how media portray the war and how the focus is always on the U.S. army and not on the Iraqi soldiers. Perhaps also derived from his experience of game playing, he is interested only in winning the game or the battle.

Figure 5-5 Ian's Dinosaur: "If the dinosaurs came back,
dryptosaurus would go to war with Iraq."

To sum up the meanings Ian created in his drawing, he used words as the secondary reinforcing tool (i.e., "usa") to set up a war scene in motion (i.e., "Let's go!" and "Let's kick butt!"). He considered all the powerful features of dinosaurs to be what strong soldiers need to win battles. He made a clear statement that dinosaurs would be *kick-butt* soldiers in the war.

*3. Jeff's Dinosaurs*: One thing I observed while Jeff created his dinosaur page (Figure 5-6) is that he drew first and then wrote the sentence later. It is important to know that drawing is Jeff's first step of meaning-making because (a) drawing seems to be a direct mode of thinking process for Jeff, and (b) drawing is the primary medium of meaning-making, while writing is secondary for summarizing but not fully covering the rich meaning contained in his drawing.

Jeff presents a fairly complex picture here and we need to go step by step in order to see what he tries to achieve. Let us start by looking at the dinosaurs: (a) the two big ones (the black one on the left and the white one on the right), (b) the small one next to the black dinosaur, (c) the two small ones on the right corner, and (d) the one flying by the black dinosaurs.

**Figure 5-6 Jeff's Dinosaurs: "If the dinosaurs came back,
they could eat grows [gross] food.**

These dinosaurs' diets are depicted. The black one is omnivorous and it eats all sorts of things, dumping into its mouth "liver," key, locks, and so forth. The big dinosaur on the right can devour bigger things, such as the car inside its stomach. The little one next to the black dinosaur is carnivorous because it eats only "liver." The two little ones on the right corner are herbivorous because they eat "leaf." The flying pterosaur is carnivorous, too, but it mainly eats fish. What is the underlying meaning of representing different diets among different dinosaurs? One way to interpret what Jeff achieves is that he expands the conventional categorization of dinosaurs based on their diet (i.e., omnivore, carnivore, and herbivore) and connects it with the modern recycling concept of how we sort out trash (i.e., keys, locks, cars, leaves, animal liver, fish). Jeff thinks dinosaurs can help us deal with the recycling issue. Although he tries to summarize the main idea in one sentence—"If dinosaurs came back, they could eat growss [gross] food"—we see more rich and detailed meanings depicted in his drawing.

Another interest for Jeff is the dinosaurs' extraordinarily huge size. He expresses hugeness of dinosaurs in three ways: (a) the size ratio difference between people and the two big dinosaurs, (b) the big long ladder in the middle of the two, and (c) the white dinosaur's spine functioning as another ladder on which people can climb to reach its mouth. This also implies that dumping trash into the dinosaurs' mouths is not an easy task because of their colossal bodies. At the same time, their huge bodies function to gulp down large amounts of garbage. Jeff's new meaning of dinosaurs is derived by situating their size and diet in the modern concept of recycling.

## How Big Is Big?

The following two drawings continue the concept of dinosaurs' immense size but in a different way. The setting in which these two pictures were created by Peter and Jeff was me drawing along with them. They both showed me how they represented the size of their dinosaurs. Both were sitting by me and drawing for fun in the rug area of the classroom. In the following analysis, I would like to focus on how children design their graphic text as an invitation to evoke the audience's imagination and ask the audience to make their own meaning based on their drawing. It seems an ultimate way of expressing themselves not only in conveying the meaning but also in arousing the viewer's semiotic sensitivity to interpret what the viewer sees and/or feels through their graphic text.

While some children were circling around me drawing, Peter asked me, "Do you know how big a hasarysaurus is?" I told him I did not know and asked him, "Can you show me how big it is?" When I said "show me," I meant any information that he could find from any dinosaur encyclopedias in the classroom, but Peter took it upon himself to define how big the dinosaur was. He replied, "Ok," and then grabbed a piece of paper, flopped down on the carpet, and started drawing. Jeff, sitting next to Peter, also joined the discussion and claimed, "Oh, I know. I know. I know how big the dinosaur is." Both of them tried to show me how big the dinosaur is through drawing.

*1. Peter:* A couple of minutes later, Peter sat up straight and showed me what he meant by "big" (see Figure 5-7). Instead of directly telling me the size of the dinosaur, he showed me the height of the trees and volcano around the dinosaur with a measurement key at the bottom corner on the right and thus gave me some clues to figure out how big the dinosaur was by comparing and contrasting the surrounding objects with the dinosaur. This way of representing the size with real objects is a technique Peter borrowed from the information books such as dinosaur encyclopedias or Eye-Witness series of prehistoric life.

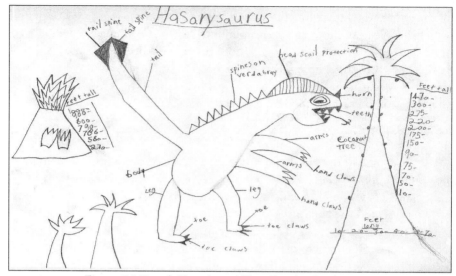

**Figure 5-7 Peter's Drawing of How Big the Dinosaur Is**

There are several aspects to the orchestration of his text. First, in terms of the directionality of the text, there are several ways to conceptualize it. We may say that the directionality is from the right to the left, starting from the big tree, the dinosaur, and then the volcano. It may indicate the order of Peter's thinking process and also the direction he intends for the viewer to start reading his text from by comparing the big tree with the dinosaur first and then contrasting the dinosaur's size derived from the tree height with the volcano. Notice that the size of the volcano appears smaller on the paper than the big tree and the dinosaur. Another possible way to interpret it is that Peter is showing the contrast between the foreground and the background in which things in the foreground appear bigger visually. Thus, we can also say that the directionality of Peter's meaning-making is from the front to the back. Or we may also interpret that the directionality is from the left to the right because the dinosaur is facing the right. Either way of explaining the direction of the text does not affect the meaning Peter tries to make. His primary focus is, as the title on top of the picture shows, "Hasarysaurus" in the center of the text with extra detailed information of its body parts.

In addition to the concrete objects (the big tree, the dinosaur, and the volcano) applied to represent the concept of being "big," number is another important medium to show the size of the dinosaur. Without the numbers keyed on the tree and the volcano, the picture may mean to inform us about something other than the dinosaur's size. Moreover, using a tree and a volcano as objects to reference, the dinosaur's size reflects a deliberate choice for two reasons: (a) both the tree and the volcano are considered big and thus are compatible objects for referencing the size of the dinosaur, and (b) both are significant elements of the dinosaurs' ecosystem as the former represents parts of their diet or habitat, or both, while the latter is regarded as a possible factor for their extinction.

2. *Jeff:* Jeff explained his drawing (Figure 5-8) to me, "The dinosaur is huge because its foot print can fit a city, many houses, trees and roads." Peter commented, "But where is the dinosaur?" Jeff answered, "It's too big. You can't see it."

**Figure 5-8 Jeff's Drawing of How Big the Dinosaur Is**

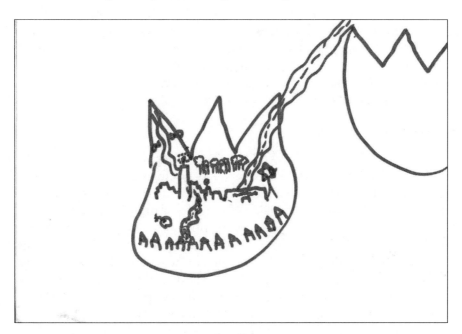

While Peter uses concrete objects and numbers to illustrate how big the dinosaur is, Jeff preserves the abstract concept of hugeness by not showing the dinosaur. For him, this is the ultimate expression of hugeness by not framing its limitation. "You can't see it" achieves the proximal essence of being huge. Although Jeff maintains the abstraction of how big a dinosaur can be, he does use concrete objects to make his point that it is the size of a city or town people live in. However, Jeff keeps pushing the viewer's imaginative semiosis to understand his ultimate expression of hugeness. As his picture depicts, footprints are the only clue he provides, which is a very small part of the information we can get about the dinosaur. This very partial information is also closely related to our everyday life because the dinosaur's footprint is, according to Jeff, about the same size as a city or town we live in with trees, houses, neighborhoods, and roads. Jeff's expression of hugeness is similar to the way we try to define the concept of "universe." That is, we live in the universe and we are part of it, but neither can we see it nor can we frame the boundary of it. And this is an *expression* of hugeness!

As Jeff claims, his sense of the dinosaur's size is too big to see or to draw on the paper. All he can show are the dinosaur's footprints. Each footprint can contain a city and there is a highway connecting the city footprints. Some may argue that Jeff is exaggerating the size of the dinosaur, but I think he successfully conveys the concept of hugeness in his own way and reaches its proximate sense. It is not his intention to provide a "correct" or "precise" answer as to the real size of the dinosaur. Rather, he uses drawing to explore how far he can go toward the idea of hugeness. He keeps the abstraction of hugeness within concrete and intimate everyday spatial experiences: a city. His new definition of "big" is being something enormous that we are simply a part of and thus cannot see or circumscribe its limitation.

## A Letter to the President

It was mid-October and the class was writing letters to the U.S. soldiers for Thanksgiving. While the whole class was busy writing letters to the soldiers, I could not help but notice Tammy's letter full of colorful words and pictures. I walked toward her table and said, "Wow, nice pictures!" Tammy was busy switching between markers, drawing, and writing her letter. She talked to me with her eyes staring at her letter and continued drawing and writing, "I am writing the letter to the president." She then turned toward her neighbor and borrowed a blue marker. Out of curiosity, I asked, "Really? What do you want to tell him?" She replied, "Well, I am done with the real letter to the soldiers, but I am writing a letter to President Bush myself. And and I want to say 'peace' to him." I was excited to witness this social practice that the seeds of critical thinking were sprouting in Tammy's mind and turning into action. I replied, "That's neat." Then she left her table. I quickly jotted down this wonderful literacy event in which Tammy decided to carry out something on her own, something "extra" to the assigned schoolwork.

Tammy came back to her table with another piece of paper stripped from a notebook and started to draw. She drew a big circle and many little circles around it. My persisting curiosity continued urging me to ask her what she planned to do next with the letter to the president of the United States. She explained, "I am drawing 'peace'. A lot here. This is the second page." The following is Tammy's two-page letter for the President (Figure 5-9).

Structurally speaking, the letter follows the conventional format (the beginning and the end of a letter) and the marginal area of the letter is decorated with pictures (butterflies, hearts, stars) to mark the central area as the focal point of the letter. Moreover, for Tammy, the colorful decoration in the marginal area of the letter is to highlight the significance of the content that she wants to draw to the president's attention.

**Figure 5-9 Tammy's Letter to the President**

> **Dear PreisDent**
> **Bush   DO NOT GO to**
> **war   it is BaD**
> yoU soD [should]  notis [notice] that
> you are Doweing [doing]
> a BaD Ting   HalP
> peaec   love [Tammy]

The second page follows the same structural design—a big peace sign in the middle surrounded by many small ones. The first page uses written words to tell the president her opinion about the war and the second page reinforces her meaning and concern for peace by using a symbol. The strong assumptions in the letter are that the president is responsible for the war, that the president should think more about it, that the war is bad, and that the president needs to keep "peace" in mind.

Tammy's view reflects the controversial issue broadly debated in media. However, her action seems more important than what she represents in the letter. Her decision to carry out something on her own reveals her view that writing letters to the president is as important as writing letters to the soldiers. This literacy activity of writing letters to the soldiers inspires Tammy to make her own decision and create her own literacy experience. But how far did her action go? During lunch break, Tammy walked toward me and said, "You can have the letter if you want." I was surprised and honored by her offer. I asked her, "You don't want to send it to the president?" She said, "It's ok" and then ran out for recess. Why did Tammy give me the letter instead of sending it to the president? I have several speculations.

The supposition is that writing belongs to the official schoolwork and is important while drawing or doing whatever one wants is unofficial and not that important. The implicit official assumption about children's drawing probably makes Tammy think that her drawing or action outside the curriculum is insignificant. Although her action leads her toward an expression of herself in terms of her view about the war, this action of meaning-making may not become an *experience* for Tammy in Dewey's sense. Tammy might even forget that she ever wrote a letter to the president because this letter was never sent. Since I was the only person who showed curiosity and concern in the process of her action, she might have felt that I should be the one to keep the letter because I *cared* about what she had been doing.

Another possibility is that Tammy must conform to what others are doing in the classroom. Everybody in this class writes a letter to the soldiers but no one writes to the president. Therefore, as Tammy implies, "It's ok" not to send the letter to the president because no one is doing that. Since nobody is doing that except Tammy, "It is ok" to give the letter to me. Or "It's ok" because the teachers will not check or care about it.

Perhaps Tammy's letter also answers my question at the beginning of this chapter: why do children's rich semiotic powers dwindle as they stay longer in school? After all, what else could be more detrimental to a child's creativity as well as identity than her learning to think that what she does and can achieve are not important?

## Kate's Drawn and Told Story versus Her Written Story

Now let us come back to Kate's drawn and told story at the beginning of this chapter. There is still a parenthetical question not answered: Should Kate be considered an author? All the above discussion about children's expressing through drawing has tried to reiterate the fact that meaning-making is a complex process that involves multiple sign systems. Thus, Kate's drawn and told story is as valuable as those written ones.

I showed Kate's flower story to the teachers and one of them commented, "Hmm, we need to get her write something. She still struggles with reading and spelling." Perhaps the teacher sees only that Kate cannot write but not her creative ideas expressed in her drawn story. Figure 5-10 is Kate's written story, *A Trip to Florida*, in her 2nd grade. As the teacher told me, Kate made big progress in spelling and experienced the power of writing.

How does Kate construct meaning and experience texts differently in her two stories (Figure 5-1 and Figure 5-10)? I will let readers make that judgment. There are two points I would like to make by comparing her two stories.

First, despite the fact that the flower story is fictional and the story of the trip is personal memoir, the former somehow mysteriously tells me more about who Kate is. What I am arguing here is that when one puts more expression into a story, it brings her audience closer to her. By drawing a story, Kate liberates her experience from the routine and explores new ways to mean through expressing herself. Writing is another way of experiencing print and a new way Kate has been learning to mean and create expressions. But how will she develop her creative expression through writing? The answer requires another long period of exploration. By simply comparing her first written story about a trip with her drawn story, the former seems lacking in vitality and creativity. Perhaps I am prejudiced by the experience of working with Kate, because I have watched her enjoying the process of drawing stories and not stopping to draw until the teachers asked her to put the markers away. I am also biased by the Kate I know, who is full of imagination and energy in creating through graphic forms. I somehow fear that this part of Kate might disappear gradually as the other forms of knowledge in school demand her to focus solely on spelling, writing, and testing. This also triggers the next point I want to make about sign-making.

My second point is to question why Kate's fictional story seems to reveal more about her than her personal story about a trip. If identity claims are defined as statements showing who one is, how can one's personal experience tell us less than one's fictional imaginative story?

**Figure 5-10 Kate' Story:** *A Trip to Florida*

I have no quick or easy answer to the question. One thing for sure is that one's identity claims involve a complex structure of expressing the self. And identity claims can be expressed in different forms that show us who one is as well as what one achieves in the process of meaning-making. Drawing allows us to observe how a child's thinking process actually occurs in constructing texts and how a child claims her identity in the process of acting, imagining, and creating.

## Discussion

This chapter is an invitation for teachers and educators to take a closer look at what children have achieved (or try to achieve) in their drawing and to reflect on the complexity of the meaning-making process when children construct texts. First, by placing Kate's drawn story at the beginning and her written story at the end, I want to bring up questions about (a) what might have been lost on her way to becoming literate, (b) whether or not her written story is simply a product of school literacy, and (c) how her way of meaning-making may have been marginalized in school. The teachers' comments seem to contrast with my doubts. According to the teachers, Kate had changed from "struggling with reading and spelling" to making progress in writing. For me, the creative part of her identity as an author seems to be missing and is, perhaps, compromised under the frame of what counts as literacy in school. This is when children's identity construction becomes identity compromising.

Second, children use drawing as a tool to help their meaning-making reach its fuller sense. What they draw strongly reflects their gender identity and motivated interests in building up friendship. We see how the girls' self portraits and the boys' depictions of various action scenarios in their pen pal letters reveal their gender distinctions. Also friendship is defined differently in the boys' and the girls' worlds.

Third, children's drawings are their implicit ways of negotiating space for constructing their identities in school activities. Written words are structurally rule-governed and may prevent young children from taking risks in constructing texts. For instance, one child may want to write a story about crocodiles. Later, he may drop the idea and pick an easier topic to write about because writing a story about crocodiles is difficult. Drawing, on the contrary, opens up a horizon of possibilities for children to reshape, relate, select, and distinguish in the process of meaning-making. Jeff's re-creation of pirates unifies the conflicting features—evil and good, selfish and generous, and so forth—as his new definition. Both Ian and Jeff re-create the meaning of dinosaurs by assigning them new functions in the modern world. Ian considers dinosaurs to be good *kick-butt* soldiers in the war in Iraq. Jeff believes that dinosaurs will help us sort out our recycling problems.

Fourth, drawing creates a series of semiotic interactions between the sign-maker and the viewer in which the representation is an invitation for viewers to make their own meaning from the drawing. At the same time, this is also the sign-maker's ultimate way of self-expression by evoking the viewer's semiotic capacity. Peter uses real objects referenced with numbers to indicate the size of the dinosaur. Viewers need to analyze and compare these references to figure out how big the dinosaur is. Jeff shows partial information about the dinosaur and arouses viewers' imagination to paint the whole picture of the dinosaur themselves. His ultimate expression is to invite us to define hugeness in our own way through his drawing.

Fifth, Tammy's letter to President Bush makes us believe that children need a supportive environment in school to carry out their own decisions in making meaning and to encourage them to put literacy into action by interacting with the world. Their creative actions also provide valuable implications for teachers in adjusting a curriculum, understanding individual potential, and assisting them to become critical thinkers and independent learners.

Finally, as Harste et al. (1984), Dyson (1989, 1993, 1997), Kress (1997, 2003), and other researchers have already informed us how children make meanings with various sign systems and in multimodal ways, what other new dimensions about literacy can we learn from the children in this study? My primary concern is that literacy is a mode of action that does not only keep learning or exploring new ways to express meaning, but should also preserve and value what children are already capable of doing. As children engage themselves in drawing, what they are showing us is simply that they want to stay on something that they are happy to do and capable of doing.

A critical issue that awaits educators is to figure out how to help children continue developing their rich semiotic power and make verbal forms of meaning-making a "plus to" and not a "minus from" their creativity. Besides, literacy is not only about meaning-making but also, more importantly, about self-expression. It is a lifelong process of cultivating one's mind, exploring one's potential, responding to the dynamics of one's environments, and valuing who one is. Following Dewey's (1934) sense, literacy becomes a significant experience when one's identity is not reduced or sacrificed in the process of meaning-making. It is an act of making identity claims and the children in this study use drawing to compensate for written words and reach self-expression in their own way.

In a sense, what children are trying to do through drawing is to create the kind of experiences that make them feel good about themselves. Thus, literacy should also be the kind of action that will create positive feelings toward oneself, satisfy one's need, and reach one's satisfaction in meaning-making. As popularly defined, literacy is social practice, but only when one's expressive action is coherent and well supported by one's social environments can we say that this social practice does justice to one's identity.

Drawing is a spontaneous action as well as an expression that children enjoy doing. It is an improvised, unpredictable and yet structurally meaningful kind of action as well as intelligence. It is a kind of expression that is framed not simply as situated identity but rather a situated creativity in which children desire to maintain as well as re-create the self in the process of action.

# CHAPTER SIX

# Gender Identity

In the previous chapters, I left some parenthetical questions on gender issues untreated. In Chapter Three, we explored how boys try to build solidarity and collective identity in their peer culture. In Chapter Five, we also saw how gender identity affects children's literacy practice (i.e., the drawings from their pen pal letters) and how friendship is defined differently between boys and girls. In this chapter, I would like to focus on this intriguing part of children's identity—gender. The discussion centers particularly on how peer rules are developed differently in the boys' and girls' worlds and on the role that the official school agenda plays in shaping their gender identities. I discuss some current research on gender issues in the school context as well as the theoretical underpinnings that guide the exploration of gender construction. Then I delve into the examination of how the boys and girls divide conflict, integrate, and make use of each other as a medium for asserting their gender power.

## Research of Gender Identity

Originally belonging to the psychological domain, the issue of gendered childhood has been approached and reexamined by different disciplines. Anthropological research emphasizes the different roles, functions, and responsibilities boys and girls have in the social structure (i.e., families, communities). It has derived a general conclusion that girls' childhood ends sooner than boys' and that girls spend significantly more time than boys helping the mother with housework and taking care of younger siblings (Chagnon, 1968; Mead, 1928; Wolf, 1972; also see Montgomery, 2005). However, as Montgomery (2005) argues, the anthropological approach tends to ignore or downplay the children's perspective in the process of constructing and negotiating gender identity.

Early childhood studies attempt to reexamine how children construct their peer culture and gender identity in their own way (Yelland & Grieshaber, 1998; Kamler, 1999; MacNaughton, 2001; Blaise, 2005). These studies suggest that children use their understanding of gender discourses in various social contexts to regulate social order and gender roles in school. In addition to exploring how gender is created, taken up, and performed in school, some early childhood studies also reveal how everyday teaching practices influence or reinforce the gendering of young children's identities (Schlank & Metzger, 1996; MacNaughton, 2001).

Cultural studies and sociological research about gender identity indicate the hegemonic forces of masculinities constraining and pressuring boys to behave "manly" as members of the "manhood" by assimilating the male codes of being macho, tough, defiant, rough, and violent (Willis, 1977; Best, 1983; Connell, 1989; Thorne, 1993; Gilbert & Gilbert, 1999; Chambers et al., 2004; Robinson, 2005). Any nonhegemonic ways of doing male gender would result in a devastating and painful experience under the system of hegemonic masculinities (Renold, 2004). Renold (2004) argues that masculinities are "actively constructed and defined in relation to and opposition against an Other, which can include girls, 'emphasized femininities' and gay and non-hegemonic masculinities" (p. 249). In a way, not only girls but particularly boys themselves are the victims of this heterosexual hegemonic discourse in which what it means to be a "guy" and how to behave as a "guy" are strictly rule-governed. Girls, under the power of male dominance, seem to have more freedom to do what they want or try out any strategies to negotiate and practice power through and over the male discourses. This is discussed in greater detail later in this chapter.

In childhood sociological research, researchers (Thorne, 1993; Corsaro, 1985, 1997; Boyle et al., 2003; Swain, 2005) point out that *doing* gender is not only socioculturally determined but also individually experienced and collectively manipulated by children in their own peer culture where different versions of masculinity and femininity are adopted, produced, and re-interpreted. Boyle et al. (2003) explore how the gender "borderwork" is strongly implicated in the games children play during recess. Swain (2005) notes that the gender division is interpreted by the boys in the study as "difference" rather than as "opposition" and argues that "rather than maintaining there were two detached and discrete worlds, there are two complementary gendered cultures sharing the one overall school world which, in turn, are intersected and further shaped by a series of other structural factors" (p. 87). As Swain's (2005) study shows, boys are disinterested in or detached from girls because playing with girls or associating too closely with them would jeopardize their male gender and would exclude them from the peer group. In other words, "girls" or the "other" that is not boys exist side by side with the hegemonic masculinities: "the 'other' was always present and acted to control boys' behaviors even when the real others were not there" (Swain, 2005, p. 81).

The gender confinement in which boys and girls tend to segregate from each other, as Aydt and Corsaro (2003) point out, "derives from compatibility of interest among members of the same sex" (p. 1307). The division between girls and boys is largely the result of different interests developed, rewards gained when playing with same-sex playmates, and frustration generated when playing with opposite-sex playmates. Moreover, they argue that children's gender construction is far more complex than the usual depiction of the traditional binary of the gender system. Instead of showing the stereotypical gendered behaviors or segregation, their study purports "how widely boy-girl interaction varies in different peer cultures and that gender segregation is something that is socially negotiated through peer interaction rather than a universal, individualistic process" (Aydt & Corsaro, 2003, pp. 1329-1330). The following is an interesting example in their study about how two young girls, Anita and Sarah, uniquely interpret and reproduce gender discourse while chasing two boys:

> As they run, the two girls start to pull up their shirts and say, "You want to see my bra?" Anita says, "I have a bra for my belly button" as she holds up her shirt. Sarah then turns to the researcher and says, "I really have a bra at home!" Here the girls use their knowledge of secondary sex characteristics (breast and bras) to tease their male classmates. (p. 1307)

This is also an example of how girls exercise power over boys and manipulate gender difference to tease boys.

Challenging the effect that schooling has as a process of naturalizing gender identities, literacy researchers (Davies, 2003a, 2003b; Anggard, 2005) as well as critical and feminist pedagogists (Markowitz, 2005; Kamler, 1999; Davies, 1997; Freire, 1973) explore how children construct gender through talking, reading, and writing and challenge ideological assumptions about power, knowledge, and authority. Davies (2003a) claims that deconstructing gender can be done in the school context by introducing children to a new discourse that deconstructs the ideological assumptions:

> "[A] discourse which enables them to see for themselves the discourse and storylines through which gendered persons are constituted to see the cultural and historical production of gendered persons that they are each caught up in. In this different approach, children can be introduced to the possibility, not of learning the culture, or new aspects of it, as passive recipient, but as producers of culture, as writers and readers who make themselves and are made within the discourses available to them. (p. 2)

Despite the fact that language and other forms of text are imbued with gender discourses, gender usually is the major tool children use to create stories for their own purposes (Dyson, 1997; Anggard, 2005). In this chapter, I would like to focus on how the boys and girls construct their gender identity against and through each other. As you will see, my analysis emphasizes the girls, first, to counterbalance my previous analysis in Chapter Three that emphasized male peer culture and, second, to reveal how the girls assert or exercise power over boys by applying male discourses and sharing the official authority in school.

## Post-Structuralists' Thoughts on Gender Identity

As research shows, gender is rooted deeply in children's daily social practices and they learn how to "do" gender well by the age of three (Aydt & Corsaro, 2003; Thorne, 1993). Thus, how boys and girls (should) act differently is not simply the outcome of school culture but reflects the broader sociocultural structure of gender roles reproduced and interpreted in the adult world. In the children's world, gender becomes the medium of how they assert power, divide themselves from the other, and build up the collective identity as well as solidarity among peers. Any attempt at deviating from the normative axis of gender division would jeopardize one's own sense of being and sometimes even become the target of peer hostility. As Butler (1990/1999, 2004) and Foucault (1997) assert, gender is the "effect" of cultural construction and a binary hegemonic system in which heterosexuality, reproductive bodies, and medico-legal jurisdiction are maintained and policed.

Butler argues that gender identity or categorization is constructed in discourse by the acts one performs. That is, "gender identity is a sequence of acts" (Salih, 2002, p. 45). As Salih (2002) explains, Butler's notion of performativity,

> "It's a girl!" is not a description of a state inscribed in nature, but a performative act, "an interpellation that initiates the process of 'girling,' a process based on perceived and *imposed* differences between men and women, differences that are far from 'natural.' (p. 89)

Thus, for Foucault and Butler, if gender is a cultural construct that is "done," then it can also be "undone" or deconstructed. Critical pedagogy and critical literacy are developed based on the tenet of deconstructing the norms monitoring our daily social practices and trying to educate students to maintain a critical as well as transformative relation to these social regulations dictating what is and what is not legitimate.

In a sense, gender is a cultural construct produced and maintained by the social norms that, on the one hand, explicitly define as well as divide people into categories of male and female and, on the other hand, implicitly lay out the structure of power relations underlying the "doing" of gender. However, gender is also the locus of one's social identity that intimately defines one's own being and reproduces general patterns and divisions in one's lifeworld.

This leads to a discussion of Butler and Foucault's theoretical insights in guiding the exploration toward the notion of gender construction. First, gender is defined by Butler (2004) as a set of relations. Second, these social relations are also normative regulations in which one's self-determination is practiced and recognized. Drawing from the Hegelian tradition linking desire with recognition, Butler (2004) argues that if human "desire is always a desire for recognition...as socially viable beings...then recognition becomes a site of power by which the human is differentially produced" (p. 2). The kind of person one desires to become is constrained by normative power legitimizing "who qualifies as the recognizably human and who does not" (Butler, 2004, p. 2). The objective of the gay/lesbian movement is an example of how people want to be recognized as valuable and respected by fighting against the gender binary that is discursively naturalized, culturally restrained, and heterosexually mobilized. Applied to the current study, what a boy or a girl should or should not do in school is also monitored under the hegemonic binary of heterosexuality implicated in the peer norms.

Foucault and Butler suggest that gender is a set of possibilities as well as a process of doing, shaping and re-making in an infinite repetition of linguistic institutions or discourses. Thus, gender terms or signifiers (i.e., male/female, masculine/feminine, etc.) are "never settled once and for all but are constantly in the process of being re-made" (Butler, 2004, p. 10). Foucault (1997) argues that people should not become trapped in issues of gender or sexual orientation, nor should gender be merely a struggle with government or legal institutions in power relations. Rather, people can and should be free from the shackles of gender binary because gender is *made* and not destined, discursively limited but not pre-given as an absolute biological "truth" of science. His genealogical inquiry of "the techniques of the self" tries to elaborate on the more fundamental question of how the legitimate form of knowledge is discursively produced and maintained:

> The guiding thread that seems the most useful for this inquiry is constituted by what one might call the 'techniques of the self,' which is to say, the procedures, which no doubt exist in every civilization, suggested or prescribed to individuals in order to determine their identity, maintain it or transform it in terms of a certain number of ends, through relations of self-mastery or self-knowledge. (Foucault, 1997, p. 87)

Butler (1999) also questions the "category" of women and the constitution of a subject and argues that

> "Gender" ought not to be conceived merely as the cultural inscription of meaning on a pre-given sex (a juridical concept); gender must also designate the very apparatus of production whereby the sexes themselves are established. As a result, gender is not to culture as sex to nature; gender is also the discursive/cultural means and established as "prediscursive," prior to culture, a politically neutral surface on which culture acts." (p. 11)

Thus, we can say that gender is not only a proliferation of possibilities, but it is also the inception of interrogation as well as transformation of power relations instigated in language use, political institutions, and the structure of gender construction.

Conceptualizing gender as a set of possibilities is crucial for this study to downplay the traditional binary of boys versus girls, and to foreground the girls' power, strategy, and perseverance when positioning themselves against the boys. Specifically, the girls in this study try different ways to *do* their gender strategically and to integrate with the boys and, thus, open up more possibilities for their gender identity, while most of the boys try hard to secure their male discourse and prevent the girls from breaking into the cocoon of male power.

Gender (as well as identity) is a paradoxical and dialogical construct with constant synthesis of the known and the unknown, social structure and individual agency, and the "I" who is and the "I" who is not. It is not another binary structure as the gender discourse, but the Hegelian unity of the "me" and the "not me." In this case, "I" and "not I" are unified as one, instead of two separated entities. De Beauvoir (1973) asserted that "one is not born a woman, but, rather, becomes one" (p. 301, as cited in Butler, 1999, p. 12). In other words, gender is discourse that is made. Also, it is not a free choice for a human but a system of naming and categorizing as the absolute legitimate form of being. As argued above, gender is a set of norms that constitute an "I" (or a subject) and in order to live in the social world, this "I" depends on the social systems as well as institutions to exercise its agency. One obvious example is that social actors are constrained by and dependent on language, one of the common institutions, to restore their agency and freedom in daily social practices.

Butler (2004) depicts paradox as the condition of the formation of our social identity:

> If my doing is dependent on what is done to me or, rather, the ways in which I am done by norms, then the possibility of my persistence as an "I" depends upon my being able to do something with what is done with me... My agency does not consist in denying this condition of my constitution. If I have any agency, it is opened up by the fact that I am constituted by a social world I never chose. That my agency is riven with paradox is the condition of its possibility. (p. 3)

This is how the children in this study constantly apply the norms operating in school to define themselves and, at the same time, to fight against what has been done to them by these norms (see Chapters Two and Three). In this chapter, this kind of paradox residing in gender construction guides us to think about how girls rely on the gender binary as an internal coherence to assert their gender power, while simultaneously trying to emancipate themselves from the conventional shackles of gender division.

For Foucault, gender is the grammar of sex and a hegemonic restraint of discourses suppressing the possibility of one's own being. He conceptualized gender not only as a set of possibilities but also as a freedom of choice and creativity (Foucault, 1997). For Butler (1999), gender is neither a noun nor an attribute but an incessant process of doing and deferring, and "a permanently available site of contested meaning" (p. 20). In a sense, both Foucault and Butler assume that after removing the institutional constraint of gender, there lies a universal sense of "a person" or an "I" that is free from the binary system of male-female, men-women, and boys-girls. The question is whether we can restore that sense of being through education by showing how girls and boys are equal as "a person," and whether school as an institution can allow children to exercise their self-determination and open up more possibilities for their identities.

Now, I would like to examine how children *do* their gender in the conventional binary structure and what other insights can be drawn from their ways of doing gender that deconstruct our stereotypical notion that girls are subordinate to boys in the power structure, that girls are weaker while boys are stronger, or that girls are submissive and boys are dominant.

## Gender Division, Conflicts, and Integration

### How Girls and Boys Become Popular Differently

"Body" is the primary site of gender division because male and female are biologically different. This "difference" becomes the most unshakable norm of gender construction that determines how one should look and become "normal" corresponding to one's sex. Thus physical size and appearance are the essential ways that boys and girls differentiate each other. Linda provides her insight about physical difference in terms of charisma between girls and boys:

> **Linda:** Well, like basically, the big kids are the ones who are popular and since for girls they know fashion and act like Bratz and stuff. The girls who are like Bratz and stuff, they'll get popular... That's usually for girls, if they are rich, they get popular. But for boys who like just play with basketball and are good at sports, they are usually the popular ones.

Physical size and appearance, as defined and "made" by gender discourse, are the fundamental components used by most children to define who is popular and who has charismatic power. As Linda depicts, it seems that for boys, being "big" or tall is a major way of showing physical strength through sports; for girls, they have to "know fashion and act like Bratz" to become popular. To achieve that, girls need to be "rich." As Linda explained to me, Bratz was the number one toy of the year and the Bratz Company beat the Barbie Company, a surprising indicator of just how much children know about the game/toy industry. All the media corporations advertise trendy images of fashion and beauty that manipulate children's gender identity. These media/advertising cultures become a major resource for their identity construction, in which their lifeworld is driven by media systems in which one is largely defined by what sorts of materials one has or how much one can afford to buy trendy items. The communicative action for reaching an understanding among people is short-cut by system relations, and the interaction among peers relies on the kinds of resource (e.g., money and power) one has, what kind of games or toys one is playing, or what kind of clothes one is wearing. According to Linda's account, we can see that those media products dictate the female body and define what counts as beauty.

What is worth noticing is how Linda pointed out the different ways of being popular between girls and boys. The boys assert their charismatic power through sports or doing what they are good at, while the girls need what is "outside" themselves (e.g., trendy clothes) to become attractive. In the previous chapter, I already pointed out that literacy capacity is one crucial criterion in the boys' peer culture but not in the girls'. What a girl is capable of doing seems to have little to do with her charisma, when the only way of becoming popular is through physical attraction. This is why feminist and post-structuralist theories try to free the "body" discursively confined by hegemonic cultural heterosexuality.

Rose and Kate also concurred:

> **Rose:** Well, popular students um like ~ on TV and stuff, they, they wear flashy clothes and they put on sparkly make-up.

**Kate**: I am one of the popular students... because I am pretty and I have nice clothes... Andy is popular... Oscar is popular and Sally is popular... All the people that are nice and pretty and have good clothes and are cool are popular.

Again, wearing "flashy clothes," putting on "sparkly make-up," and being "cool" are all related to the "body" appearance from these girls' perspectives. This also reflects what feminists and post-structuralists argue: gender is a social construct as well as a cultural contest of meaning rather than a fact simply determined in a natural or biological sense. However, Linda tried to get away from the Bratz-doll image when defining herself and criticized those who purposely behaved like a Bratz doll:

They [the popular girls] look thumbs-down... They have eye shadow, lipsticks, necklaces. They are just like Bratz dolls or show girls. They get really short skirts... They wear high heels or flip-flops... and you can almost see their underwear 'cause their skirts are so short... well, actually that's kind of how Bratz dolls look like. So they will just show their underwear and they will just copy that and try to copy Bratz and that's all they care about...and they make sure not to get their clothes dirty and if someone pours off ~ say, uh, a [?], they would just scream and run away like 'Ahhhhh' (Screaming), freaking out...They're just like ~ very girly. And I am not very girly. I am a tomboy, so I am tough...And they do not really like fighting and stuff, which I kind of really do. And they would try ~ like they would spend time walking and talking... if they step on anything, they just freak out basically.

Linda remained critical toward these fashion outfits for decorating a female body and making a girl become popular. Moreover, she described herself as a *tough* "tomboy" who liked "fighting" and contrasted herself with those who wear "high heels," "flip-flops," and super short skirts barely covering their underwear and "freak out" easily. We can see how Linda uses male discourse (i.e., "tough," "fighting") to differentiate herself from the other Bratz-doll girls. This is one way the girls in this class try to escape from the traditional female image as weak, vulnerable, and a doll-like pretty. I will discuss more about how girls assert gender power in a later section.

## Boys and Girls Usually Do Not "Hang Out"

Let us hear another long comment from Linda about why boys and girls should not "hang out" in school:

**Linda**: ... me and Andy, we draw a picture and then um Andy and Oscar are friends and then like Oscar doesn't like me to do stuff with Andy, so ~ 'cause he thinks Andy and he is not really like me so then um ~ Andy has to talk to Oscar and explain everything about what Andy and I did. And it's kind of like something that I called "boy trials" because like he [Oscar] has to ask all these questions and stuff... I saw [?] like

Oscar had been talking to Andy and basically he just got into trouble with Oscar because Oscar does not like other people to do stuff with his best friend [Andy]... And
like girls and boys if they hang out, it's really weird. In school, it's really weird when a
girl hangs out with a boy, you know, and a boy hangs out with a girl... It's just like --
it's really HARD um to get to have a friend that's a boy if you are a girl and if you are
a boy, it's really hard to have a friend that's a girl 'cause you like -- get bugged all the
time in class and that's one reason why kids do not do that.

It is a common phenomenon during childhood construction of gender
identity for children to gravitate to the same sex group—boys play with boys
and girls play with girls. Most children, particularly girls, shared similar views
with Linda during interviews. As most of them told me, boys and girls just did
not (or perhaps should not) hang out together. Some boys even considered it
as an absolute rule between boys and girls. Once this gender boundary is set
up, any action such as a boy hanging out mostly with girls that crossed it
would be either defined by the peer norms as something of a boyfriend-
girlfriend relationship or the boy will be sanctioned by the peer group.

Linda's experience of trying to cross the gender boundary and become
friends with Andy turned out unsuccessful. To summarize the main issues
here, Linda encountered three major problems: first, she felt the difficulty of
becoming friends with boys in school because the only legitimate relationship
between a boy and a girl is a "romantic" one; second, she was excluded from
the male peer culture strictly controlled by male discourse because the law-like
male regulation is deeply rooted in the boys' world; third, she witnessed the
consequences of Andy hanging out with her and how he was sanctioned and
interrogated (i.e., "boy's trials") by his peers, which indicates the great peer
pressure against making friends with girls in the boys' world.

Furthermore, it is "weird" when a boy "hangs out" with a girl unless they
are ready to either accept the normatively assumed kind of relationship (i.e.,
boyfriend-girlfriend) or "get bugged" all the time by their peers. During interviews, almost every child knows who has a boyfriend or a girlfriend in the
classroom. Apparently, many children admit or are tacitly forced to accept this
norm that boys and girls cannot develop a friendship and that they can become only a boyfriend or a girlfriend to each other. This is also how children
adopt themes from the adult world and recreate them to form their own peer
rules. Andy told me, "I'm not going out with girls until I get married." Sally
asserted, "I will have a real boyfriend when I am in 6th grade." For the children, marriage or having girlfriends/boyfriends should be "age-appropriate"—
another concept reinterpreted from the adult world.

The following is an example of how the boys, Andy and Oscar, talked
about their "girlfriends," which shows that this quasi-romantic kind of relationship is the major legitimate form of social integration between the boys

and girls in this class. During the interview, I asked Oscar straightforwardly about his "girlfriends" in this classroom. Andy took up my role as an interviewer most of the time:

> **Interviewer:** Let's talk about girls you know in this class.
> **Oscar:** Girls? (Looking at Andy, smiling and seeming a bit timid)
> **Andy:** Why are you looking at me?
> **Oscar:** Girls ~ (Looking at Andy and still laughing)
> **Andy:** Do you have any friends that are girls? (Andy re-phrased the question in a way that Oscar might not feel embarrassed).
> **Oscar:** I have a friend named~ the girl is Molly.
> **Andy:** And Sandra. More? (Andy pushed Oscar to spell out more as if he already knew about all Oscar's girlfriends).
> **Oscar:** Kristen.
> **Andy:** More? (Andy took my role to interview Oscar. I just listened and laughed with both of them).
> **Oscar:** Kate.
> **Andy:** More?
> **Oscar:** Sally.
> **Andy:** And Mrs. Jones (Andy teased Oscar).
> (Then, Oscar grabbed the tape recorder and ran to another corner and whispered something in the recorder. Andy was laughing as if he already knew what Oscar was going to say.)
> **Oscar:** (Whispering in the tape) Secretly, I love Molly.

## Enclosure of Male Discourses

From Linda's experience, we already see that the boys' peer culture seems exclusively for boys; girls are usually not allowed to join or are simply excluded. When I interviewed the boys about why they never played with the girls, most of their reactions were either shaking their head or just replying "no," seemingly implying that there is no need to discuss this question or that this is an "absolute" tenet in the boys' world—boys simply do not play with girls and there is no need to explain why. This is why the data appearing in this chapter are mostly about the girls' experiences of being refused by the boys during interaction. The following examples show how the boys in this classroom try to defend their male enclosure as well as discourse when the girls join their discussion.

*1. Ian and Edward Excluded the Girls' Involvement in Discussing Games:* Ian and Edward were working on the game column for the classroom newspaper. Vivian tried to join their conversation.

> **Ian:** ...What is, what is your favorite board game? I already introduced mine.
> **Vivian:** My favorite board game is "Candy land."

Ian: No, not yours; what's his. (Raising his voice)
Edward: My favorite board game is um ~ I don't know yet. I have a lot of game...

Ian is telling Vivian that this was his and Edward's column and that he was only interested in Edward's favorite board games, not hers. Raising his voice warns Vivian not to get involved in their discussion and Vivian's attempt to join the boys failed.

Another example is of Ian, Peter, and Edward talking about PlayStation 2; Paula and Michelle joined their conversation:

Ian: What do you~ hey, do you have PlayStation 2?
Edward: No—
Peter: You never play PlayStation 2? (Seeming surprised)
Edward: Well, I've played it but I don't have it.
Paula: I play video games with my brother.
Edward: I play Gameboy.
Michelle: Well, guess what? I have a GameCube.
Edward: Is that your brother's?
(Michelle was silent.)

When Paula said that she played video games with her brother, the three boys tacitly assumed that the video games belonged to her brother. However, when Michelle claimed that she herself owned a GameCube, Edward immediately wanted to clarify her statement by asking whether it belonged to her brother. Edward's question was responded to by Michelle with silence, which terminated the continuous interaction between them. Michelle's silence seemed to tacitly protest Edward's reaction and claim that girls can also own a GameCube and/or the conversation is about me, Michelle, not my brother. This is how most boys consider video games or any game devices—as an exclusive male discourse that girls can access only through their brothers.

*2. Ted Challenged Kate's "Knowledge" about PlayStation 2:* This is another example of how Ted tried to defend and secure this "absolute" male knowledge about video games by interrogating Kate about her game knowledge.

[1] Ted: Oh yeah? I bet you DO NOT have a Nintendo, a PlayStation cube, a PlayStation 3, Gameboy cards—
(As far as I know, there is only PlayStation 2, but no PlayStation 3. Nor have I heard of PlayStation cube. I think what Ted means is Nintendo GameCube)
[2] Kate: My brother does.
[3] Ted: Oh! NO. I am talking about YOU don't have those.
[4] Kate: I have PlayStation 2 and PlayStation 1, PlayStation card—
[5] Ted: PlayStation color? Hehehehe~ (Seeming to twist what Kate said)
[6] Kate: And Nintendo 2.
[7] Ted: How much dollars?

[8] **Kate**: What?

[9] **Ted**: How much dollar~money did you pay?

[10] **Kate**: (Thinking for a while) Thousand bucks.

[11] **Ted**: Ha-ha-ha. Liar! (Making a mocking face when teasing and then immediately turning into a stern face when saying "Liar")

[12] **Kate**: No, I am not a liar (Saying it calmly and twisting her pencil).

[13] **Ted**: Yeah? I could ask your mom any time.

[14] **Kate**: You have no clue of my mom's phone number. You don't know my phone number.

[15] **Ted**: Oh yeah? The school PHONE BOOK. Hee-he-he (Laughing). Gotcha.

[16] **Kate**: You do NOT~ You can't go to the school phone book.

[17] **Ted**: Oh yeah? I have one at my HOUSE!

[18] **Kate**: No, you do not (Saying it calmly). My mom does not live in town.

[19] **Ted**: Your dad's phone number is in the phone book. It's the same. HA-ha (Giving a Bart Simpson's laugh).

[20] **Kate**: (Kate was quiet. Her parents are divorced. She seemed to avoid explaining that to Ted and tried to change the subject). Do you know a remote control bed?

[21] **Ted**: My grandma has that.

Both Kate and Ted based their argument on the same normative ground acknowledging that video games are a part of male discourse. Ted claimed this through his male gender, and Kate asserted her access to the male discourse through her brother. Ted's interrogation is possibly motivated by his attempt to prove that Kate did not know or perhaps should not have anything to do with video games. Kate would not surrender to Ted's bombardment with a series of questions and she adjusted her previous ground by shifting from stating "My brother does" [2] to "I have PlayStation 2 and PlayStation 1, PlayStation card" [4]. However, Ted tried to twist Kate's word "PlayStation card" into "PlayStation color" [5] as if to make fun of Kate that she had no idea about PlayStation cards and that girls know only about "color" and nothing about a game "card."

It seems to me that both Ted and Kate boasted about their knowledge of video games. Ted sort of invented many game devices here, such as "PlayStation 3" or "PlayStation Cube" that are unheard of in the game industry. His game knowledge provided him resource and power to "boast" the way he wanted and Kate seemed to have no clue about how to challenge him, but Ted did. He asked Kate how much money she paid for those game devices and when Kate randomly said a number [10], "Thousand bucks," Ted was laughing aloud because it proved him right that Kate did not know anything about video games and that she was a "liar" [11].

Kate defended herself that she was not a liar, and Ted continued to threaten her that it was not difficult to find out whether she was a liar or not because he could check with Kate's parents in person or call them. "Gotcha"

[15] is Ted's way of claiming his triumph in this argument as if he successfully saved the boys' face by securing the male discourse on the matter of video games from the girls' invasion. Facing Ted's nonstop challenges as well as avoiding the topic of her parents' divorce, Kate's tactic is to change the topic from video games to something else—"a remote control bed" [20], a more neutral and gender-free topic.

# Ways of Asserting Power

Here I apply the metaphor of a "wall" and "war" derived from the children's talk to depict how the girls and boys express aggression and assert power differently.

## The Girls' *Wall* and the Boys' *War*

1. *Tammy and Vivian's "Wall"*: During the writing workshop, Tammy and Vivian sat at the same table writing and drawing together. Nick came to the table, and Vivian immediately held a book open and placed it in the middle of the table.

> **Vivian:** This is my wall and you are not supposed to break it, ok? (Commanding firmly and loudly)
> **Nick:** Ok (Saying it with tears circling in his eyes).
> **Tammy:** This is the girl's wall and you cannot break it (Concurring with Vivian and also placing another book adjacent to Vivian's).

This is how Vivian and Tammy marked their "girl territory" when boys approached. Nick was probably scared by their sudden aggression. However, this kind of girl aggression was rare during my prolonged observation in this classroom. Explicitly showing one's anger or aggression is not a major way for the girls to assert their gender power. The most "hostile" argument between the girls, according to my field notes, occurred when Julia asked Rose to leave her table. Rose refused and replied, "Free country," implying that people can sit anywhere they want to. According to Julia, her argument with Rose started way before this event, but I have no idea exactly what happened between them, and Julia did not want to explain further, saying, "it's difficult to explain." This is an example of how the tension between the girls is somehow opaque.

Vivian and Tammy's metaphor shows that the girls' peer culture is somehow behind the "wall" and cannot be directly approached or detected. In the previous chapter, I also briefly mentioned that the girls' interaction is not as direct as the boys', either verbally or physically. Simmons (2002, 2004) points out that most girls are conventionally educated to be "nice" and thus lack strategies to deal with peer conflict. This aggression becomes a set of secret codes between girls to attack each other in an indirect and vicious manner under the camouflage of their female "niceness." Examples as such are many and yet not obvious. For instance, once Kate and Nina got into a fight about who should get the chair for the teacher. Both were pushing each other with their elbows and trying to grab the chair. Kate explained to me, "We want to get the chair for Mrs. Jones." Another example is that I constantly noticed that some girls who are otherwise good friends would stop talking to each other for quite a long time. There seemed to be some hostile undercurrents within their friendship, but no one yelled or argued in public about it. Avoiding confrontation or hiding their anger seems a common way for girls to deal with their social relationships in school.

*2. Boys' War*: Compared to the girls, the boys seem to provide more examples on expressing their aggression in different social practices, including the literacy activities. Let us hear the conversation between Josh and Edward:

> **Josh**: I will not let go of the chair. What do you think you have to do? What do you think would happen if I don't let go of the chair? (Josh seemed half challenging and half joking with Edward).
> **Edward**: I will immediately cut your fingers off.

Expressing aggression overtly is usually the boys' way. Some of these talks are playful and nonaggressive, for the primary purpose of talking aggressively is to engage other peers and build up solidarity. Whenever there is an indoor recess, the boys in this class would build their "army base" and "forces" with wood blocks in the classroom. "Let's destroy the enemy," "kill them all," "Dadadadadadadada..." (Making the sound of a machine gun), and other such expressions of bravado are examples of boy talk in their imaginary battles.

In Chapter Four, I discussed boys' expression of their aggression in their imaginary superhero stories as a way of empowering themselves to control and deal with their problems in real life. Newkirk's (2002) study argues that there is "no evidence showing that students who employ violence in their stories actually commit violence" (p. 94). He also asserts that boys' desire for action, conflict, and violence is restricted and sometimes aestheticized "within a system of comprehensive rules" (p. 103). In particular, a violent game is enjoyable because it is bound tightly in a fairly "controlled environment" (p. 103) that the boys try to master. The following is an example of how Edward aestheticized the war scene with humor in his self-created storybook.

**Edward**: My book is called *Army Explosives*... Well, um...there's this Japanese army and ...we launched a jet in one of the towers on the air cafeteria [aircraft carrier] and um~ And this is funny~ hehehehe (laughing)... In this funny part, this guy was told not to launch himself, but he launched himself in the jet, and he, well, he was fine. He put the hood of his jet up. He took away this grenade and he went like, "BYE-BYE" (screaming in a high-pitched tone). He throws the grenade and shows the confidence while he throws it away. And he makes this huge hole in the commander's submarine for the Japanese and it sinks... I think it just gets all that water in and it goes "Shooooo...Waaaaaa..." (Making the sounds as if the submarine was gradually sinking and people were drowning and screaming).

Edward's primary purpose of writing this "war" story is not to emphasize the violence or the destructive weapons of the war, but to stress the "fun" part of the war by humorously creating a scene in which a soldier made a hilarious mistake and accidentally sank his commander's submarine. Thus, we need to rethink and interpret male aggression carefully and avoid traditionally associating the male with aggression or the female with submission. Aggression may be what boys' action appears to be, but it is not their primary purpose; girls may seem nice but their covert aggression could be more powerful than the boys'.

The following is another example of a boy's "aggressive" talk:

**Andy**: I don't really like school... [I want to] tear down all the schools in the whole universe... I'll build um~ school with preschool only. I really like kindergarten. That's the only grade I like... On the rug procedures, I just hope to change "no talking" into "just talking", (?), "sitting on the bottom" into "lying down," and~ and "keeping hands to yourself" into "slapping people"... Oh, I also wish you can do anything you like, tearing down the new shelves, knocking out those~ I wish there's no teacher... No teachers in the whole school besides the lunch lady... [I hope to find] books that talk about sloppy behaviors and drawing.

I have mentioned before that Andy was a very well-behaved student according to the teachers and during my almost two-year friendship with him, despite the fact that he struggled a lot with his schoolwork. Although his talk is full of seemingly destructive action (i.e., tearing down, slapping, and knocking out) and his rebellious way of revolutionizing school, his underlying motivation for this vicious talk is to show his frustration but not aggression, negotiation but not destruction.

To summarize the main point here, the boys' way of showing aggression is different from the girls', but this gender difference should not be seen in the conventional way of regarding overt aggression as more powerful or vicious and covert aggression as weaker or less destructive. Simmons (2002) argues that female aggression is as guilty and destructive as male aggression. Moreover, the boys' actions expressed through their talks or writings are usually obvious, violent, active, and playful; it is their way of rallying solidarity among peers. The girls' action, on the contrary, is opaque, reserved, and serious, which is the primary tactic used to hide their anger and minimize drawing public attention to their aggression. Having said that, I do not intend to naturalize this gender difference or excuse the boys' aggression. Rather, we need to deconstruct the conventional image of male aggression and female niceness. Male aggression may not be as powerful as we used to think, nor should female aggression be exonerated from its niceness.

## Conforming to and Challenging the Teacher's Authority

In this part, I focus my discussion on how the girls and boys react to official authority in relation to their gender power. Generally speaking, most girls in this class consider conforming to or exceeding the teacher's expectations as success while most boys tend to challenge the official authority as a way to have fun or strengthen their male solidarity. The girls also seem to understand the importance of official rules from the teacher's perspective. The following two examples show how girls conform to the official standards and take the position of the teacher while commenting on the classroom discipline.

*1. Paula, Gina and Julia's views about the responsibilities of a student*

> **Paula:** Um, well, good students would follow lots of directions. They wouldn't tease or make fun of or talk with their friends in class. They would listen to the teachers and pay attention to what everybody says and what their opinions are. They would read a lot and spell a lot and challenge themselves, work very hard and do their best. And um they would be productive. They would share what they're learning with everyone. And they would try it a lot, a lot, a lot until they really get it; maybe just like from the North Pole to the South Pole or something. They would work through but they would try to do their best and work really hard... they wouldn't put up with it.

> **Gina:** If I want to be a good student, I would just try it to be my personal best and if I couldn't like figure out this one thing, I would just persevere and would listen to my teacher and I would try really, really hard.

> **Julia:** If I could make new rules in our classroom, it would probably be that you should always listen to the teachers and no talking when someone else is speaking. And you have to raise your hands when you are gonna talk... It's like all the basic rules that a classroom has because when I grow up, I want to be a teacher.

Their recursive phrases—such as  following directions, paying attention, reading and spelling a lot, working really hard, being productive, doing one's

best, working through without giving up, persevering, and the like—reflect the
official values and discourses in school. Paula created an active metaphor—
going "from the North Pole to the South Pole"—to depict the meaning of perseverance when encountering difficulties in school. Julia takes the position of
a teacher to emphasize the importance of obeying rules in the classroom. Although this is usually how the girls comply with the official standards in
school, I argue that their compliance is also the main tactic to secure identity
as well as to claim power and privilege in school.

I have already discussed how the girls in this class gain more trust from the
teachers to carry out challenging tasks and that they are more likely to receive
public praise or rewards from the teachers. The official authority is usually
their resource for power and whenever there is an argument between the boys
and girls, the girls would be more likely to get the teacher's support. This may
be the result of their compliance to the official agenda.

## 2. Bob, Tim and Greg's collective action

The boys, on the contrary, are blunt in expressing their opinions about official
rules. Sometimes, they would complain directly if the rule was not fair. Whenever possible, they would protest the teacher's authority in a playful manner.

Bob, Tim and Greg were punished by writing their names on the board
because they talked too loud during the work time. They were not allowed to
sit next to each other as the class rule indicates—"Do not sit with your friends."
During the community circle time, the teachers asked each child to sit on the
rug and share their goal(s) for the week with the whole class.

> **Teacher**: Bob, share with us your goal.
> **Bob**: I don't have a goal.
> **Teacher**: Ok, think of one and we will come back to you later.
> ...
> **Tim**: I don't have a goal (Tim and Bob looked at each other and laughed).
> ...
> **Teacher**: How about Greg?
> **Greg**: I don't have a goal (Greg looked at Tim and Bob and three of them laughed).
> **Teacher**: Think about your goal (Then, the teacher asked the next student).

Their collective action by saying "I don't have a goal" seems to be their playful
defiance to protest the teacher's authority.

Another example of this was the teacher punishing the whole class by taking away three points from the bonus recess because some children were still
talking. Some girls warned the class to keep quiet, "She (the teacher) is taking

points away. She is taking points away. Shhh, Shhh, Shhh..." Nick questioned the teacher bluntly, "Why did you take the points away? It's not my fault. I did not talk." The teacher answered, "The class is a community and each of you is responsible for it." Nick still mumbled, "It's not fair." Again, we see the different reaction between Nick and the girls.

Also, once during Read Aloud, the teacher read two chapters of a story but many children wanted to hear more; "More, please; read more, more...," some children whined. Suddenly, several boys (Oscar, Eric, Tim, Greg, Bob, etc.) initiated a rhythmic chant that was similar to slogan shouting during a public strike, "We want more! We want more! We want more! We want more! ..." The teacher asked them to be polite to the story reader, or there would be no story time anymore in the future. The protest dwindled after the teacher's warning.

The three examples above are the typical ways of how the boys in this class overtly negotiate with the official agenda in school. The girls, on the other hand, conform, acquire, understand, and support the official authority. In a sense, the girls share power with the official system in school while the boys try to work that system; the girls are more likely to get rewarded while the boys are more likely to be punished—as a result of their constant challenges to the teacher's authority. In the following discussion, I will elaborate more on how the girls share and extend the official power in school when interacting with the boys.

## Asserting Gender Identity through the Opposite Sex

This section is about female attraction, victory, and perseverance through "conquering" the boys in different ways. Asserting one's gender identity through the opposite sex is particularly obvious in the girls' action when asserting their gender power. The boys become the medium for them to construct their identity. Of course, the constructing process is not free of disturbances and tensions. The following three examples show how girls empower themselves through (a) fighting against the boys by applying male discourses and (b) sharing and extending the official power in unofficial settings.

*1. Linda knew that she was attractive to "the most powerful kid" in class*

> **Linda:** Oscar wants girls to notice that he is like the PERSON who is basically a big guy. He wants us to notice that HE is the person that girls should like...and he knows that I am kind of smart and he knows that I am looking for a boy to play with. And he is trying to get me to do stuff with him and to like him... Well, basically, he is the most powerful kid ...Oscar said to me in music class like yesterday; he said, "You have

to do what I say and must listen to me because I am older and bigger than you."... I said, "NO! I do not because I can do my own things and you are not in charge here." So and sometimes with him, he's not going to get bugged and you got to keep on basically fighting back. You know what I mean... I got practiced 'cause at my house, my big brother, he's kind of like that and like so I practiced on him and so I know how to handle it... Oscar likes Molly. He also likes me... Well, basically, he is my enemy and he'll try to get me into an argument. Then he gets to show he is boss more and that's one way he gets more, you know, popular and more people to like him and stuff like that...I just figured that out. He likes me a lot, and he is basically, focusing on me, trying to get my attention, and trying to get me to like him, which is not going to happen.

First of all, Linda is confident that she is attractive to Oscar because she considers herself "kind of smart" and keeps on "fighting back" Oscar's attempt to get her attention. Second, she affirms that she is somehow familiar with the boy's way of bugging and threatening because she "practices on" her brother and knows "how to handle it." Third, "enemy" is the metaphor Linda uses to refer to "the most powerful kid," Oscar, in this class. She positions herself as a "heroic" character in this gender "battle" who is smart, brave, unyielding, and yet attractive to her enemy. Finally, despite these characteristics, Linda claims victory through her persistent resistance as well as resilience against the enemy's constant nagging, bossing, and bullying.

## 2. Kate's muscle and headband

Kate, Max, Ron, and the other girls sat at the same table during the work time. Kate rolled up her sleeve, bent her elbow, and showed her upper arm to Max and Ron, "Touch this. These are all muscles." Max poked with his finger. Ron poked with his pencil. Kate smiled and seemed proud. Kate applied conventional male discourses here (i.e., muscles, strength) to show the boys her power and asked them to feel her strength. Moreover, instead of asking the other girls to feel her muscles, Kate seems to consider that the boys' compliance would make her strength more convincing.

Another example is how Kate tried to mix the typical female and male gender roles by improvising her headband into a "beard" and forcing a boy to put on her headband. It was the writing workshop time. Kate, Max, and Kevin were constructing their story web on the same table. Kate played with her headband and put it around her face and chin as if it were her "beard." Max saw it and commented, "You're not a man. You don't want to have a beard." Then Kate forced Kevin to put on her headband by pressing it really hard on his head. Kevin struggled and screamed, "No, no, no..." Max laughed and said, "Whoa, that's for girls, not for boys!" Kate kept trying to force Kevin to put on her headband even though he tried to fight against her persistence. Finally, Kate made it and said, "See? He used it." To use her headband as a beard may be how Kate experiments or challenges the issue of the gendered "body." Moreover, Kate forcing Kevin to use her headband seems to prove to Max that boys and girls are not that different, that boys can use girls' stuff, and that girls can be as strong as or even stronger than boys.

### 3. Linda, Vivian, and Tammy scolded the boys' mischief

The following long episode shows the scene in which two boys, Greg and Eric, were creating funny songs about their family during the work time and two girls, Linda and Vivian, were observing and trying to join in. Linda's attempt to join the boys was ignored. Vivian scolded the boys for their mischief but it turned into an argument. By showing this long episode, I want to emphasize three points: (i) the process of how Greg and Eric created their funny rhyming songs, (ii) the language used that gave rise to Linda and Vivian's scorn for the boys' improper song-making, and (iii) the copresence of the girls' "silence" and observation during the whole process of the boys' action that seemed to try to find a proper tactic to join in but failed. The lines in bold in the episode below are the songs the boys made.

[1] **Greg**: (Hitting the table with pencils as if playing a drum and singing with a self-created melody) **My mom is 41; she looks a little fun.**

[2] **Eric**: Hehehehehehehe (Laughing aloud).

[3] **Greg**: I got lots of songs about my mom.

[4] **Eric**: Sing the second one.

[5] **Greg**: **My mom is 42. She looks so big and blue** (Hitting the table as if it were a drum with pencils while singing). I just made a song about my dad the day before yesterday. **My dad is 4—my dad is 22; he looks so big and huge. My mom is 22; she looks a lot like you...**

[6] **Eric**: Hehehehe... (Laughing). Do when she's 47.

[7] **Greg**: Ok. **My dad is 47; he's gonna go to heaven.**

[8] **Eric**: ...How about my brother? He's 10.

[9] **Greg**: **My brother is 10; he likes to hug the hen.**

[10] **Eric**: Hehehehe... **My grandma's 62; she looks sad and huge.**

[11] **Greg**: **My grandma's 41; she look—she has a hamburger bun.**

[12] **Eric**: Hehehehe...

[13] **Linda**: Now. Everybody here can stop doing that and work on the questions.

[14] **Greg**: I already have 4 questions down.

[15] **Eric**: Me, too.

[16] **Linda**: **My little sister is 5; she lives in a bee hive** (Linda joined them but was ignored).

[17] **Greg**: **My sister is 45; she lives with bees in a hive.**

[18] **Eric:** Hehehehehe.. (Still laughing)

[19] **Greg: My mom rides a horse; she's going to be a hoarse.** You know what that means? "Hoarse" means sick.

[20] **Eric:** She's going to be a HORSE? (Eric might not know the word "hoarse.")

[21] **Greg:** This is my mom singing now. This is my mom singing after she got a hoarse (He sang in a harsh, low voice).

[22] **Eric: My mom is 21; she likes to lick her bun.** Hehehehehe... (Laughing)

[23] **Greg:** This is my mom singing after she got a hoarse. **My dad is—My husband is 42; I hate him and I hate you** (Singing with harsh sound). Hehehehe...

[24] **Eric:** Hehehehe...that's great.

[25] **Greg: My gerbil is 22; it writes with pencil, too.** You made one, Eric.

[26] **Eric:** Hehehehehe...Uh (thinking) wait.

[27] **Greg:** That's your song "wait"?

[28] **Eric:** Hehehehehe... no, no, hehehehehe....

(Mrs. Jones came and asked them to be quiet by saying "Shhhh—")

[29] **Greg: My dad can't hear with his ears; he drinks a lot of beer.**

[30] **Eric:** Hehehehe...he drinks a lot of beer.

[31] **Linda:** Hey, Greg, how about I tell your mom that song? How about I tell your dad about that song? (Seeming to indicate that the songs Greg was making were not appropriate and his parents would not be happy when they heard those songs. Both Greg and Eric lowered their voices and tried to giggle as quiet as they could).

...

[32] **Eric: My dad—wait. My dad is scary; he likes to be—he likes to be—**

[33] **Greg: He likes to be furry.**

[34] **Eric:** No, hehehehehe....**He likes to be buried.**

[35] **Greg: My dad is very hairy; he looks so big and scary. My dad is so so hairy; he wants to be a canary.** You know what a canary is?

[36] **Eric:** A bird.

[37] **Greg: My dad is such a fairy; he eats a lot of berries.**

[38] **Eric:** Hehehehehe... buried.

[39] **Greg:** "Berries" not "buried" (Emphasizing the ending sound).

[40] **Linda:** Belly.

[41] **Greg:** What? (Greg did not hear what Linda said and asked her again, but was interrupted by Eric).

[42] **Eric: My dad is so hairy; he wants to be—** (thinking)

[43] **Greg: A canary.**

[44] **Eric:** No. **My dad is so hairy; he likes to be buried.....**

[45] **Vivian:** Hey! (Staring at Greg)

[46] **Greg:** What?

[47] **Vivian:** Stop it! (Asking Greg to stop making those silly songs)

[48] **Eric:** Ok (Eric complied immediately).

[49] **Greg:** You stop it! You stop coming over here (Arguing with Vivian and asking her to leave).

(Vivian left and walked toward Mrs. Jones. After a while, Mrs. Jones made an official announcement.)

[50] **Mrs. Jones:** I just heard a big complaint and a lot from this group right over here (Pointing to Greg and Eric's table).

Greg and Eric were making silly songs about their families. Notice how the male solidarity was working here through joking and teasing themes from the adult world, such as "going to heaven [7]," "husband-wife" relationships [23], aging and death (i.e., being buried) [34, 44]. Also, finding words that rhyme in a funny way is their major concern during song-making and thus choosing a morally appropriate word is beyond their consideration. This, however, caught Linda and Vivian's attention, and they tried to intervene in the boys' "inappropriate" behavior.

Linda extended the official surveillance by reminding the boys that they were supposed to finish writing their questions in their journals [13]. The boys tacitly acknowledged her claim and told her that they already finished working on that. Linda [16] tried to join the boys' song-making. Greg responded by re-wording Linda's song [17] but this did not last long. Linda was somehow excluded by the boys' enclosure. She observed silently until she tried another tactic [31] by applying moral surveillance to raise the boys' conscience on their "improper" manner of teasing their parents. Again, Greg and Eric acknowledged Linda's statement by significantly lowering their voices, but the male solidarity still excluded her. She kept observing and trying to break through the male barrier. Linda tried again [40] by joining the boys' rhyming (i.e., "berries," "buried," and "belly"), and when Greg seemed to show some interest in letting Linda join in [41], he was stopped by Eric's song [42].

Vivian observed the whole process of interaction and how Linda failed to stop the boys' inappropriate behavior. She tried a more severe tactic by taking the teacher's role and warning the boys in a harsh yelling tone [45, 47]. Eric, as a 1st grader, immediately complied [48] under the power of $2^{nd}$ grader Vivian's scolding, but Greg considered her action as provoking a fight with him and thus responded to Vivian's challenge by yelling back and chasing her away [49]. Failing in this tactic, Vivian went to Mrs. Jones and reported the boys' mischief. Mrs. Jones responded to Vivian's complaint [50] and gave them a warning.

This exemplifies how girls in this classroom sometimes try to join the male discourse or break through the male enclosure by extending the official surveillance while interacting with boys. Unfortunately, this does not seem to work well. Vivian failed to make Greg comply with her quasi-official authority, but she reclaimed power by reporting to her powerful ally, the teacher.

Sometimes the girls also take up the teacher's role in an official setting. An example occurred once when it was Fred's author celebration. He was sitting on the author chair and reading his story, *The Little Bear*. After Fred finished reading his story, Bob commented straightforwardly, "Mrs. Jones, his story is too short. I thought there was going to be more. It's like only two pages." While Mrs. Jones was busy taking a picture of the author, Tammy turned around, stared at Bob, and said seriously, "The story is good. It's really nice." Then she started applauding for Fred. The other students also clapped their hands showing that they agreed and supported Tammy's comment. Tammy tacitly took on the teacher's role by trying to make Bob feel that he should respect the author regardless of the length of the story and that it was impolite to comment that the story was too short after the author shared his story with the class.

## Discussion

I have examined how the girls and boys do their gender under the binary system of gender discourses in this classroom. First, I discussed how a "body" is gendered. Linda used "Bratz-dolls" as the metaphor to show how girls become popular and powerful through the materials outside their body while boys need to be physically big and tall to do sports well for asserting their charismatic power. However, Linda applied male discourses (i.e., tough, tomboy, fighting) to define herself and asserted her gender power in contrast to the Bratz-doll girls.

Second, I explored the gender division strictly monitored by the peer rules in this class and found that the major social integration between the boys and girls is through developing a sort of romantic relationship legitimated by the peer culture. Children adopted the adult theme of romance into their peer culture and many of them considered that hanging out with the opposite sex should be age-appropriate. Also, when one has a friend of the opposite sex, he or she must be ready for the public comment in this class.

Third, I discussed how most of the girls actively attempted to break through the gender barrier between boys and girls while the boys try to secure their male territory (i.e., topics about video games, male enclosures) from the girls' invasion. In a way, the boys are caught up in their own hegemonic male discourses while the girls seem to be flexible and have more choices to explore different ways of doing gender (e.g., Kate's beard and muscles).

Fourth, I tried to deconstruct the conventional image of male aggression and female submission by showing how the girls express their aggression in a reserved, opaque, but serious way, while acting aggressively is the fundamental way of how the boys interact with peers. Their seemingly aggressive talk or action is how they build up male solidarity, express their humor, or show their frustration. I argue that female aggression could be more serious and "destructive" and we should not mistakenly consider boys' overt aggression as more powerful and girls' covert hostility as weaker.

Fifth, I also investigated how the children respond to official authority differently to exercise power. I argue that boys challenge the official authority while girls share or try to assume the teacher's authority. Specifically, the girls' compliance to the official standards is their major way of constructing identity as well as asserting power. The teacher is their most powerful "ally" in school when confronting with the boys. Most of the boys, on the contrary, choose to rebel against the official authority by overtly challenging or violating the rules. Furthermore, the girls tend to extend the official surveillance by constantly taking up the teacher's role when interacting with the boys in unofficial settings. This also shows another way of how the official agenda is reproduced by the girls when exercising power over the boys.

In the final chapter, we will listen to the children's version of what constitutes a wonderful day in school. I will review the main arguments proposed and conclude the study by offering possible implications for current research in education.

# CHAPTER SEVEN

# Conclusion

### A Wonderful Day in School

**Andy**: It would be party all day. I don't like reading and writing. I want to draw. My favorite part in school is lunch and gym. I wish there's no teacher. No teachers in the whole school besides the lunch lady...

**Kate**: I like to wander around the school and do some fun stuff like playing in the park, reading books in the library and going to my old class.

**Ian**: I really really like this class. There sin't a lot I don't like about it, but I think we should be allowed to go outside. And like if we have the writing workshop really long time, if we could have half day for that, it would be pretty fun.

**Ted**: Um...no homework. All the school does is play, recess, and eat lunch. I wish all the authors would make the books a little bit funnier and writing workshop all day.

**Jeff**: It will uh probably you will get to draw all day and if it's Thursday or Wednesday, I hope spelling test would be cancelled. And I wish we would have like an activity that I might get more friends. Um I have a good lunch and not have any work to do.

**Bill**: A wonderful day would be uh everybody is quiet during work time and then we have a bonus recess at the end of the day. You can do something you like.

**Tammy**: A wonderful day um... the rule is gonna to be changed. Yeah, change the rule into talking to your neighbors and you can do whatever you want. You can draw, extend recess and you wouldn't have to do math. You can do anything you want. You can wear your pajamas to school.

These are some children's versions of what a wonderful day in school would be like. In Bakhtin's (1984) notion of *carnival ambivalence*, the children's complaints, mockery, playful jokes, abusive expressions, and imagination regarding the kind of school life they want are like their unofficial *folklore cultures*:

> [Their unofficial folklore cultures are] sharply distinct from the serious official, ecclesiastical, feudal, and political cult forms and ceremonials. They offered a completely different, non-official, extraecclesiastical and extrapolicial aspect of the word, of man, and of human relations; they built a second world and a second life outside officialdom. (p. 197)

In children's carnival-like temporary liberation from routine regulations, forms of speech and meaning are challenged, discarded, and yet transformed; tensions are aroused to break as well as to renew the life cycle; new insights about education are extracted with the clash of the real and the ideal. Thus, to ignore children's unofficial voices about what kind of school they want to have is to see a distorted view of school culture.

This study shares the same argument with Pollard, Thiessen and Filer (1997):

> [T]aking pupil perspectives seriously can contribute to the quality of school life, the raising of standards of educational achievement and understanding of many important educational issues. We would also argue the converse, that to ignore or underplay the significance of pupil perspectives can undermine the quality of school life, learning achievements and the development of understanding. (p. 1)

One might argue that the children's versions of a wonderful day in school are simply complaints that they always whine about and what they want is just more playing, less working, or even no school at all. If these are typical impressions you get after hearing from these children, then you may want to think about why it is so and how we can make learning a fun experience for every child in school. I hope this study will provide a new start for different possibilities of exploring identity issues in early childhood education and evoking a more creative thinking and application in curriculum, policy, as well as implementation.

In the following discussion, I review some of the major themes of children's learning experiences and identity construction that I have examined in each chapter. As my reflections and discussions unwind with the children's idea of a wonderful school day, I hope to initiate dialogues among children, teachers, educators, policy-makers, those who care and struggle to provide quality education, and those who believe in a standardized curriculum, instruction, and assessment. It is an invitation for all of us to reflect on the kind of schooling and learning environment that shapes the children's sense of the self, and to continue improving our education and believing that we can make a difference in children's lives.

## Summary and Suggestions for Future Studies

### Two Dominant Social Identities and the Concept of Negation

In Chapter Two, I tried to elicit how the children defined who they are through the two dominant social identities in school, being a successful student and being a popular student. The children's narratives revealed the struggles they confronted and that their sense of the self was restricted and misrepresented by the generalized other in school. Deriving from their endeavor to construct a valid self are three ways of positioning themselves as well as each other in school:

- Conforming to the norms
- Striving to be the dominant group
- Negotiating and fighting against the norms

My findings suggest that the children's desire for reconstructing the unity of a meaningful self is projected in their language use through negation or saying NO to the discourses operating in the classroom. The concept of *negation* is the language pattern embedded in the children's narratives when telling their stories in school. Negation, however, can also be viewed as a mechanism of exclusion (Vitanza, 1997). As Vitanza (1997) elaborates:

> By saying NO, we would purchase our identity. Know ourselves. By purifying the world, we would exclude that which, in our different opinions, threatens our identity. (pp. 12–13)

I have pointed out how most of the children criticized the popular students in this class who became the dominant and privileged group in this class. Mysteriously, none of the children regarded themselves as belonging to the snobbish popular group in the class. Even though Ian identified himself as popular among peers, he insisted that he was a "nice guy" to be with and he was definitely not related to the "mean," "hot-shot," "bragging" popular students who hurt people's feeling. Then who are those mean popular students? Why does the negative idea toward popular students keep showing up in the children's narratives?

Vitanza's (1997) idea of a "mechanism of exclusion" may suggest another way to understand *negation* embedded in the children's narratives:

> To hold a dialogue is to suppose a third man and to seek to exclude him; a successful communication is the exclusion of the third man. The most profound dialectical problem is not the problem of the Other, who is only a variety... of the Same, it is the problem of the third man. We might call the third man, the demon, the prosopopeia of noise... Dialectic makes the two interlocutors play on the same side, they do battle together to produce a truth on which they can agree, that is, to produce a successful communication. In a certain sense, they struggle together against interference, against the demon, against the third man. (Serres, 1982, p. 67; cited from Vitanza, 1997, pp. 21–22)

Perhaps by creating this imaginative third party and then excluding it, the children are able to justify their action choices and repair their identity, oppressed by the unfair school norms that they have little control over.

Furthermore, identity construction seems a process of contradiction within the self. While the children are eager to express their discontent and challenge the normative regulation in school, they also strive to conform and sometimes even passively succumb to it. Some children felt spiteful toward the popular students and tried to differentiate themselves from them; but, at the same time, not being one of the popular students somehow threatened their identity. We desire sameness from the society we belong to, but we also yearn for difference that makes us each a unique individual distinct from the other. If contradiction is one component of identity construction, then it requires further research to explain the discrepancies between one's identity claims (i.e., who one is) and one's action choices (i.e., what one actually does).

To conclude our discussion, an emergent framework can be derived from the concept of negation that constitutes three interpretive dimensions of identity construction:

(1)  Linguistic structures embedded in one's narratives
(2)  Mechanisms of inclusion and exclusion that rationalize one's action
(3)  Contradictions rendered within the making of the self

### Classroom Culture

In Chapter Three, I have attempted to map a larger picture of the classroom culture that situates as well as shapes the children's routine actions and identity formation. I focused on the three structural aspects of the classroom culture: (1) the official, (2) the unofficial, and (3) the discrepancies between these two. The three of them constitute a reproductive loop of the life cycle in the classroom that conditions as well as shapes the children's identity trajectories in school.

Even though the children had brought up many issues about the official agendas they disagreed with, underlying these complaints were the challenges that the teachers were facing in school. These challenges await further investigation by teachers and educators:

• Is student resistance an unavoidable part of a classroom culture?
• Does this mean that teacher discourse is constantly in conflict with student discourse when both teachers and students struggle with identity as well as control in school?

- How should this issue of conflicting discourse be addressed in teacher education where a major part of a teacher's job is to deal with students' resistance?
- What are the possible strategies that teachers could use to detect and avoid discrepancies between the official agendas and the unofficial discontentment unintentionally resulting from the curriculum and instruction practices?

I will provide some suggestions in the subsequent discussion.

## Becoming an Author

Chapter Four centered on the identity that is important for most children in this classroom—being an author who writes and creates her own story. Empowered by the ownership through creating their novelistic discourses, they use language to craft new meanings derived from their life memories and experiences in their book. As authors who make their own books, these children also *author* and outgrow themselves by encountering others and recreating others' utterances through an endless expansion of meaning-making in a continuous dialogic process.

Extending the argument that being an author is how the children create their own way to express meaning and live in the world, writing stories is also their favorite literacy activity in school, where their agency and the teacher's instruction find a common ground. Thus, the writing workshop plays a significant part in many children's school life. It is also the time when the teachers are involved minimally, permitting the children to have maximum control and freedom to explore, create, and make their "OWN THING" through writing their own books. The writing workshop is also the one official feature of the classroom that many children would include in a "perfect school."

One area worth examining is how this *freedom* of being an author may extend its influence into other aspects of children's learning in promoting self-esteem in school where teachers and students are co-constructors and explorers in a curriculum. While freedom of choice seems crucial for many students in text construction and learning, it still remains instructionally challenging for teachers to provide enough flexibility as well as to maintain order in the classroom and monitor every child's progress and needs. Research on classroom management needs to explore how the notion of *freedom* and *flexibility* can be best applied in a curriculum that establishes children's sense of agency and allows them to take more responsibility for their own learning in school.

## Complexity and Multiplicity of Meaning-Making

Chapter Five was an invitation to re-examine the complex process of the children's text construction embedded in their graphic design. The exploration started from Kate's drawn and told story and then contrasted it with her written story. The purpose of this is to remind us that many children use different sign systems to compose stories, which also suggests that the identity of being an author should not be reduced to or prioritized to a form of literacy in school. Different forms of meaning-making should not change the way we assess and value children's creativity and efforts in constructing texts.

Although the writing workshop is the favorite literacy activity for many children, some are still marginalized by the writing program if putting words down is the *only* legitimate form of literacy in school. Moreover, Dyson (1993) disagrees with a rigidly structured writing program that presupposes a "process." She reminds teachers to reflect on the writing workshop program implemented in the classroom:

> In such a [process] pedagogy, there is an emphasis on children as "real" authors who make decisions about what and how they are going to write. However... process pedagogy is undergirded by an imaginative universe rooted in a dichotomous view of "oral" and "literate" texts, and more generally in a narrow conception of school literacy. (p. 50)

A structured process in a writing program may violate the complex nature of the meaning-making process. It may stop children from taking risks and limit a variety of possibilities in text creation. What they end up writing may be simply to produce or reproduce an accepted version of school literacy. Some children need more structure and some don't in constructing texts. However, if we agree with Dyson (1989, 1993), Harste et al. (1984), and Kress (1997) that drawing, talking, and playing are more primordial forms of meaning-making and that human thought and expression involve multiple sign systems, then we should create writing programs that are inclusive and creative for all children to experience success, take risks, and become authors in their own way.

One thing struck me about the teachers' comments on Kate's drawn story. In a sense, they focused only on her inability to write out her ideas in words, but they completely ignored her creative ideas expressed through her drawings. I suggest that teachers need to notice and teach to the children's strengths and believe that each child can learn but, perhaps, in different ways. Dozier, Johnston, and Rogers (2006) argue that we create different labels to categorize children who experience difficulty acquiring literacy:

The labels many children bear before coming to our program are not helpful in solving the problems they might face. Quite the reverse: the labels often lead our teachers to begin teaching in ways responsive to the label rather than the student, thus impressing the label's imprint even deeper. (p. 24)

Thus, we need to change our way of looking at Kate's drawing from "she still struggles with reading and spelling" to "she has great artistic talents and creative ideas in her book, and I need to help her see how she can write out her ideas and find out the kinds of support she needs in the process."

To sum up the findings in Chapters Four and Five, I propose a curriculum model (Figure 7-1) that excludes the binary opposition between the official and the unofficial, teachers and students, the capable and the less capable. The official and the unofficial are not two independent entities. Rather, they are collaborative components of a unity that lays the foundation for successful learning and teaching.

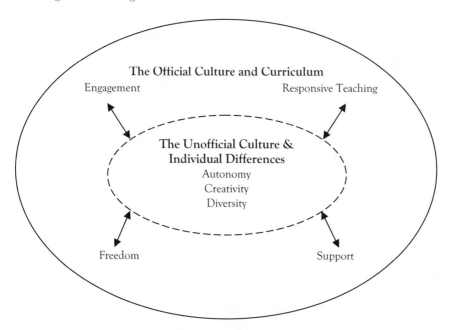

Figure 7-1 An Inclusive and Supportive Curriculum Model

The dotted line surrounding the children's unofficial domain of intelligence indicates that each child is able to maneuver between curriculum expectations and individual goals, build on knowledge base through transaction between the old and the new, and relate the self with the other and the world. An inclusive curriculum and a supportive official school environment provide children with a safe space in which individual differences, autonomy, creativity, and identity are allowed to develop and connect to the instructional objectives. The classroom culture generated from such a curriculum will:

- provide children with ample freedom to explore different possibilities of life experience
- engage children in quality and creative learning
- support and encourage children to realize their full potential
- satisfy and value each individual's needs and differences through responsive and sensitive teaching.

## Reexamining the Relationships between Gender and Power

Considering gender as a cultural and ideological construct, I have tried to reinterpret the binary system of gender identity in Chapter Six by comparing the boys' blunt and explicit actions expressing their anger or making seemingly aggressive jokes among male peers with the girls' compliant and implicit practices of negotiating power that actively participate in male discourses and strategically share authority with the teachers. Further, I have argued that the girls' covert aggression probably carries more powerful and political implications in shaping both official and unofficial culture in school than the boys' overt and defiant aggressiveness that mainly operated within the arena of their male discourses.

Future studies that examine gender identity need to pay more attention to structural changes in our society when gender evolves and becomes an identity choice rather than a restriction and the resulting implications for education. Moreover, while our society becomes more egalitarian about gender, there seems to be a rising problem with an increasing crime rate and a growing tendency for physical violence specifically in female teenage groups (Garbarino, 2006). We may wonder why femininity becomes such a polarized social phenomenon in adolescent girls who used to be locked up in the traditional notion of being "ladylike," "nice," or "nonaggressive" and now have turned to crime and physical aggression that traditionally belonged to masculinity. This may also help us understand the kind of egalitarian society we are creating to accommodate gender difference and some potential threats embedded in our society.

# From *A Day in the Classroom* to *A Wonderful Day in School*

> **Oscar:** A wonderful day um... we have lunch, recess, team reading and gym. I don't want to do anything but eat, drink, and gym. Oh, and art class. That's all. Or maybe we can eat lunch whenever we want. Like every time when we feel hungry, just go to lunch and we don't need to wait until lunch time. And we go outside and play whenever we feel like it. During lunch time, if you want bacon, you get bacon. If you want pancakes, you get pancakes. If you want waffles, you get waffles. If you want apples, you get apples. If you want ice cream, you get ice cream. If you want milk shake, you get milk shake. If you want...

The story of the children's school life started from Chris and Oliver's official version of *A Day in the Classroom* and ended with Oscar's imaginative mockery of *A Wonderful Day in School*. I had been analyzing the children's daily routines and examining different dimensions of how they actively constructed their identity in school. One thing we can be sure about is that these children certainly have something to say about their school life. They imagined quite a different vision of school life from the one they actually lived. Although their goofy day in school is mostly about more free time to do what they want, work less, and have more fun, these children are still hard-working "busy beavers" in school. Their passion for writing, drawing, and creating all kinds of literacy artifacts shows that their imaginative minds are always ready to learn and create new things in school. Even though they have some complaints about the classroom rules and propose various ways to change them, one undeniable fact is that they love their teachers, struggle to learn, and try their best to live a successful life in school.

I have emphasized that the ultimate purpose of the study is to let the children's perceptions and voices of schooling be heard. I consider them valuable resources for teachers to construct a "fun" curriculum that allows children freedom to learn "what they want" and eliminate meaningless worksheets or practices.

Many children shared Linda's view about what they hope to have in school:

> **Linda:** Uh a wonderful day in school would be that you can have friends to play around during recess, and you get to draw and play with friends. And you can do anything you want and you can just be yourself. I just want to be just ME, myself.

From the children's stories, two primary urges appear that most of them would like to fulfill and maintain in school: (1) making changes, and (2) being themselves. These are certainly at the core of many pressing issues in our educational system that teachers, educators, researchers, and policy makers should strive to explore and find ways to improve.

Perhaps, before thinking about what can be done or changed in our educational system, we should critically reflect on as well as courageously admit what we still fail to accomplish in making school a place for *every* child to learn and grow. I believe children's perceptions of schooling and their learning experiences are good places to start thinking about what sets us back from making a difference in current education.

# Bibliography

Adler, A. P., & Adler, P. (1998). *Peer power: Preadolescent culture and identity*. New Burnswick, NJ: Rutgers University Press.

Allen, G. (1993). Traditions and transitions. In P. Cook (Ed.), *Philosophical imagination and cultural memory*. Durham, NC: Duke University Press.

Andrews, M. (2002). Introduction: Counter-narratives and the power to oppose. *Narrative Inquiry*, 12, 1–6.

Anggard, E. (2005). Barbie princesses and dinosaur dragons: Narration as a way of doing gender. *Gender and Education*, 17(5), 539–553.

Appiah, K. A. (2005). *The ethics of identity*. Princeton, NJ: Princeton University Press.

Apple, M. W. (1979). *Ideology and curriculum*. Boston: Routledge & Kegan Paul.

Apple, M. W. (1999). *Power, meaning, and identity: Essays in critical educational studies*. New York: Peter Lang Publishing.

Atwell, N. (1998). *In the middle: New understanding about writing, reading, and learning*. Portsmouth, NH: Boynton/Cook.

Aydt, H., & Corsaro, W. A. (2003). Differences in children's construction of gender across culture. *American Behavioral Scientist*, 46(10), 1306–1325.

Bakhtin, M. M. (1976). The art of the word and the culture of folk humour. In H. Baran (Ed.), *Semiotics and structuralism: Readings from the Soviet Union* (pp. 284–296). White Plains: International Arts and Sciences Press.

Bakhtin, M. M. (1981). Discourse in the novel (C. Emerson & M. Holquist, Trans.). In M. Holquist (Ed.), *The dialogic imagination: Four essays by M. M. Bakhtin* (pp. 259–422). Austin, TX: University of Texas Press.

Bakhtin, M. M. (1984). *Rabelais and his world* (H. Iswolsky, Trans.). Bloomington: Indiana University Press.

Bakhtin, M. M. (1986). The problem of speech genres (V. W. McGee, Trans.). In C. Emerson & M. Holquist (Eds.), *Speech genres and other late essays* (pp. 60–102). Austin, TX: University of Texas Press.

Bakhtin, M. M. (1990). Author and hero in aesthetic activity (V. Liapunov, Trans). In M. Holquist & V. Liapunov (Eds.), *Art and answerability: Early philosophical essays by M. M. Bakhtin* (pp. 4–231). Austin, TX: University of Texas Press.

Bakhtin, M. M. (1993). Toward a philosophy of the act (V. Liapunov, Trans.). In V. Liapunov & M. Holquist (Eds.), *Toward a philosophy of the act* (pp. 1–75). Austin, TX: University of Texas Press.

Bean, T. W., & Moni, K. (2003). Developing students' critical literacy: Exploring identity construction in young adult fiction. *Journal of Adolescent & Adult Literacy*, 46(8), 638–648.

Best, R. (1983). *We've all got scars: What girls and boys learn in elementary school*. Bloomington, IN:

Indiana University Press.

Blaise, M. (2005). *Playing it straight: Uncovering gender discourses in the early childhood classroom.* New York: Routlege.

Bloome, D. (1987). Reading and writing as social process in a seventh grade classroom. In D. Bloome (Ed.), *Literacy and schooling.* Norwood, NJ: Ablex.

Borgaard, B. O. (1999). Peirce on abduction and rational control. *Transactions of the Charles S. Peirce Society, 35*(1), 129–155.

Bowles, S. & Gintis, H. (1976). *Schooling in capitalist America: Educational reform and the contradictions of economic life.* New York: Basic Books.

Boyle, D. E., Marshall, N. L. & Robeson, W. W. (2003). Gender at play. *American Behavioral Scientist, 46*(10), 1325–1345.

Britsch, S. J. & Meier, D. R. (1999). Building a literacy community: The role of literacy and social practice in early childhood programs. *Early Childhood Education Journal, 26*(4), 209–215.

Broughton, M. A. & Fairbanks, C. M. (2003). In the middle of the middle: Seventh-grade girls' literacy and identity development. *Journal of Adolescent & Adult Literacy, 46*(5), 426–435.

Bruner, J. (1990). *Acts of meaning.* Cambridge, MA: Harvard University Press.

Bruner, J. (2002). *Making stories: Law, literature, life.* Cambridge, MA: Harvard University Press.

Burgess-Macey, C. (1999). Classroom literacies: Young children's explorations in meaning making in the age of the literacy hour. *Reading, 33*(3), 120–125.

Busser-Webb, K. (2001). I won't tell you about myself, but I will draw my story. *Language Arts, 78*(6), 511–519.

Butler, J. (1999). *Gender trouble.* New York: Routledge.

Butler, J. (2004). *Undoing gender.* New York: Routledge.

Calkins, L. M. (1994). *The art of teaching writing.* Portsmouth, NH.: Heinemann.

Carspecken, P. F. (1996). *Critical ethnography in educational research: A theoretical and practical guide.* New York: Routledge.

Carspecken, P. F. (1999). *Four scenes for posing the question of meaning.* New York: Peter Lang Publishing.

Carspecken, P. F. (2001). Critical ethnographies from Houston: Distinctive features and directions. In P. F. Carspecken & G. Walford (Eds.), *Critical ethnography and education* (pp.1–26). Oxford, UK: Elsevier Science Ltd.

Carspecken, P. F. (2002). The hidden history of praxis: Theory within critical ethnography and the criticalism/postmodernism problematic. In Y. Zou & E. T. Trueba (Eds.), *Ethnography and schools: Qualitative approaches to the study of education* (pp. 55–84). Lanham, MD: Rowman & Littlefield.

Carspecken, P. F. (2003). Ocularcentrism, phonocentrism and the counter Enlightenment problematic: Clarifying contested terrain in our schools of education. *Teachers College Record, 105*(6), 978-1047.

Chagnon, N. A. (1968). *Yanomamo, the fierce people.* New York: Holt, Rinehart and Winston.

Chambers, D., Tincknell, E. & Van Loon, J. (2004). Peer regulation of teenage sexual identities. *Gender and Education, 16*(3), 397-415.

Collins, J. & Bolt, R. K. (2003). *Literacy and literacies: Texts, power, and identity.* New York: Cambridge University Press.

Comber, B. (2000). What really counts in early literacy lessons? *Language Arts, 78*(1), 39–49.

Comber, B. & Wells, P. (2001). Critical literacy finds a "place": Writing and social action in a low-income Australian grade 2/3 classroom. *The Elementary School Journal, 101*(4), 451–464.

Connell, R. W. (1989). Cool guys, swots and wimps: The interplay of masculinity and education. *Oxford Review of Education*, 15(3), 291–303.

Cook-Gumperz, J., & Corsaro, W. A. (1986). Introduction. In J. Cook-Gumperz, W. A. Corsaro, & J. Streeck (Eds.), *Children's worlds and children's language* (pp. 1–11). New York: M. de Gruyter.

Cook-Gumperz, J., & Kyratzis, A. (2001). Child discourse. In D. Schiffrin, D. Tannen, & H. Hamilton (Eds.), *A handbook of discourse analysis* (pp. 590–611). Malden, MA: Blackwell.

Cornett, C. E. (1998). *The arts as meaning makers*. Upper Saddle River, NJ: Prentice Hall.

Corsaro, W. A. (1985). *Friendship and peer culture in the early years*. Norwood, NJ: Ablex.

Corsaro, W. A. (1997). *The sociology of childhood*. Thousand Oaks, CA: Pine Forge Press.

Corsaro, W. A. (2003). *We're friends, right? Inside did's cultures*. Washington, DC: Joseph Henry Press.

Corsaro, W. A., & Emiliani, F. (1992). Child care, early education, and children's peer culture in Italy. In M. Lamb & K. Sternberg (Eds.), *Child care in context: Cross-cultural perspectives*. Hillsdale, NJ: Lawrence Erlbaum.

Craib, I. (1998). *Experiencing identity*. Thousand Oaks, CA: Sage.

Crossley, M. (2000). *Introducing narrative psychology. Self, trauma and the construction of meaning*. Buckingham, U.K.: Open University Press.

Dakos, K. (2003). *Put your eyes up here: And other school poems*. New York: Simon & Schuster.

Daniel, D. H., Beaumont, L. J., & Doolin, C. A. (2002). *Understanding Children: An Interview and observation guide for educators*. New York: McGraw-Hill.

Davies, B. (1997). Constructing and deconstructing masculinities through critical literacy, *Gender and Education*, 9(1), 9–30.

Davies, B. (2003a). *Shard of glass: Children reading & writing beyond gendered identities*. Cresskill, NJ: Hampton Press.

Davies, B. (2003b). Working with primary school children to deconstruct gender. In C. Skelton and B. Francis (Eds.), *Boys and girls in the primary classroom*. Berkshire, UK: Open University Press.

De Beauvoir, S. (1973). *The second sex*. (E. M. Parshley, Trans.). New York: Vantage.

Denyer, J., & LaFleur, D. (2001). The Eliot Conference: An analysis of a peer response group. *Voices from the Middle*, 9(1), 29–39.

Denzin, N. K. (2003). Performing [auto] ethnography politically. *The Review of Education, Pedagogy, and Cultural Studies*, 25, 257–278.

Derrida, J. (1967/1974). *Of grammatology* (G. C. Spivak, Trans.). Baltimore, MD: Johns Hopkins University Press.

Derrida, J. (1967/1978). *Writing and difference* (A. Bass Trans.). Chicago: University of Chicago Press.

Derrida, J. (1973). *Speech and phenomena and other essays on Husserl's theory of signs* (D. B. Allison, Trans.). Evanston: Northwestern University Press.

Dewey, J. (1922/1983). Human nature and conduct, In J. A. Boydston (Ed.), *John Dewey: The middle works* (Vol. 14). Carbondale, IL: Southern Illinois University Press.

Dewey, J. (1934). *Arts as experience*. New York: Perigee.

Dewey, J. (1952/1989). Modern philosophy. In J. A. Boydston (Ed.), *John Dewey: The later works* (Vol. 16). Carbondale, IL: Southern Illinois University Press.

DiLeo, J. H. (1983). *Interpreting children's drawings*. New York: Brunner/Maze.

Dozier, C., Johnston, P., & Rogers, R. (2006). *Critical literacy critical teaching*. New York: Teachers College Press.

Dunn, J., Cutting, A. L., & Fisher, N. (2002). Old friends, new friends: Predictors of children's perspective on their friends at school. *Child Development*, 73(2), 621–635.

Durkheim, E. (1984). *The division of labor in society* (W. D. Halls, Trans.). New York: Free Press.

Durkheim, E. (1995). *The elementary forms of religious life* (K. E. Fields, Trans.). New York: Free Press.

Dyson, A. H. (1989). *Multiple worlds of child writers: Friends learning to write*. New York: Teachers College Press.

Dyson, A. H. (1993). *Social worlds of children learning to write in an urban primary school*. New York: Teachers College Press.

Dyson, A. H. (1997). *Writing superheroes: Contemporary childhood, popular culture, and classroom literacy*. New York: Teachers College Press.

Dyson, A. H. (2000). Linking writing and community development through the children's forum. In C. D. Lee & P. Smagorinsky (Eds.), *Vygotskian perspectives on literacy research* (pp. 127–149). New York: Cambridge University Press.

Eisner, E. W. (2002). *The arts and the creation of mind*. New Haven, CT: Yale University Press.

Fairclough, N. (1992). *Discourse and social change*. Cambridge, MA: Polity.

Fasoli, L. (2003). Reflections on doing research with young children. *Journal of Australian Research in Early Childhood*, 28(1), 7–11.

Finders, M. J. (2000). "Gotta be worse": Negotiating the pleasurable and the popular. *Journal of Adolescent & Adult Literacy*, 44(2), 146–149.

Fiske, J. (1998). Audiencing: Cultural practices and cultural studies. In N. K. Denzin & Y. S. Lincoln (Eds.), *The landscape of qualitative research: Theories and issues* (pp. 359–378). Thousand Oaks, CA: Sage.

Forman, E. A., & Cazden, C. B. (1994). Exploring Vygotskian perspectives in education: The cognitive value of peer interaction. In R. B. Ruddell, M. R. Ruddell, & H. Singer (Eds.), *Theoretical models and processes of reading* (pp. 155–178). Newark, DE: International Reading Association.

Foucault, M. (1979). *The history of sexuality*, vol. 1: An Introduction. London: Allen Lane.

Foucault, M. (1997). Subjectivity and truth. (R. Hurley et al. Trans.). In P. Rabinow (Ed.), *Ethics: Subjectivity and truth*. New York: New Press.

Foucault, M. (2000). Extracts from Foucault's theory (P. Rabinow & J. D. Faubion, Trans.). In J. D. Faubion (Ed.), *Power: Essential works of Foucault 1954–1984*. New York: New Press.

Freebody, P., Luke, A., & Gilbert, P. (1991). Reading positions and practices in the classroom. *Curriculum Inquiry*, 21(4), 435–457.

Freeman, M. (1993). *Rewriting the self: History, memory, narrative*. London: Routledge.

Freeman, M. (2002). Charting the narrative unconscious: Cultural memory and the challenge of autobiography. *Narrative Inquiry*, 12(1), 193–211.

Freire, P. (1970). *Pedagogy of the oppressed*. (M. B. Ramos, Trans.). New York: Continuum.

Freire, P. (1973). *Education for critical consciousness*. (M. B. Ramos, Trans.). New York: Seabury.

Freire, P., & Macido, D. (1987). *Literacy: Reading the word and the world*. Westport, CT: Bergin & Garvey.

Gadamer, H. (1982). *Truth and methods*. New York: Crossroad.

Galda, L., & Beach, R. (2001). Response to literacy as a cultural activity. *Reading Research Quarterly*, 36(1), 64–73.

Gallas, K. (1998). *"Sometimes I can be anything": Power, gender and identity in a primary classroom*. New York: Teachers College Press.

Garbarino, J. (2006). *See Jane hit: Why girls are growing more violent and what we can do about it*. New York: Penguin Press.

Gardner, H. (1980). *Artful scribbles*. New York: Basic Books.

Gardner, H. (1990). *Art education and human development.* Los Angeles, CA: J. Paul Getty Trust.

Garrison, J. (2001). An Introduction to Dewey's theory of functional "Trans-Action": An alternative paradigm for activity theory. *Mind, Culture, and Activity,* 8(4), 275–296.

Gee, J. P. (1989). Literacy, discourse, and linguistics: Introduction. *Journal of Education,* 171(1), 5–17.

Gee, J. P. (1992). What is literacy? In P. Shannon (Ed.), *Becoming political, too: New reading and writings on the politics of literacy education* (pp.21–28). Portsmouth, NH: Heimemann.

Gee, J. P. (1996). *Social linguistics and literacies: Ideology in discourses.* Philadelphia, PA: Falmer Press: Taylor & Francis.

Gee, J. P. (1999). *An introduction to discourse analysis: Theory and method.* New York: Routledge.

Giddens, A. (1971). *Capitalism and modern social theory: An analysis of the writings of Marx Durkheim and Max Weber.* London/New York: Cambridge University Press.

Giddens, A. (1984). Social science as a double hermeneutic. In G. Delanty & P. Strydom (Eds.), *Philosophies of social science: The classic and contemporary readings* (pp. 400–404). Philadelphia, PA: Open University Press.

Giddens, A. (1991). *Modernity and self-identity.* Stanford, CA: Stanford University Press.

Gilbert, R., & Gilbert, P. (1999). *Masculinity goes to school.* Sydney: Allen & Unwin.

Giroux, A. H. (1981). *Ideology culture and the process of schooling.* Philadelphia, PA: Temple University Press.

Giroux, A. H. (1983). *Theory and resistance in education: A pedagogy for the opposition.* New York: Bergin & Garvey.

Giroux, A. H. (1988). *Schooling and the struggle for public life: Critical pedagogy in the modern age.* Minneapolis, MN: University of Minnesota Press.

Giroux, A. H. (1998). Are Disney movies good for kids? In S. R. Steinberg & J. L. Kincheloe (Eds.), *Kinderculture: The corporate construction of childhood.* Boulder, CO: Westview Press.

Giroux, A. H. (2000). *Stealing innocence: Youth, corporate power, and the politics of culture.* New York: St. Martin's Press.

Giroux, A. H. (2001). Cultural studies as performative politics. *Cultural Studies Critic Methodologies,* 1(1), 5–23.

Giroux, A. H., & Shannon, P. (1997). Cultural studies and pedagogy as performative practice: Toward an introductin. In A. H. Giroux & P. Shannon (Eds.), *Education and cultural studies: Toward a performative practice* (pp. 1–9). New York: Routledge.

Godley, A. J. (2003). Literacy learning as gendered identity work. *Communication Education,* 52(3/4), 273–285.

Goffman, E. (1961). *Asylums.* Garden City, NY: Anchor.

Goffman, E. (1963). *Behavior in public places.* New York: Free Press.

Goffman, E. (1974). *Frame analysis: An essay on the organization of experience.* Cambridge, MA: Harvard University Press.

Goodman, N. (1976). *Languages of art.* New York: Hackett.

Goodnow, J. (1977). *Children drawing.* Cambridge, MA: Harvard University Press.

Graham, R. J. (1999). The self as writer: Assumptions and identities in the writing workshop. *Journal of Adolescent & Adult Literacy,* 43(4), 358–364.

Gramsci, A. (1977). *Pasado y presente.* Gariel Ojeda Padilla, Mexico: Juan Pablos Editor.

Graue, M. E., & Walsh, D. J. (1998). *Studying children in context: Theories, methods, and ethics.* Thousand Oaks, CA: Sage.

Graves, D. H. (1983). *Writing: Teachers and children at work.* Exeter, NH: Heinemann.

Graves, D. H. (1994). *A fresh look at writing.* Portsmouth, NH: Heinemann.

Gutierrez, K., Rymes, B., & Larson, J. (1995). Script, conterscript, and underlife in the classroom: James Brown versus "Brown v. Board of Education." *Harvard Educational Review*, 65, 445–471.

Habermas, J. (1984). *The theory of communicative action: Reason and the rationalization of society.* (Vols. 1; T. McCarthy, Trans.). Boston: Beacon.

Habermas, J. (1987). *The theory of communicative action: Reason and the rationalization of society.* (Vols. 2; T. McCarthy, Trans.). Boston: Beacon.

Hall, S. (1996a). The question of cultural identity. In S. Hall, D. Held, D. Hubert, & K. Thompson (Eds.), *Modernity* (pp. 596–634). Malden, MA: Blackwell.

Hall, S. (1996b). Introduction: Who needs "identity"? In S. Hall & P. du Gay (Eds.), *Questions of cultural identity* (pp. 1–17). Thousand Oaks, CA: Sage.

Halliday, M. A. K. (1978). *Language as social semiotic.* London: Edward Arnold.

Hamilton, M. (2000). Expanding the new literacy studies: Using photographs to explore literacy as social practice. In D. Barton, M. Hamilton, & R. Ivanic (Eds.), *Situated literacies: Reading and writing in context.* New York: Routledge.

Hanninen, V. (2004). A model of narrative circulation. *Narrative Inquiry*, 14(1), 69–85.

Harste, C. J., Woodward, V. A., & Burke, C. L. (1984). *Language stories and literacy lessons.* Portsmouth, NH: Heinemann.

Harste, J. & Manning, A. (2001). "I just want to raise a nice boy!": Being critical and political. *Talking Points*, 13(1), 9–14.

Heath, S. (1983). *Ways with words.* New York: Cambridge University Press.

Heffernan, L., & Lewison, M. (2000). Making real-world issues our business: Critical literacy in a third-grade classroom. *Primary Voices K-6*, 9(2), 15–21.

Heffernan, L., & Lewison, M. (2003). Social narrative writing: (re)constructing kid culture in the writer's workshop. *Language Arts*, 80(6), 435–443.

Heidegger, M. (1962). *Being and time.* New York: Harper & Row.

Herder, J. G. (2002). Letters for the advancement of humanity. In M. Forster (Ed.), *Herder philosophical writing.* Cambridge, U.K.: Cambridge University Press.

Hicks, D. (2000). Self and other in Bakhtin's early philosophical essays: Prelude to a theory of prose consciousness. *Mind, Culture and Activity*, 7(3), 227–242.

Holmes, R. M. (1998). *Fieldwork with children.* Thousand Oaks, CA: Sage.

Holquist, M. (2002). *Dialogism.* New York: Routledge.

Husserl, E. (1962). *Ideas: General introduction to pure phenomenology* (B. Gibson, Trans.). New York: Collier.

Husserl, E. (1970). *The crisis of European sciences and transcendental phenomenology* (D. Carr, Trans.). Evanston, IL: Northwestern University Press.

Janks, H. (2000). Domination, access, diversity and design: A synthesis for critical literacy education. *Educational Review*, 52(2), 175–186.

Jenkins, R. (1996). *Social identity.* London: Routledge.

Joas, H. (1995). *The creativity of action.* Chicago: University of Chicago.

Jones, G. (2002). *Killing monsters: Why children need fantasy, super heroes and make-believe violence.* New York: Basic Books.

Jordan, E., Cowan, A., & Roberts, J. (1995). Knowing the rules: Discursive strategies in young children's power struggles. *Early Childhood Research Quarterly*, 10, 339–358.

Jordan, M., Jensen, R., & Greenleaf, C. (2001). "Amidst familial gatherings": Reading apprenticeship in a middle school classroom. *Voices from the Middle*, 8(4), 15–24.

Josselson, R. (2004). The hermeneutics of faith and the hermeneutics of suspicion. *Narrative Inquiry*, 14(1), 1–28.

Kamler, B. (1999). *Constructing gender and difference: Critical research perspectives on early childhood.*

Cresskill, NJ: Hampton Press.

Kamler, B. (2001). *Relocating the personal: A critical writing pedagogy.* Albany: State University of New York Press.

Kincheloe, J. L., & McLaren, P. (2002). Rethinking critical theory and qualitative research. In Y. Zou & E. T. Trueba (Eds.), *Ethnography and schools: Qualitative approaches to the study of education* (pp. 87–126). Lanham, MD: Rowman & Littlefield.

Klepsch, M., & Logie, L. (1982). *Children draw and tell.* New York: Brunner/Mazel.

Kress, G. R. (1997). *Before writing: Rethinking the paths to literacy.* New York: Routledge.

Kress, G. R. (2001). "You've just got to learn how to see": Curriculum subjects, young people and schooled engagement with the world. *Linguistics and Education,* 11(4), 401–415.

Kress, G. R. (2003). *Literacy in the new media age.* New York: Routledge.

Kress, G. R., & Jewitt, C. (2000). Knowledge, identity, pedagogy: Pedagogic discourse and the representational environments of education in late modernity. *Linguistics and Education,* 11(1), 7–30.

Kyratzis, A. (2004). Talk and interaction among children and the co-construction of peer groups and peer culture. *The Annual Review of Anthropology,* 33, 625–649.

Lakoff, G., & Johnson, M. (2003). *Metaphors we live by.* Chicago: University of Chicago Press.

Lancia, P. J. (1997). Literacy borrowing: The effects of literature on children's writing. *Reading Teacher,* 50(6), 470–475.

Lancy, D. F. (2001). *Studying children and schools: Qualitative research traditions.* Prospect Heights, IL: Waveland Press.

Lankshear, C., Gee, P. J., Knobel, M., & Searle, C. (1997). *Changing literacies.* Bristol, PA: Open University Press.

Larson, J., & Gatto, L. A. (2004). Tactical underlife: Understanding students' perceptions. *Journal of Early Childhood Literacy,* 4(1), 11–41.

Lemke, J. (1988). Genres, semantics, and classroom education. *Linguistics and Education,* 1, 81–99.

Lemke, J. (1995). *Textual politics: Discourse and social dynamics.* London: Taylor & Francis.

Lensimire, T. (1994). *When children write: Critical re-visions of the writing workshop.* New York: Teachers College Press.

Lensimire, T. (2000). *Powerful writing, responsible teaching.* New York: Teachers College Press.

Lewis, C. (2001). *Literacy practices as social acts: Power status and cultural norms in the classroom.* Mahwah, NJ: Lawrence Erlbaum Associates.

Lewison, M., Flint, A., & Van Sluys, K. (2002). Taking on critical literacy: The journey of newcomers and novices. *Language Arts,* 79(5), 382–392.

Luke, P. (1988). The non-neutrality of literacy instruction: A critical introduction. *Australian Journal of Reading,* 11, 79–83.

MacNaughton, G. (2001). *Rethinking gender in early childhood education.* Thousand Oaks, CA: Sage.

Malchiodi, C. A. (1998). *Understanding children's drawings.* New York: Guilford Press.

Mandell, N. (1988). The least-adult role in studying children. *Journal of Contemporary Ethnography,* 16, 433–467.

Mansfield, N. (2000). *Subjectivity: Theories of the self from Freud to Haraway.* Washington Square, NY: New York University Press.

Markowitz, L. (2005). Unmasking moral dichotomies: Can feminist pedagogy overcome student resistance? *Gender and Education,* 17(5), 39–55.

Marshall, J. (2000). Research on response to literature. In M. L. Kamil, P. B. Mosenthal, P. D. Pearson, & R. Barr (Eds.), *Handbook of reading research: Vol. 3.* Mahwah, NJ: Lawrence

Erlbaum.

McCarthey, S. J. (2001). Identity construction in elementary readers and writers. *Reading Research Quarterly*, 36(2), 122–151.

McCarthey, S. J. (2002). *Students' identities and literacy learning.* Chicago, IL: NRC.

McDaniel, C. (2004). Critical literacy: A questioning stance and the possibility for change. *The Reading Teacher*, 57(5), 472–481.

McFarland, D. A. (2001). Student resistance: How the formal and informal organization    of classrooms facilitate everyday forms of student defiance. *American Journal of Sociology*, 107(3), 612–678.

McLaren, P. (1986). *Schooling as a ritual performance: Towards a political economy of educational symbols and gestures.* London ; Boston : Routledge & Kegan Paul.

McLaren, P. (1993). Critical literacy and postcolonial praxis: A Freirian perspective. *College Literature*, 19/20 (3/1), 7–27.

McLaren, P. (2003). Critical pedagogy: A look at the major concepts. In A. Darder, M. Baltodano, & R. D. Torres (Eds.), *The critical pedagogy reader* (pp. 69–96). New York: RoutledgeFalmer.

Mead, G. H. (1932/1980). *The philosophy of the present.* Chicago: University of Chicago Press.

Mead, G. H. (1934). *Mind, self, and society.* Chicago: University of Chicago Press.

Mead, M. (1928). *Coming of age in Samoa.* London: Pelican.

Mladenov, I. (2001). Unlimited semiosis and heteroglossia (C. S. Peirce & M. M. Bakhtin). *Sign Systems Studies*, 29(2), 441–461.

Montgomery, H. (2005). Gendered childhoods: A cross disciplinary overview. *Gender and Education*, 17 (5), 471–482.

Morrow, R. A., & Torres, C. A. (1995). *Social theory and education: A critique of theories of social and cultural reproduction.* Albany: State University of New York Press.

Myers, J., & Beach, R. (2001). Hypermedia authoring as critical literacy. *Journal of Adolescent & Adult Literacy*, 44(6), 538–546.

Newkirk, T. (2002). *Misreading masculinity: Boys, literacy, and popular culture.* Portsmouth, NH: Heinemann.

Peirce, C. S. (1958–1960). *Collected papers, vol. 1–8.* C. Hartshorn & P. Weiss (Eds.), Cambridge, MA: Belknap Press of Harvard University Press.

Peirce, C. S. (1985). Logic as semiotic: The theory of sings. In R. E. Innis (Ed.), *Semiotics: An introduction anthology (pp. 1–22).* Bloomington, IN: Indiana University Press.

Piaget, J. (1954). *The construction of reality in the child* (M. Cook, Trans.). New York: Basic Books.

Pollard, A., Thiessen, D., & Filer, A. (1997). Introduction: New challenges in taking children's curricular perspectives seriously. In A. Pollard, D. Thiessen & A. Filer (Eds.), *Children and the curriculum: The perspectives of primary and elementary school children* (pp. 1–12). Bristol, PA: Falmer Press.

Poole, D. A., & Lamb, M. E. (1998). *Investigative interviews of children.* Washington, DC: American Psychological Association.

Ray, K. W. (1999). *Wondrous words: Writers and writing in the elementary classroom.* Urbana, IL: NCTE.

Ray, K. W., with Cleaveland, L. B. (2004). *Writing workshop with our youngest writers.* Portsmouth, NH: Heinemann.

Renold, E. (2004). "Other" boys: Negotiating non-hegemonic masculinities in the primary school. *Gender and Education*, 16(2), 247–266.

Robinson, K. H. (2005). Reinforcing hegemonic masculinities through sexual harassment: Issues of identity, power and popularity in secondary schools. *Gender and Education*, 17(1),

19–37.

Rowe, D. W., Fitch, J. M., & Bass, A. S. (2001). Power, identity and instructional stance in writers' workshop. *Language Arts*, 78(5), 426–434.

Ryan, M., & Anstesy, M. (2003). Identity and text: Developing self-conscious readers. *Australian Journal of Language and Literacy*, 26(1), 9–22.

Salih, S. (2002). *Judith Butler: Essential guides for literacy studies*. New York: Routledge.

Schaefer, R. (1992). *Retelling a life*. New York: Basic Books.

Schlank, C. H., & Metzger, B. (1996). *Together and equal: Fostering coopterative play and promoting gender equity in early childhood programs*. Boston: Allyn and Bacon.

Schrauf, R. W. (2000). Narrative repair of threatened identity. *Narrative Inquiry*, 10(1), 127–145.

Sebeok, T. A. (1999). *Signs: An introduction to semiotics*. Toronto: University of Toronto Press.

Sedgwick, P. R. (2001). *Descartes to Derrida: An introduction to European philosophy*. Malden, MA: Blackwell.

Serres, Michel. (1982). *Hermes: Literature, science, philosophy*. Baltimore: Johns Hopkins University Press.

Shannon, P. (2002). Critical literacy in everyday life. *Language Arts*, 79(5), 415–424.

Shor, I. (1999). What is critical literacy? In I. Shor & C. Pari (1999). *Critical literacy in action: Writing words, changing worlds*. Portsmouth, NH: Boynton/Cook.

Short, K. G., Harste, J. C., & Burke, C. (1996). *Creating classrooms for authors and inquirers*. Portsmouth, NH: Heinemann.

Simmons, R. (2002). *Odd girl out: The hidden culture of aggression in girls*. Orlando, FL: Hardcourt.

Simmons, R. (2004). *Odd girl speaks out*. Orlando, FL: Hardcourt.

Smith, F. (1994). *Writing and the writer*. Hillsdale, NJ: Lawrence Erlbaum.

Sobieraj, S., & Laube, H. (2001). Confronting the social context to the classroom: Media events, shared cultural experience, and student response. *Teaching Sociology*, 29, 463–470.

Spradley, J. P. (1980). *Participant observation*. New York: Holt, Rinehart and Winston.

Steinberg, S., & Kincheloe, J. L. (1998). Introduction: No more secrets—kinderculture, information saturation, and the postmodern childhood. In S. R. Steinberg & J. L. Kincheloe (Eds.), *Kinderculture: The corporate construction of childhood*. Boulder, CO: Westview Press.

Street, B. (1984). *Literacy in theory and practice*. New York: Cambridge University Press.

Stryker, S. (1980/2002). *Symbolic interactionism*. Caldwell, NJ: The Blackburm Press.

Stryker, S. (1994). Freedom and constraint in social and personal life: Toward revolving the paradox of self. In G. M. Platt & C. Gordon (Eds.). *Self, collective behavior and society: Essays honoring the contributions of Ralph H. Turner* (pp. 119–138). Greenwich, CT: JAI Press.

Stryker, S. (2000). Identity theory. In E. F. Borgatta & R. J. V. Montgommery (Eds.), *Encyclopedia of sociology* (pp. 3095–3102). New York: Macmillan.

Stryker, S., & Burke, P. J. (2000). The past, present and future of an identity theory. *Social Psychology Quarterly*, 63(4), 284–297.

Stryker, S., & Vryan, K. D. (2003). The symbolic interactionist frame. In J. Delamater (Ed.), *Handbook of social psychology*. New York: Kluwer Academic/Plenum Publishers.

Sugaman, S. (1987). *Piaget's construction of the child's reality*. Cambridge, NY: Cambridge University Press.

Swain, J. (2005). Sharing the same world: Boys' relations with girls during their last year of primary school. *Gender and Education*, 17(1), 75–91.

Swift, S. (2005). Kant, Herder, and the question of philosophical anthropology. *Textual Practice*, 19(2), 291–238.

Thorne, B. (1993). *Gender play: Boys and girls in school*. Buckingham: Open University Press.

Toohey, K. (2001). Disputes in child L2 learning. *TESOL Quarterly*, 35(2), 257–278.

Tugendhat, E. (1986). *Self-consciousness and self-determination* (P. Stern, Trans.). Cambridge, MA: MIT Press.

Valeski, T. N., & Stipek, D. J. (2001). Young children's feelings about school. *Child Development*, 72(4), 1198–1213.

Vitanza, V. J. (1997). *Negation, subjectivity, and the history of rhetoric*. Albany: State University of New York.

Vygotsky, L. S. (1978). *Mind in society: The development of higher psychological process*. Cambridge, MA: Harvard University Press.

Warton, M. P. (2001). The forgotten voices in homework: Views of students. *Educational Psychologist*, 36(3), 155–165.

Weber, M. (1978). *Economy and society*. G. Roth & C. Wittich (Eds.). Berkeley: University of California Press.

Wells, G. (1986). *The meaning makers*. Portsmouth, NH: Heinemann.

Wertsch, J. V. (1985). *Vygotsky and the social formation of mind*. Cambridge, MA: Harvard University Press.

Widdershoven, G. (1993). The story of life. Hermeneutic perspectives on the relationship between narrative and history. In R. Josselson & A. Lieblich (Eds.), *The narrative study of lives*, (Vol. 1, pp. 1–20). London: Sage.

Wiley, N. (1994). *The semiotic self*. Chicago, IL: University of Chicago Press.

Williams, B. T. (2003/2004). Heroes, rebels, and victims: Student identities in literacy narratives. *Journal of Adolescent & Adult Literacy*, 47(4), 342–345.

Willis, P. (1977). *Learning to labor: How working class kids get working class jobs*. New York: Columbia University Press.

Wilson, C. & Powell, M. (2001). *A guide to interviewing children: Essential skills for counselors, police, lawyers, and social workers*. New York: Routledge.

Winterbourne, N. (1996). Writing pictures, painting words: Artists notebooks in literacy workshops. In R. S. Hubbard & K. Ernst (Eds.), *New entries: Learning by writing and drawing*. Portsmouth, NH: Heinemann.

Wittgenstein, L. (1953). *Philosophical investigations* (G. E. M. Anscombe, Trans.). Oxford, U.K.: Blackwell.

Wolf, M. (1972). *Women and the family in rural Taiwan*. Stanford, CA: Stanford University Press.

Wortham, S. (2000). Interactional positioning and narrative self-construction. *Narrative Inquiry*, 10(1), 157–184.

Yelland, N. & Grieshaber S. (1998). Blurring the edges. In N. Yellan (Ed.), *Gender in early childhood* (pp. 1–14). New York: Routledge.

Zwiers, M. L. & Morrissette, P. J. (1999). *Effective interviewing of children: A comprehensive guide for counselors and human service workers*. Philadelphia, PA: Accelerated Development.

# Index

# RETHINKING CHILDHOOD

JOE L. KINCHELOE & GAILE CANNELLA, *General Editors*

A revolution is occurring regarding the study of childhood. Traditional notions of child development are under attack, as are the methods by which children are studied. At the same time, the nature of childhood itself is changing as children gain access to information once reserved for adults only. Technological innovations, media, and electronic information have narrowed the distinction between adults and children, forcing educators to rethink the world of schooling in this new context.

This series of textbooks and monographs encourages scholarship in all of these areas, eliciting critical investigations in developmental psychology, early childhood education, multicultural education, and cultural studies of childhood.

Proposals and manuscripts may be sent to the general editors:

> Joe L. Kincheloe
> c/o Peter Lang Publishing, Inc.
> 29 Broadway, 18th floor
> New York, New York 10006

To order other books in this series, please contact our Customer Service Department at:

> (800) 770-LANG (within the U.S.)
> (212) 647-7706 (outside the U.S.)
> (212) 647-7707 FAX

Or browse online by series at:
> www.peterlang.com